The Mismeasure of Orcs

ALSO BY ROBERT T. TALLY JR.
AND FROM McFARLAND

*Representing Middle-earth: Tolkien,
Form, and Ideology* (2024)

The Mismeasure of Orcs

*A Critical Reassessment of
Tolkien's Demonized Creatures*

ROBERT T. TALLY JR.

McFarland & Company, Inc., Publishers
Jefferson, North Carolina

LIBRARY OF CONGRESS CATALOGING-IN-PUBLICATION DATA

Names: Tally, Robert T., Jr. author
Title: The mismeasure of orcs : a critical reassessment of Tolkien's demonized creatures / Robert T. Tally Jr.
Description: Jefferson, North Carolina : McFarland & Company, Inc., Publishers, 2025. | Includes bibliographical references and index.
Identifiers: LCCN 2025009033 | ISBN 9781476694351 paperback ♾
    ISBN 9781476655635 ebook
Subjects: LCSH: Tolkien, J. R. R. (John Ronald Reuel), 1892-1973—Criticism and interpretation | Tolkien, J. R. R. (John Ronald Reuel), 1892-1973—Characters | BISAC: LITERARY CRITICISM / Science Fiction & Fantasy | LCGFT: Literary criticism
Classification: LCC PR6039.O32 Z8345 2025 | DDC 823/.912—dc23/eng/20250310
LC record available at https://lccn.loc.gov/2025009033

ISBN (print) 978-1-4766-9435-1
ISBN (ebook) 978-1-4766-5563-5

© 2025 Robert T. Tally Jr. All rights reserved

No part of this book may be reproduced or transmitted in any form or by any means, electronic or mechanical, including photocopying or recording, or by any information storage and retrieval system, without permission in writing from the publisher.

Front cover image from Adobe Firefly

Printed in the United States of America

*McFarland & Company, Inc., Publishers
    Box 611, Jefferson, North Carolina 28640
        www.mcfarlandpub.com*

For the many....

Debout, les damnés de la terre du milieu,
Le monde va changer de base.
Nous ne sommes rien, soyons tout!

Table of Contents

Preface and Acknowledgments — 1
Introduction: Always the Poor Uruks — 7

1. **"As real a creation as anything in 'realistic' fiction": J.R.R. Tolkien's Vision of the Orcs** — 17
   "A good name for these creatures" — 19
   "The hideous race" — 24
   "Orcs behind every tree" — 29
   "The rising tide of 'orquerie'" — 32
   "Seeing good in Carthaginians" — 36

2. **Breeding Orcs: Origins, Revisions, and Speculations in the "Silmarillion"** — 39
   Mockery of the Elves: The First Appearances of Orcs in *The Silmarillion* — 41
   "The Shadow that bred them can only mock, it cannot make" — 46
   Hearts of Granite: Early Origin Stories — 47
   "Orcs are not Elvish": Revisionist Visions in Tolkien's Later Writings — 51
   "The whole of 'Middle-earth' was Morgoth's Ring" — 57

3. **Great Goblins: Orcs in *The Hobbit*** — 62
   "Goblins, hobgoblins, and orcs of the worst description" — 63
   The Golfimbul Paragraph: Establishing Orcs in Middle-earth — 65
   "Down, down to Goblin Town": The King Under the Misty Mountains — 71
   Beorn's Captives; or, the Quality of Mercy — 80
   "This is how it fell out": Orcs in Council and at War — 82
   The Orphaned Bolg — 89

Table of Contents

**4. They Are Coming: The Resurgence of Orcs in
   *The Fellowship of the Ring*** — 92

"The old bogey-stories": An Abundance of Monsters — 93
The Squint-Eyed Southerner: Bree, Cosmopolitanism, and Xenophobia — 97
Drums in the Deep: The Orcs of Moria — 102
Yrch! Orcs Abroad — 105

**5. The Fighting Uruk-Hai: Orcs, Geopolitics, and the
   Utopian Impulse in *The Two Towers*** — 109

"Orcs travel fast": *Entrelacement* and Political Geography — 110
The Common Speech: Orcs in Debate — 115
"The Whiteskins will catch you and eat you": Orcs in Flight — 120
Helm's Deep, Isengard, and Ithilien: Orcs (and Men) in Battle — 123
"No big bosses": Orcs in Conversation — 131

**6. Don't You Know We're at War? The Ends of the Orcs
   in *The Return of the King*** — 140

Drûgs Are Not Orcs: Varieties of the Humane in the Siege of Gondor — 141
Gothmog and the Mouth of Sauron; or, the State of Mordor — 145
"Where there's a whip there's will": Traversing the Plains of Gorgoroth — 151
Witless and Purposeless: An Unlikely Demise of the Orcs — 156
"Orc-Talk": In the Aftermath of the War of the Ring — 160

Conclusion: In a Hole in the Ground There Lived an Orc — 166
Notes — 173
Bibliography — 187
Index — 193

Preface and Acknowledgments

Fiery the Angels rose, & as they rose deep thunder roll'd
Around their shores: indignant burning with the fires of Orc
—William Blake

A memorable strip from *Existential Comics*, the philosophy-themed webcomic series created by Corey Mohler, features an alternative vision of The Council of Elrond, in which Elrond tries to convince Michel Foucault, Noam Chomsky, and Franz Fanon that the One Ring must be destroyed. Foucault demurs, noting that such a choice is only desirable if one wishes the maintain the current political hierarchies and asserting that "the power of Sauron is but one vector in the power relations of Middle-earth," while "the institutions of the elves both predate and surpass Sauron in their scope and magnitude." Chomsky chimes in, citing a worldwide poll of "all the peoples of Middle-earth" (i.e., orcs, men, hobbits, dwarves, trolls) which found that the elves themselves were deemed "the greatest threat to world peace"; naturally, he adds, the media in Rivendell did not report it. Chomsky goes on to say that Sauron is not nearly the menace he is made out to be, and points out that "Mordor was at peace for 1,500 years before Ar-Pharazôn landed with the largest army of Númenóreans ever assembled," invading and destroying the "peaceful, sovereign nation." Fanon takes up this thread by observing how the orcs, reduced to poverty and "excluded from the advanced society of the elves," quite understandably accepted a "strong leader who promises to give them some kind of dignity." When Elrond objects that "the orcs are corrupted beyond redemption" and "must be destroyed to protect the free people of Middle-earth," Fanon seizes upon the ideological and propagandistic use of "free people," a category that never includes the orcs even though they are no less "free" than men under the dominion of Denethor and Théoden or elves under the rule of Galadriel and Elrond. Hence, Fanon says, "'Freedom' isn't a political situation, but rather a racial one. [...] The orcs are defined to be a lesser race, so can only reach salvation through being subordinated to the elves." Then, with the enthusiastic support of Chomsky, Fanon proposes that they form a party of revolutionaries whose task will be to travel throughout the world, sowing the seeds of revolution to end all domination, "to ensure that the people, be they men, elves, or orcs, or anything else, will be able to govern themselves." A diminutive, armor-clad Karl Marx shows up at that point, vowing, "You have my ax!" as an obviously vexed Elrond murmurs, "That is not how I thought this would go."[1]

The humor of all this comes simultaneously from its juxtaposition of politically leftist philosophers with the fantasy realm of Elrond *and* from its reversal of expectations of how the moral (and also political) system of Middle-earth operates. It is funny because readers of J.R.R. Tolkien's works are not supposed to think in those terms about such matters. That Sauron, his subjects, and those in his employ are "evil" is taken for granted within *The Lord of the Rings*, although little thought is given to the particular political perspective from which this moral judgement derives: to wit, that of the "high" elves and the descendants of the Númenóreans, ancestral elites who rule the "free world" without any sort of democratic checks or balances whatsoever and who seem intent on preserving their *ancien régime* permanently. That many "lesser" men, along with most dwarves, hobbits, and "dark" elves, go along with Elrond, Galadriel, Aragorn, and Gandalf in this worldview only serves the interests of these powers that be. Accordingly, it should not surprise anyone to learn that those orcs, "wild" men, Easterlings, Southrons, Variags, and others whom this upper caste of hereditary elvish overlords considers enemies might not themselves feel so sanguine about elvish or elf-friends' control over the world system. From the perspective of these others, even Sauron and Saruman might appear to be preferable leaders, but it is also the case that many if not most would prefer no "big bosses" at all, as Tolkien has one of the orcs actually put it in *The Lord of the Rings*. The revisionist take on The Council of Elrond in *Existential Comics*, while tongue in cheek, nevertheless discloses some truth about the worldview of the orcs and other peoples of Middle-earth in Tolkien's legendarium.

The fact is, Tolkien himself gives us far too much information about the orcs to allow any reasonable reader to view them as innately and irredeemably evil. Far from being mere slaves to the "dark powers," orcs consistently reveal themselves to have their own personalities, families, communities, languages, and cultures, and moreover, they show that they have truly human, perhaps *all-too-human*, fears, desires, motives, goals, and feelings. At least, that is the case in those rare instances when readers are able to see them as more than mere cannon-fodder or "monsters" to be destroyed without the slightest twinge of pity, mercy, or humane feeling. Fundamentally, *orcs are people*, and though they may often seem like pretty bad people—crude, boorish, violent, uncouth, and altogether unpleasant to be around—they are nevertheless people worthy of life and liberty in the Middle-earth that is their home.

My argument in this book is thus more or less in line with that of the leftist thinkers in the *Existential Comics* strip, but with perhaps less humor. A revisionary reading of Tolkien's legendarium, including *The Hobbit* and *The Lord of the Rings*, reveals the degree to which orcs are absolutely as deserving of our sympathy and goodwill as many of the other people to be found in this world. Indeed, in their basic humanity, orcs are likely far more sympathetic to those of us who traverse this vale of tears than many of the ostensibly more heroic characters to be found in Tolkien's world. The preternatural purity and *hauteur* of some of the latter make them seem far less realistically "human" than many of the all-too-human orcs we encounter. In any event, by reading Tolkien's writings against the grain, as it were, I hope to highlight the complexities and ambiguities of the orcs of Middle-earth, thus rendering simplistic, moralizing, and frequently racist views of these characters, and of Tolkien's writings in general, more difficult to sustain.

* * *

I suppose that, in some senses, this project began some fifty years ago in my childhood, when I frequently found myself questioning the official, especially moral, line with respect to so many stories circulating at the time. It is not that I was a particularly radical child, but I was raised to be skeptical, and it probably did not help that my earliest political memories were of the Watergate hearings and dinner-table conversations about how this or that emperor not only had no clothes, but also tended to fecklessly attack others for what they were wearing. As a consumer of popular entertainments, I certainly was able to cheer for the "good guys," as it were, but I found myself quite unable to demonize the "bad guys" or to allow others' demonization of them to unduly influence me. As in sports, the best rivalries are those in which the opponent is respected as an equal, hence a worthy challenger. The adversary might need to be defeated, but never brutalized or annihilated. No one is "evil," to put it bluntly, and for the most part only those who would label their putative adversaries as such come close. Naturally, I found in the goblins of *The Hobbit* and the orcs of *The Lord of the Rings* far more interesting than the one-dimensionally evil creatures that so many fans have imagined.

I have admired and enjoyed Tolkien's work since childhood, when I first read *The Hobbit* and saw the Rankin/Bass animated film adaptation of it. Yes, I acknowledged the goblins as the "bad guys," but even then they struck me as no more inherently threatening than did the other adversaries faced along the way, including trolls, spiders, elves, and men. *The Lord of the Rings* was all the more enchanting, and for a time I became quite steeped in Tolkien's works, *The Silmarillion, Unfinished Tales of Númenor and Middle-earth*, and the expanding *History of Middle-earth* series in the 1980s and 1990s. Although my intellectual and professional trajectories took me in different directions, I never really lost touch with Tolkien, and I vividly recall having discussions with my younger brothers about these works as they were also exploring Middle-earth and its environs. I am grateful to them, Richey and Jay, for all their contributions to my thinking, and I am delighted to see another generation, featuring Arthur, Annabel, and Fiona, making their own ways into this world.

The first article I wrote on Tolkien was what became "Let Us Now Praise Famous Orcs," published in *Mythlore* in 2010. I had initially imagined it as a light, journalistic piece, a playful sort of "sympathy-for-the-devils" article suited to a non-academic audience comprising mostly casual fans and lay readers. Eventually it became more involved, and I am eternally grateful to Janet Brennan Croft, editor of *Mythlore*, as well as my anonymous referees who gave it a chance. That article is the foundation of this book project, and even though nothing in what follows reprints any previously published work, I would not have been able to write this book without that essay as an *Ansatzpunkt* for the developments that have followed from it.

I would also like to thank Robin Anne Reid, another superb scholar and critic, who has organized projects and panels over many years that I have been lucky to take part in. My second ever article on Tolkien, in fact, was published in a book she and Janet Brennan Croft co-edited, along with John Wm. Houghton, Nancy Marsh, and John D. Rateliff, *Tolkien in the New Century: Essays in Honor of Tom Shippey* (McFarland, 2014). In the years since, I have presented numerous talks on orcs and other matters at sessions organized by Robin, and I am thrilled to have my "Uruk.... We prefer 'Uruk': Representing the Orc in *The Rings of Power*" included in her new book on *Race, Racisms, and Tolkien* (McFarland, 2025). Many of my thoughts here were first mooted in the presence of Robin at events she has made happen, and I am very grateful for her insightful feedback and encouragement.

Although this book was mostly written in 2023–24, it is the result of many decades of reading, thinking, conversation, revision, and reflection, not to mention a good deal of confustication and bebothering. In the past decade in particular, I have benefited from the support of my many colleagues and friends. At Texas State University, I have had the opportunity to teach Tolkien in several classes, and I thank all my students for their energy and inspiration. Merve Emre helped me with my perverse "Song of Saruman," published in the *Los Angeles Review of Books* in 2014, another sympathy-for-the-devil article that allowed me to think more deeply about the question of orcs in Tolkien's legendarium, and I will always be grateful for her patience and kindness. In addition to those mentioned above, Bianca Beronio, Cameron Bourquein, Sara Brown, Gerry Canavan, Jane Chance, Cait Coker, Ying Fang, Dimitra Fimi, Jason Fisher, Verlyn Flieger, Peter Grybauskas, Sean Guynes, Thomas Hönegger, Fredric Jameson, Michael Moses, Joyana Richer, Norbert Schürer, Robert Stuart, Christopher Vaccaro, Phillip E. Wegner, and Jeffrey Weinstock, among many others, have been great. I thank Gary Mitchem and others at McFarland for their support of my earlier project, which became *Representing Middle-earth: Tolkien, Form, and Ideology* (2024), and for their enthusiasm for this study of Tolkien's orcs.

Above all, I am grateful for the love and support of Reiko Graham, as well as for the always enlivening presence of Windy Britches, Steve French, and Nigel Tuffnail (who mistakes himself for Tevildo, Prince of Cats, more often than he should). This book is dedicated to the largely unidentified many who struggle to make lives worth living in this, *our* Middle-earth.

Introduction

Always the Poor Uruks

Hope, pity, forgiveness, and redemption are key themes in J.R.R. Tolkien's writing, from his "Silmarillion" legends through *The Hobbit* and especially *The Lord of the Rings*, and so it is not surprising to find sympathy extended not only to the deserving "good" characters, but also to the most wretched, supposedly "evil" ones in these works. Referring to the ways that even those wholly committed to the good might be corrupted, for example, the wise lore master Elrond Half-elven asserts that "nothing is evil in the beginning," adding, "Even Sauron was not so."[1] Such an observation, coming from arguably one of the wisest persons in Middle-earth, is enough to show that "good" and "evil" are not absolute, that even one's fiercest adversaries might have redeeming qualities, that they may inadvertently serve desirable ends, and that in the fullness of time they may ultimately thus prove to have not been enemies after all. Tolkien himself insisted that he did not deal in "Absolute Evil," suggesting that even the most degraded figures could be redeemed.[2]

This is undoubtedly why *The Lord of the Rings* features so many instances in which orcs—those implacable "enemies" who might otherwise seem irredeemably evil—are treated humanely by the heroes throughout the novel.[3] Thus, for example,

> (1) when Frodo expresses his wish that Bilbo had killed a particular orc (or goblin) under the Misty Mountains when he had had the chance, insisting that the goblin "deserves death," Gandalf rebukes him, saying "Deserves it! I daresay he does. Many that live deserve death. And some who die deserve life. Can you give it to them? Then do not be too eager to deal out death in judgement. For even the very wise cannot see all ends" [I.ii.65].

Or, in the Golden Hall of King Théoden,

> (2) when Gandalf refers to a captive orc as "a snake," adding, "To slay it would be just," before counseling mercy, and suggesting he be set free and judged solely on the choices he makes thereafter [III.iii.520].

Or, in the aftermath of the Battle of Helm's Deep,

> (3) when the victorious soldiers of Rohan round up the orcs who "had given themselves up" and who "were afraid, and cried for mercy." The Rohirrim disarm these foes, making them swear an oath never to oppose them again; but they then tell the orcs "you shall go free back to your land," and the orcs "were amazed; for Saruman had told them that the men of Rohan were cruel" [III.viii.545].

Or, consider that famous moment in Ithilien,

> (4) when Sam witnesses the death of an orc warrior at the hands of a soldier from Gondor, and he wonders what the dead orc's name was "and where he came from; and if he was really evil of heart, or what lies and threats had led him on the long march from his home; and if he would not really rather have stayed there in peace" [IV.iv.661].

Or, in the moment just after the destruction of the One Ring,

> (5) when some orcs "proud and bold, in their turn now gathered themselves for a last stand of desperate battle. But the most part fled eastward as they could; and some cast their weapons down and sued for mercy" [VI.iv.949].

Or, a short time later,

> (6) when Aragon, now the crowned King Elessar, "pardoned" the orcs "that had given themselves up, and sent them away free, and he made peace" with the orcs of Harad, and he "released" the enslaved orcs of Mordor, giving them "all the lands about Lake Núrnen to be their own" [VI.v.968].

Or, finally, towards the end of the novel,

> (7) when the hobbits upon returning to the Shire encounter a particularly vicious orc doing violence there, they capture him, and though some hobbits clamor for his life, an older and wiser Frodo insists that he not be killed, saying "He is fallen, and his cure is beyond us; but I would still spare him, in the hope that he may find it" [VI.viii.1019].

In all these instances, among many others, readers bear witness to the tremendous power of pity, mercy, and basic humanity on display in Tolkien's masterpiece.

Of course, this is a ruse. Anyone at all familiar with *The Lord of the Rings* will have readily discerned that none of these examples from the novel involve orcs at all, even of each of the direct quotations is accurate. In actuality, (1) Gandalf was speaking of sparing the life of Gollum out of pity, a position that Frodo himself takes up wholeheartedly later in the novel, while neither Gandalf nor Frodo ever express any pity for orcs. In the next instance, (2) it is Wormtongue, not an orc, whose life Gandalf would spare. In the third example, (3) the men of Rohan, far from disarming and freeing the orcs as they did with the "hillmen," instead slay them all; in fact, the line just before that quoted above reads: "No Orcs remained alive; their bodies were uncounted" (III.viii.545). In the fourth example, (4) after witnessing a skirmish between Gondorian and Southron soldiers, Sam shows momentary sympathy toward a fallen Southron, a "swarthy" man whose "brown hand still clutched the hilt of a broken sword," but Sam never has sympathetic thoughts like these about any orc. Fifth, (5) during the Battle of the Morannon, we learn that—contrary to all evidence gleaned from earlier passages about orcs, their personalities, motivations, allegiances, and goals—the orcs "ran hither and thither mindless; and some slew themselves, or cast themselves in pits, or fled wailing back to hide in holes and dark lightless places far from hope," but none were considered "proud and bold," nor were any orcs thought to be worthy of "mercy," as were "the Men of Rhûn and of Harad, Easterling and Southron" (VI.iv.949). Moreover, regarding the sixth example, (6) King Elessar gave no pardon, nor any further thought apparently, to orcs, although he pardoned Easterlings, Southrons, and even the men of Mordor itself. Finally, in the seventh example, (7) Frodo in the "scouring of the Shire" wishes to spare the life of Saruman, as well as that of Wormtongue and other "ruffians," but never does he or any other "hero" urge that the life of any orc, anywhere, *ever* be spared. Remarkably, Frodo does elsewhere acknowledge the orcs' relatively humane treatment of him while he was being held captive in the Tower of Cirith Ungol, so he knows better than most about their basic "humanity," for better or worse (VI.i.914). In striking contrast to the mercy shown to "evil" *men* of all sorts and despite the presentation of orcs as fundamentally "humane" beings, which Tolkien elsewhere defines capaciously as to include all "speaking creatures,"[4] the heroes of *The Lord of the Rings* and of Tolkien's other writings never show the least sense of pity or sympathy for orcs. In Tolkien's world, as the saying goes, the only good orc is a dead orc.[5]

Such treatment of orcs might not be cause for alarm for most readers, who likely go along with the heroes' views within the narratives and thus accept the idea that orcs are irredeemably evil monsters, utterly inhuman, and therefore unworthy of the sort of sympathy reserved for one's fellow man; indeed, from the perspectives of the main characters in Tolkien's writings, orcs are unworthy of existence entirely. But, for various reasons, Tolkien himself was troubled by the moral and metaphysical implications of his use of orcs. In fact, he writes about the problems in several letters, and he even went so far as to imagine alternative origins, ontologies, and characteristics that would make their treatment in his legendarium seem less odious to his own sensibilities, as I discuss at greater length in Chapters 1 and 2. Tolkien's concerns about his depictions of the orcs related to his ethical and theological worldview, no doubt, but also to his desire for narrative consistency and coherence. The fact is, the treatment of orcs in Tolkien's legendarium does not make sense, and Tolkien knew it.

The Mismeasure of Orcs: A Critical Reassessment of Tolkien's Demonized Creatures is the work of an unapologetic orc-sympathizer. To sympathize with does not mean to praise, of course, and I do not wish to suggests that the orcs we encounter in *The Hobbit*, *The Lord of the Rings*, or *The Silmarillion* are somehow the real heroes for whom the readers should cheer to victory. It is true, I have published an article titled "Let Us Praise Famous Orcs," but readers will readily recognize the phrase as an homage to James Agee and Walker Evans's Depression-era portrait of working-class Americans, tenant farmers in the U.S. South. In fact, nearly all the orcs we encounter in Tolkien's writing appear to be of the working class, with the most visible appearing as common soldiers, but with evidence of a vast industrial and agricultural workforce almost certainly made up of orcs and other men that would be required to outfit and to sustain large armies, not to mention the many cities and countries those armies defend. And I pointedly say *"and other men"* because it is clear to me, and it became increasingly clear to Tolkien himself, it seems (if Christopher Tolkien's comments are to be believed),[6] that orcs *are* humans. Their distinctiveness from other humans ("men") in Tolkien's legendarium appears to be based largely on their behavior, but there is clearly also the racial component. Orcs are humans, but of one or more distinctive races or cultures that would differentiate them from others. As Charles W. Mills has put it, in a recent (alas posthumous) article, the orcs are "the wretched of Middle-earth."[7] The phrase, adapted from a line in the socialist anthem *L'Internationale*, is the one used by Franz Fanon as the title for his monumental study of the psychopathology of colonialism and racism. Reading critically, one can easily detect aspects of the racial, colonial, and subaltern working-class character of the orcs as they appear within Tolkien's writings as well.

One thing that becomes apparent in almost every scene in Tolkien's writings in which orcs personally appear—that is, beyond just their mentions as faceless hordes or otherwise dehumanized masses—is just how sorely put-upon they are. The orcs seem to represent an industrial working class that is well aware of how alienating and degrading that position in society can be. Even the captains, whose rank makes them superior to many troops while also serving their own "big bosses," show fear, maintain grievances, express doubt, and generally question the state of the world they are in. As one orc captain says to another in *The Lord of the Rings*, "the Big Bosses [...] ay, even the Biggest, can make mistakes. Something nearly slipped, you say. I say, something *has* slipped. And we've got to look out. Always the poor Uruks to put slips right, and small thanks" (IV.x.738). Whenever we meet them, in fact, the *poor uruks* are engaged in some difficult task or other, often under immediate threat of reprimand, injury, or death, and they certainly know it. The orcs readers encounter in Tolkien's writings are hardly the mindless demons, slaves to their evil masters' bidding, with no will of their own. On the contrary, Tolkien reveals them to have the full range of human emotions, intelligence, virtues, and flaws. In most cases, their lives are hard, and that makes them long for alternative social orders. In that sense the orcs also represent a potentially revolutionary class within Middle-earth.

My argument in favor of sympathy for orcs is not simply based on a perverse reversal of Tolkien's own moral values, and I am certainly not trying to say that orcs represent the "good guys" in Tolkien's tales of Middle-earth. Rather, what has always interested me most is the way that Tolkien himself, in *The Hobbit* and *The Lord of the Rings*, as well as in his letters, drafts, and other posthumously published materials, explicitly and implicitly emphasizes the basic humanity of the orcs, thereby drawing the reader's attention to the fact that the treatment of orcs in many of his works raise disturbing ethical questions. Tolkien was always a bit troubled by the characterization and disposition of orcs in his writings, as becomes clear from several well-known letters in which he ruminated on the matter. In his fastidiousness as a world-builder and scholar, this quandary impelled Tolkien to imagine different origin stories and ontologies for these creatures, but in the end, even he had to concede that the "orkish question" was too vexed to deal with in an adequate fashion. Unable to rewrite his mythologies and tales from scratch, Tolkien left the situation of the orcs as one among many ultimately unsolved problems in his larger legendarium. Nevertheless, in so doing, he also left open the possibility that we—that is, meticulously close readers of his texts, scholars of his legendary histories, explorers of his imagined geographies, creative thinkers, and sensitive souls—might see orcs differently, recognizing them as the people they clearly are, rather than as the monsters so many believe them to be.

I am, as I say, a notorious orc-sympathizer. "Let Us Now Praise Famous Orcs: Simple Humanity in Tolkien's Inhuman Creatures," which appeared in *Mythlore* in 2010, was in fact the first thing I ever published on Tolkien. In some respects *The Mismeasure of Orcs* is a more extensive, fleshed out version of that brief, relatively informal article. As in that essay, this book addresses one of the most troubling philosophical problems in Tolkien's entire legendarium: that is, the existence of a sentient, rational beings for whom no sympathy, mercy, or moral feeling is ever shown by the apparently "good" characters, who themselves are not troubled in the slightest by, and often take delight in, hunting, killing, and even torturing orcs. Tolkien's writings contain very little depicting the world from the orcs' perspectives, and those crucial moments in which we hear orcs speaking amongst themselves are scenes in which others, non-orcs who are utterly unfamiliar with their cultures and histories, merely overhear them talking. Examining what stories we do have of the orcs, which themselves changed over time according to Tolkien's own worries about whether orcs were "redeemable," I want to show that these "inhuman" creatures are, in fact, among the most human—perhaps "human, all-too-human," in Friedrich Nietzsche's apt phrase—to be found in *The Lord of the Rings*, among other works. Although it is not my chief focus, I also necessarily discuss race and racism in Tolkien's writings for, unsurprisingly, the presentation of orcs is particularly noticeable in that context. One cannot really help but imagine orcs in racial and racist terms, given their fundamental humanity, for better and for worse, in nearly all aspects of their characterization, and given Tolkien's rather definitive description of their appearance as "repulsive versions of the (to Europeans) least lovely Mongol-types."[8] Hence, even Tolkien likely saw orcs as more closely resembling the marauding hordes of Genghis Khan than the "demon-corpses" of *Beowulf*.

Focusing on key scenes from Tolkien's "Silmarillion" materials, *The Hobbit*, and *The Lord of the Rings*, this study attempts to uncover the richly diverse cultures, as well as the distinctive personalities of various orcs, who turn out to be a far cry from the nameless, faceless, and monstrous masses of demonized enemies they are taken to be in the popular imagination. I may at times extrapolate, speculate, or read "against the grain" of the narrative, to employ Walter Benjamin's marvelous metaphor, but throughout the book I try to emphasize the degree to which Tolkien's *own* writings reveal the nature of orcs to be altogether human, thus meriting the feelings of pity and mercy shown to such characters as Gollum, Gríma Wormtongue, and Saruman, not to mention the "human" adversaries in battle, such as the Dunlendings, Easterlings, and Haradrim. That is, even those readers who limit their attention to what is actually written by Tolkien in his own texts ought to conclude that there is far more to orcs than has traditionally been acknowledged, and that, further, the orcs are ultimately shown to be worthy of our sympathy and respect, if not our admiration. A renewed understanding of the orcs as a people results in seeing Middle-earth's history, geography, politics, and cultural anthropology in a new light.

For this reason I have chosen to organize this study along the lines of relatively close readings of portions of Tolkien's texts, rather than a more encyclopedic survey of secondary literature on orcs, a body of work that is rapidly growing. Rather than including discrete essays on race, language, culture, and so forth, for instance, I have organized the study in relation to the orcs as they appear in Tolkien's writings, although these broader issues will come up in the course of those readings. As such, I tend to focus on those scenes in Tolkien's fiction in which orcs are most visibly present or, as in some cases, when their absence is itself something of a notable "presence" in the text. Frequently quoting from Tolkien's writings, including letters and other posthumously published work, I recognize that this approach might justly be criticized as cherry-picking, but I can only plead my good intentions, while also noting that those who selectively quote other lines in opposition to such arguments are undoubtedly engaged in similarly discriminative harvestings. Creative reading, like creative writing, is often essential to understanding the world we live in and the otherworlds we can imagine, and Tolkien's own imaginative universe offers fertile grounds for interpretation.

The Mismeasure of Orcs is divided into six chapters, plus a Conclusion. Chapter 1, "'As real a creation as anything in 'realistic' fiction': J.R.R. Tolkien's Vision of the Orcs," focuses especially on Tolkien's letters and other works of nonfiction that offer insight into his vision of the orcs, both as creatures to be found in the imaginative universe and, more metaphorically, as types of people who may be found within our own, all-too-real world. Not surprisingly, Tolkien's perspective on the subject is complex and nuanced, and although he does not establish a single, definitive and unchanging image of what an "orc" is, Tolkien does offer a range of views that would suggest that he too reserves some sympathy for orcs, much as they may also offend his sensibilities.

In Chapter 2, "Breeding Orcs: Origins, Revisions, and Speculations in the 'Silmarillion,'" I explore the various representations of orcs in *The Silmarillion* as published in 1977 and in the vaster "Silmarillion" materials on which Tolkien worked for much of his life and most of which have come to light through the publication of *Unfinished Tales* and the multivolume *History of Middle-earth* series.[9] This chapter looks at Tolkien's "invention" of the orcs, particularly within the vast world of legends and tales he created, including multiple origin stories that he mooted over the years. Here I discuss sources Tolkien drew upon for his vision of orcs, such as the *orcnéas* mentioned in *Beowulf*, while also examining the ways Tolkien extrapolated upon the mythical creatures' character with reference to the world system more broadly understood.

Chapter 3, "Great Goblins: Orcs in *The Hobbit*," examines the role played by orcs, who are for the most part referred to as *goblins*, in that novel. *The Hobbit* notoriously "intruded" upon Tolkien's legendarium, inasmuch as it was never intended to be part of the world of the

"Silmarillion," but by securing many of the imaginary world's peoples, places, and events in published form, *The Hobbit* established something like a "canon" for fans and scholars of his work. That is where his orcs first appear in print, and their character in this novel helps us to understand their role in the larger geopolitical history of Middle-earth. From the brief mention of Golfimbul and the hobbits' past experience with goblins, to the encounters with the goblins of the Misty Mountains and the warfare with goblins in the Battle of Five Armies, *The Hobbit* establishes the place of orcs in Tolkien's universe. In this chapter I look at the way "goblins" are presented in the novel, particularly as this sets up our understanding of orcs in the rest of Tolkien's writings.

Chapters 4 through 6 deal with the representations of orcs in *The Lord of the Rings*, which is a single novel, not a trilogy.[10] Tolkien had subdivided the story into six "books," each containing nine to twelve chapters, plus Appendices that provided deeper insights into the historical, genealogical, linguistic, and social background to the narrative. (Indeed, Tolkien had wanted to publish the "Silmarillion" together with the novel, thus forming a complete "Saga of the Jewels and the Rings," but his publisher rejected the plan.) The decision to publish the novel in three installments in 1954 and 1955 was based on financial and commercial considerations, and Tolkien lamented that this made the story appear somewhat uneven across the volumes. Nevertheless, with nearly 1,200 pages and over 450,000 words to work with, it is convenient to follow the publisher's conventions here, so I take up the representation of orcs in *The Fellowship of the Ring*, *The Two Towers*, and *The Return of the King* respectively in these chapters. I trust readers will bear in mind the greater unity of *The Lord of the Rings* throughout.

In Chapter 4, "They Are Coming: The Resurgence of Orcs in *The Fellowship of the Ring*," I start by examining the world in which the orcs reappear in *The Lord of the Rings*. At the conclusion of *The Hobbit*, which after all was not intended to have a sequel, most of the orcs had been eliminated, and thus for some in Middle-earth, they represent "bogey-stories" told to frighten children, rather than actually existing peoples in the real world. The hobbits think that a "squint-eyed Southerner," for instance, looks "more than half like a goblin," but they have never encountered orcs in the flesh. In Moria, the company will engage with orcs for the first time, and thereafter orcs play a large role in the narrative that follows. In *The Fellowship of the Ring*, therefore, the relative absence of orcs is notable as a way of setting the stage for their more prominent roles to come.

The Two Towers features the most rich and detailed portrait of orkish characters, speech, behavior, cultures, and attitudes to be found in any of Tolkien's work, as the reader joins the hobbits in the company of actual orcs engaged in their duties and talking amongst themselves. In Chapter 5, "The Fighting Uruk-Hai: Orcs, Geopolitics, and the Utopian Impulse in *The Two Towers*," I examine these scenes—especially those in two key chapters, "The Uruk-Hai" and "The Choices of Master Samwise"—in which different orcs interact with one another, offering the reader a glimpse into the motivations, fears, hopes, and dreams of individual orcs, while also demonstrating the complexity of the geopolitical situation in which these orcs, along with the hobbits, find themselves. The conversations among the orcs reveal that they too hope for a better world, one in which they are no longer oppressed by "big bosses" and are free to determine their own paths in their pursuit of life, liberty, and happiness.

Chapter 6, "Don't You Know We're at War? The Ends of the Orcs in *The Return of the King*," deals with various encounters with orcs, among other people, during the battles depicted in Books V and VI of *The Lord of the Rings*. I discuss the curious encounter with the Drúedain, a seemingly orc-like people who are nevertheless on the side of the "good" forces, while also looking at the roles humans have in the leadership of Sauron's forces. Frodo and Sam experience first-hand the life of an orc in wartime Mordor, as they travel across the plains of Gorgoroth toward Mount Doom. After the defeat of Sauron, orcs apparently—and rather dubiously—disappear entirely, a completely unlikely scenario that has consequences for the theory of orkishness more generally. At the conclusion to *The Lord of the Rings*, the question of the role of the orcs in Middle-earth remains somewhat open.

In a brief Conclusion titled "In a Hole in the Ground There Lived an Orc" (a play on the first sentence of *The Hobbit*), I discuss the vexing issue of a world seemingly without orcs in the Fourth Age of Middle-earth. Reading the unpublished versions of "Epilogue" to *The Lord of the Rings*, which Tolkien had hoped to include in its original publication, and also "The New Shadow," a draft chapter of an aborted sequel to the novel, I explore what this orc-free epoch might look like. I conclude that orcs remain very much part of the world, of the Middle-earth in which Sam and his family dwells and of our own *oikumene*, only that these orcs have become so recognizably human that their continued *literal* demonization is no longer credible, except among the most abject and unreconstructed racists among us. Orcs are people, very much human, and indeed, a bit like hobbits, in their own ways. If they can be crude, obnoxious, violent, and even deadly, that does not so much speak to their monstrosity as to their all-too-human humanity, for these are characteristics widely found among our fellow man, after all. But as people who have been so oppressed, "the wretched of the earth," orcs also represent that revolutionary spirit that would transform societies.

Tolkien's orcs have always been more interesting, nuanced, and even sympathetic than many readers and fans have acknowledged. For all their apparent monstrosity, they are clearly people struggling to make a place for themselves in a world that denigrates them while also exploiting them, thus making them far more like the majority of humans in our world today than any putatively demonic or "evil" creatures. Emerging from their holes in the ground, orcs might help to figure forth a new system, one without "big bosses," in which the "small folk" are no longer subordinated to the great powers. Tolkien himself insists that orcs must be "redeemable," and in their redemption, perhaps, lies our own. We have nothing much to lose but our chains, and we have a world to win.

CHAPTER 1

"As real a creation as anything in 'realistic' fiction"
J.R.R. Tolkien's Vision of the Orcs

In a May 25, 1944, letter to his son Christopher, who was at the time serving in the Royal Air Force in South Africa, J.R.R. Tolkien famously wrote, "Yes, I think the orcs as real a creation as anything in 'realistic' fiction," adding, "only in real life they are on both sides, of course."[1] Some readers might be tempted to interpret this as a symbolic use of the term *orc*, and Tolkien did sometimes employ the word in a mostly metaphorical way, but here *orc* is also the designation for a certain type or temperament of human being. As I argue here and throughout this book, this is what orcs actually are in Tolkien's legendarium as well. The *orc* stands for "various modes of badness" (to use Tolkien's own phrase), which undoubtedly includes rudeness, obnoxiousness, mean-spiritedness, and even cruelty. However, there is no question that Tolkien imagines these features to be utterly human in form and in character. In Tolkien's personal view, then, orcs are not to be understood as monsters or demons, strictly speaking, but as "men." Most of them are "bad guys," to be sure, but they are "humane" nonetheless.

Tolkien was specifically responding to Christopher's complaints about his fellow soldiers and officers in the British military, which is in part what the "on both sides" comment is about. In another letter written three weeks earlier, Tolkien had conceded that, in the current world war, "we started out with a great many Orcs on our side," going on to lament that Christopher was himself "a hobbit amongst the Urukhai." This figurative employment of the term, along with the overall sentiment regarding the universality of orkishness in the world, appears again in another letter written later that same summer, in which Tolkien asserts,

> Urukhai is only a figure of speech. [...] I fear it must be admitted that there are human creatures that seem irredeemable short of a special miracle, and that

there are probably abnormally many of such creatures in Deutschland and Nippon—but certainly these unhappy countries have no monopoly: I have met them, or thought so, in England's green and pleasant land.[2]

Given Christopher's situation among orc-like British soldiers, Tolkien urges his son to develop "a little thickening of the outer skin, if only as protection for the more sensitive interior." Human creatures being what they are, Tolkien advises, thick skin "will be of permanent value in any walk of later life in this tough world (which shows no signs of softening)."[3] Learning to live with orcs, including our fellow orcs, is thus a critical part of our *Bildung* in the present age.

Perhaps it is not surprising that, at almost exactly the same time as this correspondence with Christopher was taking place, Tolkien was completing a draft of the chapter from *The Lord of the Rings* titled "The Choices of Master Samwise," which features a conversation between Gorbag and Shagrat, two orc soldiers of Mordor, who themselves complain bitterly about the war, bemoan the hardships of their duties, question the wisdom and even competence of their leadership, and long for alternative ways of living. As I will discuss at greater length later in Chapter 5, these are altogether human and humane concerns, but for now it is worth noting that Gorbag's and Shagrat's worries about the war in which they are engaged more or less mirror those of Christopher Tolkien and his father at their own wartime. Not only are there "orcs" on both sides, as Tolkien understands it, but he allows these orcs in *The Lord of the Rings* to give voice to the legitimate complaints of the common soldier, of someone positioned very much as Tolkien himself had been during World War I and as Christopher now found himself in World War II. Indeed, just as these orc captains grouse about their own "Big Bosses," Tolkien says in another letter to Christopher that summer that "the Big Folk," who "have for the most part viewed this war from the vantage point of large motor-cars," have likely planned the war effort in such a way that even in victory "ordinary people" will have no freedom left or will have "to fight for it," but will probably be "too tired to resist."[4] It is worth noting that Tolkien is here talking about the inevitable Allied victory in the war, not its defeat. It is a rather *orkish* critique, as the conversation between Gorbag and Shagrat makes clear, and yet it comes from an all-too-human perspective, that of J.R.R. Tolkien himself.

I will explore the various representations and characterization of orcs in Tolkien's legendarium throughout the book, but in this chapter, I want to focus on Tolkien's personal views of these creatures as he expressed them in letters or in other writings mostly apart from the "Silmarillion," *The Hobbit*, and *The Lord of the Rings*. Although his views about the orcs, their origins, their character, and their appearance likely changed a lot over the years, I maintain that Tolkien conceives of orcs as essentially human beings (or, at least, "humane" beings) throughout his career. If anything, orcs are not inhuman, but all-too-human, to borrow the Nietzschean expression. Of course, that does not mean that in Tolkien's mythopoesis such creatures are not also demonized. After all, one can only "demonize" those persons or things that are not already demons. The demonization of the enemy is a common enough trope in wartime, obviously, but in Tolkien's legendarium and especially in *The Hobbit* and *The Lord of the Rings*, orcs are revealed to be people … nasty, mean-spirited, uncouth, and cruel people, yes, but people nonetheless. Orcs are ontologically of the same order as elves or men, it seems, but they are often distinguished in racial (or racist) terms, along with the more general sense of these orkish people as being morally and culturally inferior. As such, their demonization comes easily to the elves, "noble" men, and hobbit-allies from whose perspective the narratives are told.

Orcs are presented within the "secondary world" created (or sub-created) by Tolkien as demon-like creatures, and Tolkien's representation of them emerges from the literary and linguistic resources made available to him as both a storyteller and as a philologist. Accordingly, then, we can learn something about the creatures based on what they are called, for the words themselves have power in determining the character of the subjects named. I begin by looking at Tolkien's use of the word *orc*, which in turn leads to a brief discussion of the racial character of the "race," before then examining Tolkien's more figurative uses of the idea of the orc as a means of criticizing his society and the times. Given Tolkien's fastidiousness as a scholar and a myth-maker, he eventually had to face a moral dilemma posed by the ways he had imagined the orcs, and I conclude this chapter with a brief discussion of Tolkien's odd mixture of ambivalence and adamancy with respect to these "bad" people.

"A good name for these creatures"

In properly philological fashion, which is in keeping with the spirit of Tolkien's own ways of thinking, perhaps we should begin by looking at the word *orc* and examining how the word is connected to the being to which it refers. This is all the more important to do, considering the terminological confusions that have arisen based on Tolkien's choice to refer to these creatures as *goblins* in *The Hobbit*, not to mention the other words that sometimes are associated with them. Among some fans especially, this had led people to think that the goblins of the Misty Mountains are a different order of being from, say, the Uruk-hai and other orcs encountered in *The Lord of the Rings*, and at some stages of his working out of things in his "Silmarillion" notes and drafts Tolkien himself seems to suggest that there are variations among these related creatures. However, ultimately Tolkien makes clear that all of these labels, while possibly designating distinctive "ranks" amongst orcs or even disparate communities or perhaps ethnicities within orcdom, still name the same type of being; that is, these are different terms used to refer to the same "race," which he preferred to call *orcs*.[5]

Tolkien asserts that he "originally took the word from Old English," citing the appearance of the word *orcneas* in *Beowulf* and "the gloss *orc* = *pyrs* ('ogre'), *heldeofol* ('hell-devil'). This is supposed not to be connected to the modern English *orc*, *ork*, a name applied to various sea-beasts of the dolphin order."[6] Needless to say, perhaps, but after the success of *The Lord of the Rings* in print, as well as throughout different media and cultural forms, readers today are not likely to confuse the *orc* with the *orca*.[7] Indeed, arguably, readers may not even be able to confuse *orcs* with *goblins* anymore, so associated is the former term with Tolkien's work.

Tolkien had used the word *goblin* in one his earliest compositions, the poem "Goblin Feet," written while he was still a student at Exeter College, Oxford, and published in *Oxford Poetry* in 1915. However, the creatures referred to in the title are not what would become orcs, but rather "gnomes" (i.e., fairies or elves). Thus, for example, it reads in part:

> O! I hear the tiny horns
> Of enchanted leprechauns
> And the padded feet of many gnomes a-coming.
> [...]
> O! the music of their feet—of their dancing goblin feet!
> O! the magic! O! the sorrow when it dies.

Undoubtedly, many of Tolkien's most ardent admirers find "Goblin Feet" charming, as even in its simplicity the poem's imagery and language already evoke those themes of nature, beauty, enchantment, and loss that would be sounded in his best-known writings to come. But Tolkien himself adamantly rejected what he had written later in life, abjuring its representations of the imaginary creatures especially. In 1971, when asked for permission to include the poem in a new anthology, Tolkien responded, "I wish the unhappy little thing, representing all that I came (so soon after) to fervently dislike, could be buried for ever."[8] Partly, no doubt, this is because Tolkien as an adult quickly abandoned his earlier fascination with diminutive "fairies" with their dragonfly wings and tinkling footfalls, and he developed the idea of elves in the form of the tall, noble, fierce, and humane beings we know from *The Hobbit*, *The Lord of the Rings*, and especially *The Silmarillion*. Partly, it may also have had to do with his rejection of certain Celtic themes (e.g., leprechauns) in favor of his goals to produce an ostensibly more English (not British!) body of legends.[9] As Dimitra Fimi's excellent study of Tolkien's legendarium puts it succinctly, this was part of Tolkien's move "from fairies to hobbits," which occurred between 1915 and the early 1930s when he began writing *The Hobbit*.[10] Thus, the goblins of "Goblin Feet" thus tell us nothing about the creatures known as *goblins* in that novel.

As I will discuss more in Chapter 2, the emergence of the creatures that will be known as *orcs* in Tolkien's legendarium appears differently in different texts written over many years, as Tolkien developed his thoughts on the matter and as he attempted to integrate and harmonize disparate names and depictions. As early as 1917, for example, there is reference to the Úvanimor "who are monsters, giants, and ogres," creatures that were "bred in the earth" by Melko (a.k.a. Melkor and, later, Morgoth). There is also mention of the Kaukareldar, "false-fairies" or "evil fays" sent by Melko to deceive humans. These may have seemed like prototypes of the orc or other enemies, but at that point "orcs" themselves, also known as "goblins," had already been mentioned as well. As Christopher Tolkien relates, the text there contains the bracketed word "Gongs," which he says "might be thought to be a name for the *Kaukareldar*," but "in the Gnomish word-list *Gong* is defined as 'one of the tribe of the Orcs, a goblin.'"[11] *Orcs*, *goblins*, and several other words are used in the early "Silmarillion" writings to refer to the same creatures, but Tolkien eventually settled on *orc* as not just his preferred term, but in his view the correct one.

Tolkien in many places explains the origins and use of the word *orc*, partly to deflect from the misunderstanding among some that he himself had invented the term, but partly to clarify what he had in mind by the word and the concept. In a 1966 letter to Gene Wolfe, who had enquired about the use of the term in *The Hobbit*, Tolkien explained, "*Orc* I derived from Anglo-Saxon, a word meaning demon, usually supposed to be derived from the Latin *Orcus*—Hell. But I doubt this, though the matter is too involved to set out here." In an earlier letter he had mentioned that "the word is as far as I am concerned actually derived from Old English *orc*, 'demon,' but only because of its phonetic suitability," and then explains that the creatures themselves "owe, I suppose, a good deal to the goblin tradition (*goblins* is used as a translation in *The Hobbit*, where *orc* only occurs once [sic], I think), especially as it appears in George MacDonald, except for the soft feet which I never believed in."[12] Elsewhere, in his "Guide to the Names in *The Lord of the Rings*," written to assist translators of the novel (at that point, only the Dutch and Swedish translations had come out), Tolkien again suggests that *goblins* in *The Hobbit* is merely used to translate of the word *orc*, but adds that "this word [goblin], and other words of similar sense in other European languages (as far as I know), are not really suitable," concluding that "*orc* seemed to me, and seems, in sound a good name for these creatures. It should be retained."[13]

Tolkien mentions the "phonetic suitability" or "sound" of the word in these examples, and his meticulous attention to languages and their histories goes a long way toward explaining his use of the word *orc* as well as his attempts to characterize the creatures to which the word refers. In a brief summary of Tolkien's method, Tom Shippey observes that "Tolkien had used the word [*orc*] in *The Hobbit*, but his regular word at that point was 'goblin.' As he built up the linguistic correspondences of Middle-earth [...] this came to seem out of place." The problem is that *goblin* "is a relatively late word in English (the *OED* cannot find a clear citation before the sixteenth century), and according to the *OED* it derives probably from medieval Latin *cobalus*—the dictionary oddly makes no attempt to link it with the German-derived 'kobold.' Tolkien preferred an Old English word."[14] In addition to avoiding the Latinate terminology, Tolkien was also concerned that, for many Europeans at least, the word "goblin" conjured up an image not very dissimilar to that of "elf," particularly when one thinks of mischievous sprites, pixies, or nymphs, and moreover, there is that Christian tradition in which all such beings are associated with demons of one sort or another. In using *orc* instead of *goblin*, Tolkien could at once adhere to his beloved northern European linguistic commitments and avoid somewhat the later associations with a Christian moral universe, which he wanted to keep outside (or at least out of view) of the main ideas of his mythology. In any case, as Tolkien stated pointedly in response to a reader who liked "goblin" better, a "preference of *goblins* to *orcs* involves a large question and a matter of taste," before adding: "Personally, I prefer Orcs."[15]

The potential etymological history of the term also reveals interesting moments in the putative genealogy of the concept. Notwithstanding Tolkien's misgivings, the word *orc* is generally thought to have derived from the Latin *Orcus*, much as did the French term *ogre*, which appears as early as Chrétien de Troyes's *Perceval, ou le Conte du Graal* (circa 1190) and is made more famous in the fairy tales of Charles Perrault (published in 1697). Orcus, an Etruscan deity, comes to be associated with "Hell," as Tolkien observed in his letter to Gene Wolfe, but like the names Pluto or Hades, it refers both to the personified god and to the infernal or underworld location. In that mythological tradition, Orcus was apparently more closely associated with *punishing* the dead, and hence Orcus has perhaps an even greater conceptual connection to violence than do Pluto or Hades, perhaps in this way prefiguring a version of Satan.[16] There is also the suggestion that Orcus may have been related, if only via transliteration, to the

Greek *Horkos*, a demon who in Hesiod is associated with punishing men who swear false oaths. Thus one may trace a distant and tortuous connection between falsehood, disloyalty, sin, punishment, and the underworld, all connected to the notion of the *orc*, etymologically speaking.

The idea that orcs might be creatures of the underworld is itself compelling, particularly as in Tolkien's writings they are frequently associated with physical spaces of subterranean darkness: caves, tunnels, mines, pits, dungeons, and so forth. We are also given to understand that orcs prefer darkness to daylight, as I discuss further below. In one early origin story Tolkien imagines, in fact, there is a suggestion that orcs were literally made out of the earth, "bred by Melko of the subterranean heats and slime," with hearts of "granite."[17] The association of orcs, as a concept and as a people, with underground spaces fits neatly with the idea of a hell-spawn or otherwise demonic race.

In speaking of the *orcneas* in *Beowulf*, the great German philologist Friedrich Klaeber concedes that "evil spirits" is not necessarily the most accurate translation, for "*Orcneas* is compounded of *orc* (from the Lat. *orcus* 'the underworld' or Hades) and *neas* 'corpses.'" Klaeber goes on to explain,

> Necromancy was practiced among the ancient Germani, and was familiar among the pagan Norsemen who revived it in England when they invaded. By this art the newly-buried dead bodies could be made to call up the spirits which had inhabited them: but of course this could, from an early Christian point of view, only be done if such spirits had been evil. *Orcneas*, then, were the evil spirits which could be conjured up from the lower world by means of necromancy.[18]

This also comports with Tom Shippey's view that *orc-neas* in *Beowulf* "seems to mean 'demon-corpses.'"[19]

Intriguingly, of course, Sauron is referred to in *The Hobbit* as the Necromancer, and presumably some forms of necromancy are among his many powers. Given Tolkien's knowledge of these sources and his explicit mention of Sauron as a necromancer, it is perhaps strange then that Tolkien did not really consider necromancy as part of the orc origins, either in the "Silmarillion" materials, in the published writings, or in letters. After all, this may have helped solve some of the moral quandaries that their "being" in the world presented. Tolkien may have had religious, philosophical, or even personal reasons for wishing to avoid the idea of orcs as zombies, mummies, or other types of reanimated corpses, but the concept of orcs as revenant elves or men, as opposed to merely being "corrupted" versions of them (and hence, victims), likely would make their cruel ill-treatment at the hands of the heroes of Middle-earth far more tolerable. In a text likely written in the late 1950s, in fact, Tolkien does suggest that the *fëa* (spirit) could be separated from the *hröa* (physical body) in some circumstances, adding "it is recorded in the histories that Morgoth, and Sauron after him, would drive out the *fëa* by terror, and then feed the body and make it a beast. Or worse: he would daunt the *fëa* within the body and reduce it to impotence; and then nourish the body foully, so that it became bestial, to the horror and torment of the *fëa*."[20] However, this idea does not appear to ever be mentioned with respect to the origin or character of orcs. In Tolkien's world, therefore, the orcs cannot really be thought of as *orcneas* or "demon-corpses."

The concept of the "orc," even in the minds of those Old English speakers who might have used the term, was rather inchoate, apparently being associated with what modern readers would call demons, giants, zombies, or evil spirits all at once. Shippey concludes that "literate Anglo-Saxons really had very little idea what orcs were at all," noting that "[t]he word was floating freely, with ominous suggestions but no clear referent." Hence, even if the name itself is rather old, we can credit Tolkien with defining, clarifying, and solidifying, if not inventing, the image of the creatures referred to as *orcs*, which have become standard features of the fantasy genre in literature, film, video games, and other media in our era. As Shippey affirms, "Tolkien took the word, brought the concept into clear focus in detailed scenes [...] and, as with hobbits, has in a way made both word and thing now canonical."[21]

"The hideous race"

Alas, a fundamental element of this now-canonical concept is deeply and abidingly racist. Anyone still denying this aspect of the conception, depiction, and characterization of Tolkien's orcs in the twenty-first century is probably somewhat obtuse, willfully deluded, hopelessly idealistic, or irredeemably compromised by commitments to ideological programs intended to support racial bigotry of one form or another. Even in an earlier period, one could read about these "swart," "sallow," "slant-eyed" creatures only so many times without feeling that their physical features were intended as racially-coded markers of their inherent evil and inferiority. That is true of many of the other human "enemies" in *The Lord of the Rings*, in fact, but with orcs, such racially coded moral opprobrium seems to be determinate of the entire race and its worth. (Notably, the "dark" Easterlings, Southrons, and even the Wild Men of Dunland are imbued with virtues denied to orcs, and they are certainly treated with more respect and mercy by Tolkien's ostensibly "good" characters.) That Tolkien himself personally held views of various peoples that were racist would hardly be surprising, not merely owing to his time, place, and social circumstances, but also owing to his worldviews more generally. That his orcs should be depicted in such racially coded terms is probably not surprising either, but there is nothing inherent in the fantasy world that required orcs to be imagined in those ways. If they be demons, for example, they could—like the balrogs, dragons, trolls, wights, or other "monsters" encountered in Middle-earth—be presented in fantastically otherworldly "evil" forms, without having to be made into "humane" beings that are then not only established as an inhuman or subhuman race but given physical features coded and easily recognized as racial stereotypes in the all-too-real world. In fact, in his writings Tolkien "humanizes" the orcs to the point that one cannot help but wonder if racial bigotry is the only thing that effectively determines their status as "evil" enemies, unworthy of pity, mercy, sympathy, or above all—considering that their bad behavior or attitudes is what so clearly marks them as "evil" in the first place—forgiveness.[22]

Although there were various origins stories that Tolkien imagined and reimagined over the years, the most prominent explanation for the existence of orcs is that they are, in fact, elves that were captured and "corrupted" by Morgoth. In *The Silmarillion* we learn that "those of the Quendi [i.e., elves] who came into the hands of Melkor, ere Utumno was broken, were put there in prison, and by slow arts of cruelty were corrupted and enslaved; and thus did Melkor breed the hideous race of the Orcs in envy and mockery of the Elves."[23] This "hideous race," according to its own origin story, is therefore made up of elves who are *victims* of the "dark powers," who were held prisoner, enslaved, and tortured. Their actual "race" is elvish, in this view, and yet even among the elves for whom this "truth" is known—"this is held true by the wise of Eressëa," after all—no sympathy, pity, or mercy is shown by elves to their orkish kinsfolk, and certainly no elven heroes express the wish to liberate, recruit, or redeem these orcs. The "sundering" of the elves who escaped Melkor's snares and those who were captured creates a putative racial difference, the basis for a racist bigotry, which is then taken to be an ontological divide. That is, orcs are not taken to be different kinds or ethnicities of elves or men, as with the various kinship groups amongst them, but a different and inherently inferior type of being altogether, a type of being, moreover, that is unworthy of existence itself. In any case, as we see throughout the "Silmarillion," *The Hobbit*, and *The Lord of the Rings*, the "good" characters within Tolkien's stories are unfazed by these family resemblances, happily destroying orcs without question or moral compunction whatsoever at every moment in which they are encountered. As I have noted elsewhere, the orcs' physical and cultural similarity to elves, humans, and even dwarves—not to mention their right as "rational, incarnate beings" to exist—suggests that the unthinking demonization of the entire race by elves, humans, and most dwarves stems, at least in part, from what Freud famously called "the narcissism of minor differences," which is to say mere racism.[24] Orcs are hated by elves and men, in part, because they are so like elves and men.

Race, racial hierarchies, and racism are thus concepts that become unavoidable when discussing Tolkien's orcs. As such, these underlie much of my discussion throughout this book, but this is not really a book about race or racism in Tolkien's life, work, or worlds. The topics have been ably addressed by such astute readers as Charles W. Mills, Dimitra Fimi, Roger Echo-Hawk, Helen Young, Robin A. Reid, Mariana Rios, Bianca Beronio, and Robert Stuart, among others, and these matters will undoubtedly receive greater attention from scholars and critics in the years to come. Stuart's *Tolkien, Race, and Racism in Middle-earth* is especially thorough in tracing Tolkien's personal racialist and racist beliefs (including potential changes thereto over time), while also exploring the relevant race theories and their adherents during and before Tolkien's lifetime, the depictions of such ideas within Tolkien's writings, critiques of the neofascist or white supremacist appropriations of Tolkien's work, and so forth. Here, I want only to register the degree to which Tolkien's vision of the orcs is characterized by race and racism, which has ramifications for the treatment of the orcs within the narrative spaces of his legendarium.

I also want to note the ambivalence and complexity on display in Tolkien's writings, for as I maintain throughout this book, Tolkien imbues his orcs with humane and human values that, perhaps unconsciously or against his own intent, render them sympathetic to sensitive readers (including Tolkien himself) if not to the "heroes" of the tales. Moreover, Tolkien found it difficult to imagine them as irredeemably "evil" and denounced the very idea of "Absolute evil." In the interstices of such spaces, there is room for hope, even for those creatures that many would abandon and abhor.

One of the most important recent studies of race and racism with respect to Tolkien's orcs was actually written in the late 1980s, but it only appeared in print in 2022. Charles W. Mills, the Marxist philosopher perhaps best known for his book *The Racial Contract* (1997), wrote but was unable to find a journal willing to publish the article, which appeared posthumously as "The Wretched of Middle-earth: An Orkish Manifesto" in *The Southern Journal of Philosophy*.[25] "The Wretched of Middle-earth" takes its title from Franz Fanon's magisterial critique of colonialism, which had employed the phrase from the opening line of the great socialist anthem, "L'Internationale": *Debout, les damnés de la terre* ("Arise, wretched of the earth"). Mills' manifesto doubles down on this

1. "As real a creation as anything in 'realistic' fiction" 27

revolutionary, Marxist heritage, showing how racism in Tolkien's world and in our own is enmeshed within systems of political, social, and economic inequality that oppress and exploit subaltern subjects and populations. Mills offers a careful, creative reading of Tolkien's writings in which he draws out the racist notions on display within the texts and their implications for readers in the real world.

Mills observes that the orcs appear in Tolkien "as a potentially insurgent lower class, a racial proletariat," and—as we see in *The Hobbit* and *The Lord of the Rings*—orcs have their own cultures, communities, mores, and morals, which render them, in anything, more uncouth than monstrous. From the perspective of elves and their supporters, however, that makes orcs worthy of extermination. Orcs are at once the industrial working class, associated with modern technology, and a primitive, "wild" race unfit for civilized societies. Their "place" is always elsewhere: orcs are both outsiders who do not belong in "our" lands and persistent threats near or within our communities, a mob threatening peace and order. Orcs likewise threaten the existing structures and relations of power, which justifies their annihilation by the heroes. Orcs are depicted as "ontological zeroes," as Mills puts it. "The pen here prepares the way for the sword"; established as "people without history," orcs are excluded from the legitimate spaces of the world, relegated to "slaves" of the dark powers, a term used with opprobrium and without pity. Hence, "[t]he literal genocide of the orcs with which the book concludes is in a sense of secondary importance to the cultural genocide that their creation signified in the first place."[26] The orcs are a racialized underclass used to reinforce racist social hierarchies. Mills ends his essay with a call for "a genuine re-seeing of the orcs of the past—and present."[27]

The racial and racist characterization of orcs as inferior humans, marked as such in part by their distinctively non-white physical and physiognomic features, occurs throughout the legendarium. But in a well-known 1958 letter, Tolkien explicitly describes the physical appearance and form of the orcs, and he does so in a way that at once highlights their fundamental humanity and emphasizes the racial dimension of their purported monstrosity. As Tolkien says, "[t]he Orcs are definitely stated to be corruptions of the 'human' form seen in Elves and Men. They are (or were) squat, broad, flat-nosed, sallow-skinned, with wide mouths and slant eyes: in fact degraded and repulsive versions of the (to Europeans) least lovely Mongol-types."[28] Tolkien's language here directly connects the features of orcs to racial characteristics among humans, not to mention culturally specific and even relativistic determinations of aesthetic value. This description merely underscores the degree to which orcs in Tolkien's world represent a "demonized enemy" rather than anything like demons in their own right. Notably, Tolkien's comments are made in the context of his critique of a film "treatment," that is, an outline of how a proposed movie adaptation of *The Lord of the Rings* would be handled. In the treatment, would-be screenwriter Morton Grady Zimmerman (whom Tolkien refers to in the letter as "Z") had depicted orcs as having "beaks and feathers," prompting Tolkien to point out somewhat acidly that "*Orcs* is not a form of *Auks*." Even this parenthetical jibe is suggestive, however, for it shows that not only did Tolkien himself picture orcs as "human" in form, but he also expected all readers to understand that this is "definitively" what orcs looked like in the novel. That is, orcs are not only *human-like*, they are recognizable *as* humans, if also "foreign" and terrifying ones. They are not inhuman "monsters," in any event, and Tolkien's exasperation with Zimmerman's apparent misreading indicates the degree to which he felt that this should have been *obvious* to anyone paying attention to the actual text of *The Lord of the Rings*.

Within the legendarium and from the perspective of elves, at least, orcs are judged to be an inferior people, even if they are also acknowledged, however grudgingly, to be people of the same basic, "humane" type. Apparently, being "corrupted" forms of life is enough to justify being unworthy of life; such corruption of the victims, far from eliciting pity, is even used to justify the merciless and mass taking of that life by the "good" people who oppose the orcs. However, it is always worth recalling that orcs in *The Lord of the Rings* frequently fight alongside and work with humans, and in *The Hobbit* we are told that goblins have made alliances with some dwarves at times, so clearly not all people feel this way about the orcs, even if all elves do. The objection to orcs on racial grounds, as with so much racist bigotry in our own "primary world," is then connected to moralizing arguments in which the inferior race is thought to be made up of "evil" people, against whom the good and pious are quite correct to righteously stand. Once the people identified as orcs are understood as such, it becomes more likely that anyone with objectionable behaviors, beliefs, morals, and so on can be treated as if part of some inhuman race of inferior beings.

Whereas once the word *orc* might have conjured up "evil spirits," demons, or perhaps even zombies, increasingly the term seems to take on a racial character that makes this demonization all the more odious. That cannot be ignored, but it is also the case that the idea of the orc came to be used by Tolkien and others to refer to "bad" people more generally. The coincidence of orkishness and racial alterity is a sign of the racism to be found in Tolkien's world, both diagetically with respect to the racialized hierarchies within Middle-earth's cultures and extradiagetically with respect to our own world. Yet Tolkien also found orkishness to be an increasingly dominant aspect of the character of many of his fellow Englishmen, proving that he could extend his disdain for orcs well beyond merely racial categories.

"Orcs behind every tree"

Although the racialized and racist characterizations of orcs in Tolkien's legendarium are undeniable and deeply troubling, Tolkien's personal views of the orcs and orkishness were not limited to simple racially defined disinclinations. As we have seen in his wartime correspondence with his son Christopher, Tolkien applied the term *orc*, for the most part figuratively, to people that he found to be despicable in various ways, particularly those who delighted in cruelty or destruction, but also many who were in his view simply uncouth, ill-mannered, or perhaps even just inexcusably "modern." Of course, there may be overlap between the racist characterizations and these morally tinged evaluations, as it is likely that Tolkien and many of his ilk found entire races and cultures in the "real" world to be more orc-like than others. But his references to white, northern European, and English orcs suggests that he also maintained an idea of the "orc" that transcended what are commonly understood to be racial differences. At its heart, the "orc" represented to Tolkien a personal "badness" that was nearly, but not totally, irredeemable.

Such distinctively orkish "badness" is also very much a matter of perspective, as many things that Tolkien found objectionable might not especially bother others nearly so much. For instance, Tolkien would imagine orcs in connection to many features of modern life that he detested, especially if they involved noise and machinery. Stuart cites two somewhat humorous examples: "Hearing the 'savage sound' of a chainsaw at work, he would exclaim 'Orcs!'"; similarly, a "motorcyclist roaring past would evoke the same outraged exclamation: 'there is an Orc!'" Stuart takes these figurative and moralizing uses of the term *orc* as evidence that Tolkien's image of such beings did not have to do with white supremacist bigotry. As he puts it, "[f]or Tolkien, modernity's apparatus of mechanized noise, pollution, and destruction was everywhere 'manned' by Orcs. Again and again, though his correspondence and in interviews, Tolkien finds Orcs resident in England and elsewhere among us."[29]

Even something so basic and arcane an Ivory Tower matter as curricular reform could be an occasion to invoke the orc bugaboo. Humphrey Carpenter, in his biography of Tolkien, recounts an episode from 1929 when, while teaching in Merton College at Oxford, Tolkien was seeking the Faculty Board's approval to modify the syllabi for his courses, a quotidian and internal issue hardly worthy of notice outside this small academic circle, yet one filled with imagined intrigue and danger. For as C.S. Lewis had written "conspiratorially" to Tolkien at the time: "Forgive me if I remind you that there are disguised orcs behind every tree."[30] Presumably, these "orcs" were not wielding chainsaws or riding motorcycles, nor would they have been brandishing scimitars while mounted upon wargs; rather, they were fellow academics considered to be "enemies" who might not approve the Tolkien's proposed changes to his courses. In some cases, that is, an "orc" might just be a person with whom one disagrees, although the inference of abiding treachery and hostility is also integral to this characterization.

Oxford dons notwithstanding, there is undoubtedly a class-based element to this attitude. Tolkien represents the values of a mostly conservative bourgeois who is not particularly impressed with the aristocrats of the realm but is fairly alarmed by emergent democratic (or anarchic) developments among the lower classes. As radical fantasist Michael Moorcock has put it very strongly,

> *The Lord of the Rings* is a pernicious confirmation of the values of a morally bankrupt middle-class. [...] If the Shire is a suburban garden, Sauron and his henchmen are that old bourgeois bugaboo, the Mob—mindless football supporters throwing their beer-bottles over the fence—the worst aspects of modern urban society represented as the whole by a fearful, backward-yearning class for whom "good taste" is synonymous with "restraint" (pastel colours, murmured protest) and "civilized" behaviour means "conventional behaviour in all circumstances."[31]

After having condemned *The Lord of the Rings* as "Epic Pooh" (a slight against A.A. Milne's beloved bear as much as hobbits, perhaps), Moorcock and his animus toward Tolkien's views may be taken with grains of salt by other scholars and fans, but the figurative use of the term *orcs*, in any case, does give credence to the sense that they represent "the mob" more generally.

Tolkien's antipathy toward democracy is well known, and he seemed to view it as little more than a form of "mob-rule," ineluctably tending to destroy the societies in which it takes root. In a letter to Christopher, Tolkien criticizes a politician ("Is he ignorant, or insincere?") for referring to Greece as "the home of democracy," noting that the term "was not in Greek a word of approval but was nearly equivalent to 'mob-rule.'"[32] Elsewhere, Tolkien wrote that he was not a *democrat*, "except that I suppose, to speak in literary terms, we are all equal before the Great Author, *qui deposuit potentes de sede et exaltavit humiles* [who has put down the mighty from their seat and exalted the humble]." Further, as he explained in another letter from 1956, "I am *not* a 'democrat' only because 'humility' and equality are spiritual principles corrupted by the attempt to mechanize and formalize them, with the result that we get not universal smallness and humility, but universal greatness and pride, till some Orc gets hold of a ring of power—and then we get and are getting slavery."[33] The sense that "we get and are getting slavery" vividly displays Tolkien's assessment of the state of both British society and the world at that time, which is to say, the postwar period of relative peace and prosperity.

Tolkien's wartime letters to Christopher offer further perspective on what he considers orkishness in this context, which extends to larger questions of modernity and what would eventually be called *globalization*. Although he insisted upon his patriotism with respect to England, and he absolutely loathed the Hitler regime (in part for its perversion of his beloved Northern mythology and lore, but also because he viewed Hitler as a "ruddy little ignoramus"), Tolkien was ambivalent about the war itself. In his letters to Christopher, it is clear he sees no "victory" that will not also destroy the world and the values he cherishes. Much of the rhetoric about "orcs" applies to the forces of modernization itself, which Tolkien assumes will only accelerate after even the victorious conclusion to the second World War. For example, in a letter dated November 29, 1943, Tolkien writes:

> My political leanings opinions lean more and more to Anarchy (philosophically understood, meaning abolition of control not whiskered men with bombs)—or to "unconstitutional" Monarchy. I would arrest anybody who uses the word State (in any sense other than the inanimate realm of England and its inhabitants, a thing that has neither power, rights nor mind); and after a chance of recantation, execute them if they remained obstinate! [...] Give me a king whose chief interest in life is stamps, railways, or race-horses; and who has the power to sack his Vizier (or whatever you care to call him) if he does not like the cut of his trousers.

Lamenting the "frightful landslide into Theyocracy," Tolkien adds that, in this era, "the special horror of the present world is that the whole damned thing is in one bag. There is nowhere to fly to." The interconnectedness of nations and peoples is part of the problem with the modern world, in Tolkien's view, which leads him to write these somewhat devastating lines: "There is only one bright spot and that is the growing habit of disgruntled men of dynamiting factories and power-stations; I hope that, encouraged now as 'patriotism,' may remain a habit! But it won't do any good, if it is not universal."[34]

Ten days later, he writes of the "terrifying" Americo-cosmopolitanism to come at the war's end, when "they have introduced American sanitation, morale-pep, feminism, and mass production" throughout the world. "At any rate, it will cut down on travel," he jokes, as "[t]here will be nowhere to go. So people will (I opine) go all the faster."[35] Later he worries that "we are attempting to conquer Sauron with the Ring. And we shall (it seems) succeed." However, Tolkien observes that such "success" will merely "breed new Saurons, and slowly turn Men and Elves into Orcs," while acknowledging that "in real life [...] we started out with a great many Orcs on our side."[36] Hence, Tolkien sees the world to come—a more cosmopolitan, international, and technologically advanced world—as a place in which all humans will ineluctably become more and more orc-like.

"The rising tide of 'orquerie'"

Tolkien's view of orcs or orkishness as being inherently linked to problems of modern industrial society arguably does not really mean he de-racializes the anti-orc position. Many of the twentieth-century critiques of modernity, especially among those launched from the right wing of the political spectrum, have associated capitalism and industry with explicitly racist ideologies, notably antisemitism, which frequently—then and now—connects the idea of a "world Jewry" (itself a racist phrase, used to displace particular Jews from whatever society in which they reside) to worldliness, cosmopolitanism, international finance, and commerce more generally. For instance, a notable contemporary of Tolkien, the influential and antisemitic philosopher Martin Heidegger, had written that "[t]he question of world Jewry's role is [...] a *metaphysical question* about the type of being that, itself uprooted [*ungebunden*], can adopt the unrooting of all beings from Being as its 'world-historical' task."[37] As Richard Wolin writes,

> In Heidegger's eyes, "world Jewry's" misdeeds did not hinge on specific wrongs perpetrated by individual Jews or Jewish groups. Instead, as the just quoted remarks confirm, the problem lay with the degenerative tendencies of "world Jewry" *as a race*. Consequently, for Heidegger, the redemption of "world history" from "world Jewry's" disintegrative influences was not primarily *a political question*. Instead, it was a matter of fundamental ontology.[38]

Orcs in Tolkien's fiction also appear as a race that is *ontologically* inferior to the other "humane" races, as Tolkien defines them (i.e., speakers of language),[39] and they are certainly imagined as having a degenerative and disintegrative influence on the societies and communities with which they come into contact.

Although in Tolkien's legendarium it is the dwarves, not the orcs, who are usually associated with Jewish stereotypes, including rather antisemitic ones (and, as Stuart has noted, even Tolkien's apparent "philo–

Semitism is just as racist as anti–Semitism, in that it ranks races hierarchically"),[40] the idea of orcs as a "type of being" that in its very existence poses a threat to the "settled" peoples otherwise secure in their respective homelands is clearly part of fabric of Middle-earth as we come to know it in *The Silmarillion*, *The Hobbit*, and *The Lord of the Rings*. I am certainly not trying to impute Heidegger's ideas to Tolkien, but in the early-to-mid-twentieth century and even continuing into the present, the critique of cosmopolitanism or worldliness from those who would defend traditional values and "organic" communities have almost never *not* also been associated with racialized or overtly racist discourses. Moreover, and needless to say (I hope), the imputation that a certain people do not "belong" in a given place ineluctably invites genocidal rhetoric and ideologies.

One aspect of this is paradoxical: orcs, like other embodiments of a fearsome, racialized "Other," are simultaneously "savage," barbaric, and uncivilized on the one hand, and technologically advanced, industrial, and "modern," on the other. As with chainsawers and motorcyclists, the orcs encountered in Tolkien's real world typically employ technologically advanced, modern machinery, which somehow make primitive, "savage sounds." In Tolkien's writings, orcs are depicted as thoroughly uncivilized, although we are also told that they are superb miners, craftsmen, and inventors of "clever" or "ingenious devices," including "some of the machines that have since troubled the world."[41] Although pictured as almost anarchic and ungovernable, as roaming bands of murderous nomads in some instances, orcs are also in the vanguard of industrialization, it seems, with elaborately complex machine cultures, complete with workshops, smithies, and armories, not to mention military regimentation, leadership, and government. Some of their actual "cities" are mentioned, but they are most frequently depicted as a globally dispersed race, either "holed" up in subterranean enclaves or wandering across lands to which they do not belong.

Not only are these orkish people seen as rootless, lacking the sort of traditional *Heimat* that grants them some geocultural identity formed by the place, but in their nomadism they represent an adulterating element that threatens to undermine the purity of the formerly isolated community, making it part of the impure world beyond. (Notably, orc strongholds like Gundabad or Moria are formerly dwarven kingdoms, which allows for readers to see orcs as invaders who do not belong even to those places that have become their "capital" cities.) In that sense, the bringing together and "mixing" of races is considered part of the baleful effects of, as well as a motor for, burgeoning modernization. Literal miscegenation, "race-mixing," is also deemed an evil, and Tolkien refers to "the interbreeding of Orcs and Men" as Saruman's "wicked deed."[42] Hence, the politically conservative or reactionary embrace of notions of racially homogeneous, "traditional" communities (like the Shire, in fact) that act as enclaves resistant to the maelstrom of modernizing developments elsewhere. In *The Lord of the Rings*, the "squint-eyed Southerner," whom Frodo thinks looks "more than half like a goblin," in Bree represents the coming of "foreign" immigrants and influence to such traditional communities, which is viewed as entirely undesirable and destructive. Later in the novel, it is proven that Saruman and people in his employ have become interested in this region, and their presence requires a "scouring of the Shire" before the War of the Ring can truly be considered at an end. That such a cleansing is not exactly "ethnic," and no orcs are present (only "orc-like" humans), does not mitigate the fact that immigrants and non-hobbits more generally are forcibly removed from the country, and later banned, by order of the King, from entering without leave, even for the purposes of commerce, presumably. This imagined community is clearly defined, in its way, in racial and indeed racist terms, regardless of whether *orcs* have become merely metaphorical. Thus, while Tolkien's own image of the "orc" as a bad person or, rather, a bad *type* of person may transcend merely racial differences, the racism implicit in even his figurative use of the term persists.

Elsewhere Tolkien demonstrates clearly that his idea of orcs is not tied to any specific racial or ethnic character, at least not exclusively, but rather orkishness has to do with class. Specifically, one might note, Tolkien objects to the mentality and attitudes of representatives of the industrial working class, although one suspects that even those workers in more artisanal or agricultural fields may be subject to his disdain, all the more so if they partake of such fruits of modernity as mass media or transit. Above all, Tolkien's conservative political views appear to underwrite his assessment of which sorts of people might be characterized as orcs, and in his generalized critique of the worldly world in the dismal age in which he lived, he found that there would be "nowhere to go to escape the rising tide of 'orquerie.'" So he put it in a 1956 letter to his son Michael, in which he expressed alarm "at the hysteria in this country," predicting that it "may well be a prelude to mob-rule!" Tolkien specifically refers to the public reaction to the Suez Crisis (i.e., the joint invasion of Egypt by Israeli, British, and French forces, which elicited well nigh global condemnation, including from the governments of both the U.S. and Soviet Union), which he worries will lead to the downfall of the Conservative government.[43] But Tolkien adds that his alarm involves "an acutely selfish aspect," namely his fear that a "Socialist government will pretty well reduce me to penury," before complaining about what he imagines as the excessive taxation on his "royalties." Tolkien offers this prospect as the principle reason why many Englishmen are fleeing "this island," before conceding that "soon there will be nowhere to go to escape the rising tide of 'orquerie.'"[44] This last reference makes clear that the orkishness in question has more to do with the politics, in particularly "liberalism" or "socialism," than with racial characteristics (though there may be a correlation between the two, of course), and that social class has far more to do with determining a given person's orkishness than many readers would readily acknowledge.

In the very next line, in fact, Tolkien identifies the type of person he has in mind when he thinks of an "orc," the member of a potential "mob" who represents both socialism and the machine age. In this case, Tolkien merges the image of the orc with a specific individual who had written him a "fan letter":

> Still you never quite know what is going on under the head of an apparent orc on a motor bike. I got a letter from a worker in Siemens factory in Woolwich thanking me for *The Lord of the Rings*, on his own behalf and three others who had read his copy! And it was the "elvish" parts that most interested him.[45]

That Tolkien was able to move so fluidly from his concerns about "mob-rule," "Socialism," taxation (principally, that of his own royalties), and "the rising tide of 'orquerie'" to a reference to a factory worker *as* an orc, capped off by his marveling over such an orc actually reading and enjoying his novel, gives us a rather good sense of the chain of associations that helped to constitute the "orc" in his mind.

The working-class status of his "fan" alone seems to have something to do with Tolkien's view of the man as "an apparent orc on a motor bike," perhaps compounded by the fact that he worked at an urban factory in southeast London. (The Siemens plant in question apparently produced massive cables for telecommunications, so perhaps that too has something to do with it; the corporation for which this English "orc" worked was literally an agent of capitalist globalization and international interconnectedness!) No doubt, following hard on his thoughts about royalties and taxation, Tolkien's exclamation point registers his amused amazement both that an "orc" should admit to sharing his copy of *The Lord of the Rings* with others who properly should have purchased copies of their own, and worse, that the "orc" should think to share this information with the author as if it were a sign of appreciation and respect. Tolkien's bemusement about this "orc" reader's interest in "the 'elvish' parts" also suggests the author's disdain for the creature, who apparently cannot fathom the degree to which this admired author is attacking his own character and way of life. But then, Tolkien was never particularly happy about the constitution of much of his fandom, as when he later said of student protesters who admired his work, "I have no wish to be read, or liked by, or even known by such folk," or elsewhere when he referred to the mostly youthful fandom in the United States as "my deplorable *cultus*."[46] With respect to the latter, Tolkien referred to "the fungus-growth of cults" in reference to "the horrors of the American scene" of his own fandom, adding: "They arise in an entirely different mental climate and soil, polluted and impoverished to a degree only paralleled by the lunatic destruction of the physical lands which Americans inhabit."[47] If anything, the peoples of the United States and perhaps especially his fans there were likely to seem like orcs or to exhibit orkishness, but irrespective of race or nationality, Tolkien identified *people*—regular, ordinary, everyday people, many even among his most ardent admirers—as orcs. Recognizing their humanity did not require him to like or even to tolerate them, of course.[48]

However, quite unlike nearly all the characters in his novels, Tolkien is not totally without compassion. In another missive from January 1945, as the Russian troops were approaching Berlin, Tolkien complains of the "appalling destruction and misery of this war," but worse, of the English "gloating" over the vanquished. "There seem no bowels of mercy or compassion, no imagination, left in this dark, diabolical hour." Recognizing that "the present situation" was "mainly (not solely) created by Germany," Tolkien nevertheless asks, "But why gloat! We were supposed to have reached a stage of civilization in which it might still be necessary to execute a criminal, but not to gloat, or to hang his wife and child by him while the orc-crowd hooted."[49] The reference to "orc-crowd" hooting, of course, refers to those who would revel in the pain and anguish of the defeated enemies. Alas, heroes like Gandalf, Beorn, Legolas, and Gimli are among those most likely to do such "hooting" in *The Hobbit* and *The Lord of the Rings*, mostly at the expense of hunted, captured, and slain orcs. To "hoot" at others' misfortunes is to be orc-like, it seems, and yet in Tolkien's view this appears to be the way of the world at present.

"Seeing good in Carthaginians"

If orcs do represent a baleful consequence of modernity, specifically the degradation of elves and men by technology and industrialization, they must also represent humanity itself as it exists in this our present world. Despite himself, perhaps, Tolkien cannot help but find ways of sympathizing with the orcs, even those who and whose orkishness he abhors, and even when he cannot manage to write characters who can be as sympathetic as himself. Were I to allow myself to speculate upon the matter, I would say that this has to do very much with Tolkien's apprehensions over modern condition in the "age of the machine," and his grudging sense that the very proponents of such "advances" are surely among its most degraded victims. This, along with his own personal experiences with war, as a soldier in one world war and as the father of a soldier in another, undoubtedly affected his sense of those characters and their ilk who largely were written to be soldiers and little more.[50] As Tolkien knew all too well, even as he complained about the "orcs" he encountered in his life and those he imagined elsewhere throughout the world, the "corruption" and "degradation" of men was common, and those affected by it were to be pitied, not demonized.

In another letter to Christopher, dated July 31, 1944, Tolkien again expresses his dismay about the conduct of the war, but notes that he must somehow remain patriotic even in his opposition to the policies of the *patria* in question: "I should have hated the Roman Empire in its day (as I do), and remained a patriotic Roman citizen, while preferring a free Gaul and seeing good in Carthaginians. *Delenda est Carthago*. We hear rather a lot of that nowadays. I was actually taught at school that that was a fine saying."[51] Alas, the Latin phrase attributed to Cato, who argued during the Punic Wars that "Carthage must be destroyed," has come to be a popular battle cry, always invoked by those who claim to speak for righteousness. The annihilation of a people, their country, and their culture might seem like a grand project, particularly in wartime, but Tolkien himself avers that one can still be patriotic while also having respect, sympathy, and pity for one's enemies. If only for the sake of his artistic, even pedantic, commitment to poetic and philosophical consistency, then, Tolkien ultimately cannot have imagined orcs as nothing more than "evil" beings in need of annihilation.

Tolkien became increasingly concerned with the moral, metaphysical, and even political problems raised by his imagined creation and characterization of orcs, as I discuss in the next chapter. As "rational, incarnate beings," orcs cannot be beyond redemption, and from a metaphysical, moral, or even political perspective, they deserve as much humane "fellow-feeling" as we would accord to other victims of repression. As Tolkien puts it, the idea that God would tolerate the corruption of elves or men into orcs "seems no worse theology than the toleration of the calculated dehumanizing of Men by tyrants that goes on today."[52] This line alone is enough to justify the opinion that Tolkien himself saw orcs as "dehumanized" humans, not as inhuman or subhuman monsters. Indeed, given Tolkien's more general sense of the dehumanizing effects of modern, technological, or machine-based societies on all people in the twentieth century, even with respect to those people who do relish their own degradation, one cannot help but think he could find reason to pity the orc.

From the philologist's expert assessment that *orc* is the appropriate name for this creature, to the racial and racist characterization of these beings, and on to the more figurative notion of a generalized social type that becomes somewhat representative of the very age in which we live, Tolkien delivers an image of the orc that is altogether human, perhaps *all-too-human* in its foibles and flaws, but nothing at all like a hell-spawn demon that must be utterly destroyed. Of course, it is not necessary that Tolkien's vision of the orcs align perfectly with that of his imagined elves, who undoubtedly perceive orcs from a vastly different historical, social, and ethical vantage point. But their judgement of a fellow "rational, incarnate being" in Middle-earth says at least as much about the elves and their moral ambiguities as it does about the orcs, and Tolkien himself provides more than enough description, narrative, and background to make readers question the "evil" attributed to the race of orcs. If anything, like Shagrat and Gorbag at the Tower of Cirith Ungol or like Christopher Tolkien stationed in South Africa in 1944, Tolkien recognizes the horrific perplexities that come with serving one's country and its "Big Folk" while trying to stay true to one's self in a world not of one's own making. In this way, as in others, orcs prove themselves to be as "real" as anyone.

CHAPTER 2

Breeding Orcs

*Origins, Revisions, and
Speculations in the "Silmarillion"*

As even casual fans of the author's work probably know, J.R.R. Tolkien's novels *The Hobbit* and *The Lord of the Rings* represent only a small portion of the vaster legends and histories of Middle-earth that he spent most of his life sketching, drafting, revising, and rewriting, material he once referred to as his "private and beloved nonsense."[1] In addition to other works that thematically lie outside this legendarium for the most part—such as *The Father Christmas Letters, Smith of Wooton Major, Farmer Giles of Ham,* or *Leaf by Niggle,* along with his academic writings, translations, and other nonfiction—the large body of notes, drafts, and materials known as the "Silmarillion" constitute the bulk of the author's productivity throughout his lifetime, arguably beginning as early as when he was a teenager but certainly by 1916 and continuing right up to his death in 1973. With the publication of *The Silmarillion* in 1977, readers got a glimpse of this vaster mythological, historical, and geographical world system, as Christopher Tolkien had organized, edited, and arranged his father's work into a relatively, if artificially, coherent narrative of events, from the mythic beginning of the world, through the three "ages" of elvish, human, dwarvish, and eventually hobbitic history leading up to War of the Ring.[2] *The Silmarillion* also provided a glancing theory of the origin of orcs in this world-system, something only hinted at in *The Lord of the Rings*.

In its organization, *The Silmarillion* nicely supplements *The Lord of the Rings*, providing much of the mythic and historical background to the events of that novel. Indeed, Tolkien himself had desperately wanted to published his "Silmarillion" alongside *The Lord of the Rings*, for he viewed them as telling a single, if very long narrative, "Saga of the Jewels and the Rings." In *The Lord of the Rings*, there is a memorable moment when Samwise Gamgee suddenly recognizes that his and Frodo's current adventure is part of the same grand tale as that of Beren and Lúthien, which took place many thousands of years earlier and was recounted in the Quenta Silmarillion (i.e., stories Sam would have presumably heard Bilbo Baggins telling when Sam was a child). Tolkien refers to this as "Sam's disquisition on the seamless web of story," and it is clear that Tolkien viewed the legendarium's many tales as parts of a greater whole.[3] In *The Lord of the Rings*, he included extensive appendices that ameliorated this problem somewhat, but beginning in the 1950s Tolkien resumed his attempt to complete and bring into publishable form his "Silmarillion" project.

One of the key elements of Tolkien's return to the "Silmarillion" materials was the apparent need to revisit the Orkish Question. That is, how to deal with the problematic construction of these enemy creatures, who at once seem so human-like but were treated in cruelly inhumane ways by even the most noble and virtuous characters? As I discussed in the last chapter, Tolkien was troubled by some of the moral, philosophical, and theological implications of the orcs as he had presented them, which led him to think further about their origin stories. For the most part, as Tom Shippey has put it, orcs served as a narrative device, "the infantry of the old war," noting that "the orcs entered Middle-earth originally just because the story needed a continual supply of enemies over whom one need feel no compunction."[4] For some writers, that would be enough, but Tolkien thought very deeply about the history of Middle-earth, its logic (and *theo*-logic, perhaps), and he could not rest easy in the thought that orkish beings could serve as mere cannon-fodder for the narrative itself. As Shippey put it elsewhere, "though he became increasingly concerned over the implications of the Orcs in his story, and tried out several explanations for them, their analogousness to humanity always remained clear."[5]

In this chapter I examine the various ways that Tolkien tried to reconcile his views with respect to this problem. I look specifically at the different ideas he developed to explain the origin and nature of the orcs in his "Silmarillion" project. I begin, perhaps perversely, with the published volume called *The Silmarillion*, since that work is best known and its depiction of orc-origins is thus nearly "canonical." Although from a scholarly perspective one could argue that the vast 12-volume *History of Middle-earth* series, plus the many other posthumously published works curated, edited, and presented by Christopher Tolkien (and now, with *The Nature of Middle-earth*, Carl F. Hostetter), supersede *The Silmarillion*, the latter work was a bestseller and has had a vast influence on the way Tolkien's universe, including its orcs, have been understood.[6] One fundamental "truth" that Tolkien never modified or abandoned is that "evil" cannot create new, living beings; only God—in Tolkien's universe, Eru—can do that, and this has significant ramifications for our conception of the orcs.

Moving backwards from *The Silmarillion*, I delve in the earlier volumes of *The History of Middle-earth*, including materials produced by Tolkien between 1916 and the mid–1930s, such as his unfinished *Book of Lost Tales* and *The Lost Road*. Around 1937, with the publication of *The Hobbit* and the demand for a sequel, Tolkien temporarily abandoned his "Silmarillion" project. He had actually hoped to publish it, first in lieu of a *Hobbit* sequel—"I cannot think of anything more to say about *hobbits* [...] But I have only too much to say, and much already written, about the world into which the hobbit intruded"—and then, when that was rejected, as *part of* the larger *Lord of the Rings*, the latter novel "requiring the *Silmarillion* to be fully legible."[7] When it became clear that this was not going to happen, Tolkien revisited and revised many of his tales, starting in the early 1950s and picking up steam throughout that decade, motivated in part by the success of *The Lord of the Rings* and by the many queries he received about its history and backstory. In the fourth and fifth sections below I examine Tolkien's revisionary writings concerning orcs and their origins from this period, which reveal to degree to which he remained troubled by the nature of these beings.

Mockery of the Elves: The First Appearances of Orcs in The Silmarillion

In brief, *The Silmarillion* offers the background history of Arda (effectively the planet Earth itself) and particularly Middle-earth (the *oikumene* or the world in which we live) extending from Creation itself and bringing the tales up to date with a chapter titled "Of the Rings of Power and the Third Age." *The Silmarillion* begins with the "Ainulindalë" or "The Music of the Ainur," which tells of how the one God-like being, Eru, gathered about him the angelic beings called the Ainur (singular Ainu) and figured forth Arda through song, which involved themes Eru himself propounded and variations provided by the disparate Ainur based on their own gifts and tendencies. Notably, the "third theme" in which were created elves and men, was propounded by Eru alone, and the Ainur had no part in it. Of note also was Melkor, perhaps the very greatest of the Ainur, who wished to dominate and control the creation for himself—that is, the fundamental sin of wishing to "be" God—and whose music thus interfered with and introduced discord into the music, as I discuss below. This is the first appearance of the *Diabolus* in Tolkien, as Melkor will become known as Morgoth, and operate as the Satan-figure in the world until his ultimate defeat at the end of the First Age.

The next section of *The Silmarillion*, the "Valaquenta," enumerates and describes the Valar, a pantheon of elite Ainur (hence god-like beings, but always under the one god, Eru) who descended to Arda and who represent the "powers" of the earth. These include Manwë (the King who delights in wind and air), his wife Varda (Queen of the stars), Ulmo (who rules waters and seas), Aulë (the craftsman), Yavanna (associated with plants and trees), and so on. Melkor is of this order as well, and indeed he is the most powerful, for he shares in or exceeds the skills of nearly all of the others; however, as the Enemy, he is not considered one of the Valar. This section also lists lesser Ainur, known as Maiar, who work with the others and who are often connected with one or another of the Valar (i.e., vassals to their lords, spiritually speaking). Hence, Gandalf will be revealed to have been a Maia "of" Manwë, and Sauron a Maia "of" Aulë before joining Melkor. We also learn that the demon-like balrogs are Maiar who were drawn to Melkor's "splendour in the days of his greatness, and remained in that allegiance down into his darkness."[8]

The vast majority of *The Silmarillion*, comprising roughly 280 of the 366 pages of narrative, is devoted to the *Quenta Silmarillion*, a vast collection of stories connected with the fate of the Silmarils, three fabulous jewels created by the elven craftsman Fëanor. These jewels, their theft by Melkor, and the subsequent quests to reclaim them become the basis for centuries of strife for Fëanor's people and others throughout the remainder of the First Age. *The Silmarillion* also includes a brief history of Númenor titled the "Akallabêth," set in the Second Age and ultimately leading to Atlantis-like destruction of the island nation, the War of the Last Alliance, the defeat of Sauron, and the taking of the One Ring by Isildur. Intriguingly enough, orcs are hardly mentioned at all in the "Akallabêth," although they were certainly a major part of the events of the Second Age; here this lack of visibility is perhaps a sign of the lack of interest in "enemy" cultures, but in any case, the presence of the orcs is not much acknowledged in the text. The word "orcs" occurs most frequently in the *Quenta Silmarillion*, but even there orcs are mostly nameless enemies, threatening from the margins of the tales or seen only as innumerable enemies to be vanquished during large battle scenes.

Indeed, *The Silmarillion* as a whole contains very little information on orcs. In contrast to both *The Hobbit* and *The Lord of the Rings*, for example, there are no scenes in which readers witness orcs talking, and little to no additional information about their lives, cultures, customs, and other activities is provided. They are presented as enemies to be feared, fought, and killed, but little else is known. In most cases, when orcs are mentioned at all, they are faceless hordes, a collective menace or vast army that seems to contain no individual personalities or characters among them. Whereas *The Hobbit* depicts interactions with orcs (or goblins), identifying and even naming individuals such as Golfimbul, the Great Goblin, Bolg, and Azog, and whereas *The Lord of the Rings* features such memorable orc characters as Uglúk, Grishnákh, Shagrat, and Gorbag, *The Silmarillion* does not mention a single *named* orc.[9]

The first reference to orcs in *The Silmarillion* occurs in the chapter titled "Of the Coming of the Elves and the Captivity of Melkor," and it provides readers with what would have been their first clear sense of an origin story for these creatures prior to the publication of the vast, multi-volume *History of Middle-earth* materials in the years to come. Fans of *The Lord of the Rings* would have surmised that orcs were corrupted versions of elves, for Treebeard (Fangorn) had told Merry and Pippin as much: "Trolls are only counterfeits, made by the Enemy in the Great Darkness, in mockery of Ents, as Orcs were of Elves."[10] Hence, it makes sense that the origin story of the orc should appear, however brief and truncated, in the section of *The Silmarillion* in which the elves make their first appearance.

The story goes that when elves, the firstborn "children of Ilúvatar," awoke, Melkor dominated Middle-earth, and the Valar decided to rescue the elves and bring them to Aman to live among them in peace and bliss. The great huntsman of the Valar, Oromë, rode to Middle-earth to summon the elves to Aman, but some were fearful or reluctant, and a number of these fell prey to Melkor. Orcs "appear" in the annals of Middle-earth in this context:

> But of those unhappy ones who were ensnared by Melkor little is known of a certainty. For who of the living has descended into the pits of Utumno, or has explored the darkness of the counsels of Melkor? Yet this is held true by the wise of Eressëa, that all those of the Quendi who came into the hands of Melkor, ere Utumno was broken, were put there in prison, and by slow arts of cruelty were corrupted and enslaved; and thus did Melkor breed the hideous race of the Orcs in envy and mockery of the Elves, of whom they were afterwards the bitterest foes. For the Orcs had life and multiplied after the manner of the Children of Ilúvatar; and naught that had life of its own, nor the semblance of life, could ever Melkor make since his rebellion in the Ainulindalë before the Beginning: so say the wise. And deep in their dark hearts the Orcs loathed the Master whom they served in fear, the maker only of their misery. This it may be was the vilest deed of Melkor, and the most hateful to Ilúvatar.[11]

It is a brief paragraph, and orcs are not mentioned again in *The Silmarillion* for several more chapters, but it gives a great deal of information that is crucial for understanding the nature of orcs, as well as the ethical and political problems associated with the characterizations of orcs in Tolkien's legendarium.

First, as Treebeard had surmised, orcs are "made" from elves. In fact, from this description, orcs *are* elves, only they have been transformed by "slow arts of cruelty" into these distinctive versions. Presumably, this would involve both physical and spiritual torture, such that the material bodies are transformed (hence, the descriptions of orkish body types and skin color) at the same time as their more intangible qualities (e.g., love of beauty, mercy, pity, etc.) would be altered as well. How such dehumanization operates in our own all-too-real world is easily understood, although the fantastic aspect of this would involve the heritability of these traits. Which brings us to a second point: "the Orcs had life and multiplied after the manner of the Children of Ilúvatar," which means they reproduced sexually. Melkor cannot create life *ex nihilo*, and we understand that the progeniture of orcs, like the progeniture of elvish or human children, operates in the usual way. As I will discuss in the next chapter, there is only one time that a "child" orc is mentioned in Tolkien's entire legendarium—Bolg, who is the son of Azog—but considering that no orc women are ever identified as such and only a handful of named orcs appear at all, perhaps this is not too surprising. However, in the famous "Letter to Mrs. Munby" from 1963, Tolkien affirmed that "[t]here must have been orc-women. But in stories that seldom if ever see the Orcs except as soldiers of armies in the service of the evil lords we naturally would not learn much about their lives. Not much was known."[12]

Although the idea that the dark powers were "breeding" orcs is raised throughout Tolkien's writings, the notion seems either metaphorical or ideological (or both), as a way of denigrating the burgeoning populations of one's enemies. More plausibly, Melkor no more "bred" orcs, in the way that a dog-breeder breeds dogs, say, than Harry Truman or Dwight D. Eisenhower "bred" Americans, leading to the "baby boom," the biggest single increase in the population of the United States in its entire history. Similarly, one can imagine the Cold War era discourse about the threat of the burgeoning Chinese or Russian populations. From the perspectives of the elves, which is the perspective of the "Silmarillion" more generally, even a small number of orcs are considered too many. Thus, the otherwise ridiculous idea that the growing population of orcs is part of an intentional, strategic effort on the part of one's adversary must be appealing, all the more so if it further allows you to dehumanize or demonize the enemies.

Indeed, the very next mention of orcs in *The Silmarillion* raises this point. The scene comes after Morgoth had stolen the Silmarils in Valinor and returned to his stronghold of Angband: "And he being freed gathered again all his servants that he could find. [...] There countless became the hosts of his beasts and his demons, and the race of the Orcs, bred long before, grew and multiplied in the bowels of the earth."[13] Notably, by separating "the race of the Orcs" from "the hosts of his beast and his demons," Tolkien affirms that orcs are neither beasts nor demons, but something else "bred long before." It is reasonable to believe that these orcs, like the elves in Beleriand or in Valinor for that matter, were simply raising families and living their lives as best as they could, whether in Melkor's absence or not.

When orcs are mentioned again in *The Silmarillion*, Tolkien speaks to the orcs' life in Beleriand, and again suggests that their origin is fundamentally elven. As Tolkien puts it,

> ere long the evil creatures came even to Beleriand, over passes in the mountains, or up from the south through the dark forests. Wolves there were, or creatures that walked in wolf-shapes, and other fell beings of shadow; and among them were the Orcs, who afterwards wrought ruin in Beleriand: but they were yet few and wary, and did but smell out the ways of the land, awaiting the return of their lord. Whence they came, or what they were, the Elves knew not then, thinking them perhaps to be Avari who had become evil and savage in the wild; in which they guessed all too near, it is said.[14]

The Avari ("unwilling") are those elves who refused the summons of the Valar, and hence never experienced the paradisiacal realm of Aman, never benefited from the tutelage of the god-like beings there, and thus remained "dark elves." Even so, in Tolkien's mythology, as elves they are still "good people" (as he puts it in *The Hobbit*), and thus, merely being among the Avari is not enough to turn one into an orc, presumably. Rather, they are thought to have been victims, taken captive, enslaved, then corrupted to form the beings known as orcs. But again, considering even the elves seem to believe that orcs are essentially victimized and corrupted elves, no sympathy is extended toward the orcs within the narratives.

The only other references to orcs in the *Quenta Silmarillion* (within *The Silmarillion*) have to do with their role as a "host" in warfare, not with their origins or character otherwise. Even so, it is clear that they are formidable, not just as "natural" menaces like wolves, but with respect to their skills in craft, weaponry, and fighting. Thus, the elves of Ossiriand were "no match for the Orcs, who were shod with iron and iron-shielded and bore great spears with broad blades." Formidable as the orkish soldiery sometimes seems, far more often they are depicted as being "slaughtered" and "hunted" even—or especially—when retreating or in flight from their adversaries.[15] Orc speech is mentioned, but no orcs are quoted in *The Silmarillion*. They are not exactly *silenced*, but neither are they given a voice. As the "infantry of the old war," their job is to fight and to die, but even so, their fundamental humanity, complete with the flaws such a state entails, of course, is on display throughout.

"The Shadow that bred them can only mock, it cannot make"

Although Tolkien mooted several possible explanations for the origins of orcs, he seemed to feel strongly that orcs were "fundamentally a race of 'rational, incarnate' creatures," and as such, they could not have been *created* by Melkor, Sauron, or other "dark" powers. Rather, orcs are understood to be *corruptions* of already existing beings, since only the one god, Eru Ilúvatar, could create living creatures and imbue them with being. As Robin A. Reid puts it, "[w]hile Tolkien's own theories about the origins and nature of Orcs changed over time, resulting in inconsistencies and ambiguities, as shown by the material in *Morgoth's Ring* (1993), one unchanging element is that only Eru could create sentient, independent, language-using beings with both *fëa* (souls) and *hröa* (bodies)."[16] Both within Tolkien's fictional world and apart from it, this principle is established. In *The Lord of the Rings*, for example, Frodo explains to Sam that "[t]he Shadow the bred them can only mock, it cannot make: not real new things of its own. I don't think it gave life to the orc, it only ruined them and twisted them; and if they are to live at all, they have to live like other living creatures."[17] Earlier, as cited above, Treebeard identified the type of creature that had been ruined and twisted to make the orcs, that is, the elves. In a letter, Tolkien suggested that Treebeard may not have been correct in this assessment,[18] but for the most part, orcs are understood to be "corruptions" of elves or else men, which Christopher Tolkien concludes was apparently his father's final verdict on the subject, as I discuss below.

The most definitive evidence of this from *The Silmarillion* comes, not in a discussion of orcs or their origins, but in the story of the making of dwarves. In "Of Aulë and Yavanna," we learn that dwarves first came into being when Aulë himself, the great craftsman-god of the Valar, decided to create them. Hence, unlike the "Children of Ilúvatar," elves and men, dwarves are presumed to have a different making altogether, which presumably would mean that dwarves are much less closely related to elves or men than orcs could possibly be. The scene takes place before the "Children" have awakened, and it seems Aulë becomes impatient:

> It is told that in their beginning the Dwarves were made by Aulë in the darkness of Middle-earth; for so greatly did Aulë desire the coming of the Children, to have learners to whom he could teach his lore and his crafts, that he was unwilling to await the fulfilment of the designs of Ilúvatar. And Aulë made the Dwarves even as they still are, because the forms of the Children who were to come were unclear to his mind, and because the power of Melkor was yet over the Earth; and he wished therefore that they should be strong and unyielding. But fearing that the other Valar might blame his work, he wrought

in secret: and he made first the Seven Fathers of the Dwarves in a hall under the mountains in Middle-earth.[19]

Although the story comes from the elvish tradition, this is arguably the genesis-story dwarves in Tolkien's world also believe.

The problem, of course, is that Aulë has no more power to create new living beings than does Melkor. Therefore, "in the very hour that Aulë's work was complete, and he was pleased, and began to instruct the Dwarves in the speech he had devised for them," Eru Ilúvatar himself intervenes, questioning why Aulë should try to do something "which thou knowest is beyond thy power and thy authority?" Ilúvatar reminds him that only he, Eru, has the ability to create new beings, and notes that all Aulë had really done was to produce puppet-like figures for him to play with, who have no "being" apart from Aulë's own thought and hand. Aulë explains why he did this, but abashed by Eru's chastisement, he offers to destroy this work:

> Then Aulë took up a great hammer to smite the Dwarves; and he wept. But Ilúvatar had compassion upon Aulë and his desire, because of his humility; and the Dwarves shrank from the hammer and were afraid, and they bowed down their heads and begged for mercy. And the voice of Ilúvatar said to Aulë: "Thy offer I accepted even as it was made. Dost thou not see that these things have now a life of their own, and speak with their own voices? Else they would not have flinched from thy blow, nor from any command of thy will." Then Aulë cast down his hammer and was glad, and he gave thanks to Ilúvatar, saying: "May Eru bless my work and amend it!"[20]

Eru actually refuses to "amend" the work—perhaps a sign that dwarves are meant to remain inferior to elves and men—but he does grant them their *being*, although he also requires that they "sleep" until after his own "children" have awakened.

What this episode underscores is that even the most powerful beings in Arda, the Valar, cannot create new sentient beings or imbue creatures with life. What this also means, of course, is that anything that in fact *has life*, has it with the tacit if not explicit approval of Ilúvatar. As Tolkien concedes, "by accepting or tolerating their making—necessary to their actual existence—even Orcs would become part of the World, which is God's and ultimately good."[21] Hence, like men and elves (and dwarves), orcs are also the "Children of Ilúvatar."

Hearts of Granite: Early Origin Stories

The Silmarillion is a remarkable work, but it is somewhat misleading to think of it is a book written by Tolkien in that same way that *The Hobbit* or *The Lord of the Rings* are books by Tolkien. To be sure, the material within *The Silmarillion* comes from Tolkien's mind and pen, but in its form, it was effectively rewritten, organized, assembled, and "normalized" by Christopher Tolkien, who put this monumental work together out of disparate notes, drafts, and other materials which his father had produced at various times throughout his life.[22] Some of Tolkien's earliest writings on these subjects go back as far as 1916 at least, and he continued working on them more or less regularly until 1937, when he turned his attention to *The Lord of the Rings*, among other matters, only to take up the "Silmarillion" project again in the 1950s. He would continue to write, revise, and rethink right up to his death in 1973. Christopher himself conceded that "it is certainly debatable whether it was wise to publish in 1977 a version of the primary 'legendarium' standing on its own and claiming, as it were, to be self-explanatory."[23] Hence the desirability of curating, editing, and publishing *Unfinished Tales* (1980) and then the multivolume *History of Middle-earth* (1983–1996), among other later works. Given the tortuous historical development of the legendarium in full, it is not really wise to ask what J.R.R. Tolkien *really* meant, as Verlyn Flieger has observed in her magisterial essay "The Arch and the Keystone," among other writings.[24] However, examining Tolkien's writings and thoughts from different moments in his lifetime can offer some sense of the developments of his ideas over that span. Needless to say, this is true of his ideas about orcs, which unsurprisingly changed over time.

Some of Tolkien's earliest thinking on these matters appears in the form of *The Book of Lost Tales*, begun around 1916–1917 and left incomplete a few years later, as he took up different modes of narrative in order to tell these and other related stories over the next twenty years, among other work he was doing during this period. In these early writings, the nature and character of orcs is not as firmly established, apart from their still being irremediably "evil," but there are intriguing variations in the legends.

First, whereas Tolkien later made quite clear that *goblins* and *orcs* were terms which refer to the same creatures, refusing to distinguish them as different orders of being—even ones so similar as elves and men, for instance—in the early writings they do seem to represent somewhat distinct races. For instance, in an early reference to dangers faced by Beren, "more fearsome still were the wandering bands of the goblins and the Orcs—foul broodlings of Melko who fared abroad doing evil work." At other times, the terms seem to be used interchangeably, as when a character declares, "It is Melko's goblins, the Orcs of the hills."[25] Another fascinating idea is that of the "false-fairies," the Kaukareldar, to which I referred in Chapter 1. These were creatures made by Melko (i.e., Melkor) in order to further sow dissension and distrust between elves and men after the Battle of Unnumbered Tears. Melko "fashioned the false-fairies or Kaukareldar in their likeness, and these deceived and betrayed men." Christopher Tolkien notes that "(Gongs)" appears in the text at that point, thus suggesting (albeit parenthetically) that a such false-fairies are themselves "Gongs." Christopher then points out that *Gongs* "might be thought to be a name for the *Kaukareldar*," but "in the Gnomish word-list *Gong* is defined as 'one of the tribe of the Orcs, a goblin.'"[26] Hence, the connection between "false" elves and orcs or goblins is made, and perhaps this is already an allusion to the later idea that orcs are in fact mutilated and "corrupted" elves.

However, famously, these earlier versions of the "Silmarillion" proffered a rather different origin story for the orcs, creatures who are referred to as "the children of Melko." In a fascinating passage from *The Book of Lost Tales, Part II*, Tolkien's narrator marvels at the idea that orcs could be confused with elves (the Noldor) by men, before describing the "true" nature and origins of such creatures:

> How it ever came that among Men the Noldoli have been confused with Orcs who are Melko's goblins, I know not, unless it be that certain of the Noldoli were twisted to the evil of Melko and mingled among these Orcs, for all that race were bred by Melko of the subterranean heats and slime. Their hearts were of granite and their bodies deformed; foul their faces which smiled not, but their laugh was the clash of metal, and to nothing were they more fain than to aid in the basest of the purposes of Melko. The greatest hatred was between them and the Noldoli, who named them Glamhoth, or the folk of dreadful hate.[27]

This is the *locus classicus* for the view that orcs were fashioned from the materials of the earth itself, "subterranean heats and slime," which suggests that they are not corrupted elves, men, or any other sort of pre-existing being. Christopher Tolkien observes that "[t]here is no trace yet of the later view" that Melkor could not create new life, only corrupt others. However, Christopher also notes that "a first hint of this idea of their origins" might lie in the passage's words about certain Noldoli being "twisted to the evil of Melko" and "mingling among these Orcs," but he concedes that "this is as it stands quite distinct from the idea that the Orcs were actually bred from Elves."[28]

Fascinating as is the idea of orcs as chthonic beings, made of the substance of the underworldly world itself and conjured into existence by the power of Melkor's craft, I am not certain that this passage establishes it. The fact that it begins by highlighting the ostensible similarities between Noldorian elves and orcs, at least to the untrained eye, suggests that these two beings are remarkably alike. That the narrator tries to explain this by imagining that some of the Noldoli could turn orc-like by "mingling" among orcs, even without any sort of torturous mutilation or interbreeding—unless that might also be implied by the use of the word *mingling*—further suggests a connection between the elves and the orcs. Indeed, in the same text, just a few pages later, there is a description of the "black elf" Meglin, whose sign was "a sable Mole," which explicitly raises the question of interbreeding: "Less fair he was than most of this goodly folk, swart and of none too kindly mood, so that he won small love, and whispers there were that he had Orc's blood in his veins, but I know not how this could be true."[29] But if being "less fair," "swart," and "none too kindly" is enough to generate such rumors about an elf, then how very different can orcs and elves actually be?

In a scene written at around the same time, Tolkien depicts a character encountering orcs for the first time. Unsurprisingly, perhaps, she "mistakes" them for humans. As Tolkien writes,

> Now on a time in an opening in the wood she descried a campment as it were of Men, and creeping nigh by reason of hunger to espy it she saw that they were creatures of squat and unlovely stature that dwelt there, and most evil faces had they, and their voices and their laughter was as the clash of stone and metal. Armed they were with curved sword and bows of horn, and she was possessed with fear as she looked upon them, although she knew not that they were Orcs, for never had she seen those evil ones before.[30]

Here again, the physical distinction between orcs and men seems negligible, a matter of aesthetics as much as anything (i.e., being "unlovely" or having unmelodious voices), hardly likely to cause a confusion between creatures made of slime and others made of flesh and bone. Even where the narrator would have us imagine these orcs as being utterly otherworldly and inhuman, they are clearly still humane enough to "pass" for human to those who encounter them. In fact, being ugly and having harsh-sounding voices, or perhaps just appearing exotic and using a foreign language, may well be signs that these orcs *are* simply humans (or elves), if strange and seemingly cruel ones, although such characteristics not uncommon among humans either.

I am inclined to think that the notion of orcs being "bred by Melko of the subterranean heats and slime" must be seen, even at this early stage of Tolkien's thinking, as symbolic or metaphorical. That is, by associating them with such underground unpleasantness, while at the same time explicitly observing their physical similarities to elves, the narrator underscores the "spiritual" differences between orcs and elves, which had far more relevance in the moral universe as *differentiae specificae* than some of the more superficial, physical or material differences. Just has having a heart made of granite and a laugh whose sound resembles the clash of metal are obviously metaphorical, I suspect that the idea of orc bodies being made from subterranean heat and slime has to be figurative as well. Their mortality alone attests to this, as so many of these stone-hearted creatures get killed by heroes with mere swords or arrows, weapons not generally known for piercing granite. Hard-hearted is a common enough saying in our own world, naturally, so it makes some sense the elves in Tolkien's mythology might imagine their enemies as having such attributes.

Perhaps the most bizarre connection, one that Tolkien would certainly wish to disavow, was the potential equation of *gnomes*, his original name for the Noldor, who are the most skilled of the elves, and *goblins*. Dimitra Fimi, in *Tolkien, Race, and Cultural History: From Fairies to Hobbits*, asserts that "it is possible that 'gnomes' and 'goblins' were originally conceived at the same beings, since the interchangeable use of both terms (together with 'leprechauns') in Tolkien's 1915 poem *Goblin Feet* supports this idea" (46). Etymologically, Fimi notes, the term *gnome* derives from a Greek root meaning "earth-dweller" (47), which could then tie the subterranean-seeming "goblins" to later conceptions of dwarves and even hobbits.[31] However much Tolkien would object to this sort of kinship later on, it seems likely that these philological and mythological associations would have informed his early thinking about orcs and their relations to other creatures in his legendarium.

Note also that the origin story involving subterranean slime and whatnot suggests that the orcs are chthonic beings, creatures *of the earth*, and thus of Creation. If it is true, as Tolkien famously put it, that "Morgoth's Ring" is Arda itself, then the beings of Arda—quite literally *of* Arda, which is to say *of* the substance of the planet—are the most "natural" beings of all, ones that almost by definition *belong* to this Middle-earth and thus have any and all of the rights to life, liberty, and the pursuit of happiness as one can imagine for such a world. Even the very early version of the orc-origin theories, then, suggests some *natural* connection to the world and emphasize the orkish resemblance to men and elves.

"Orcs are not Elvish": Revisionist Visions in Tolkien's Later Writings

In a text dating from roughly 1959 titled "Orcs," one that Christopher Tolkien refers to as "very much a record of 'thinking with the pen,'" J.R.R. Tolkien begins: "Their nature and origin require more thought. They are not easy to work into the theory and system."[32] That Tolkien even felt the need to "think with the pen" on this matter shows the degree to which the Orkish Question was vexing him. This was undoubtedly, in part, occasioned by the very earnest inquiries he received about this or that matter in the years following the publication of *The Lord of the Rings*, and as many of the letters from the 1950s reveal, the ethical, theological, and even narratological problems raised by the orcs of his tales were worth considering at some length, at least in Tolkien's view. Moreover, as he was endeavoring to bring his "Silmarillion" project at last into print, Tolkien certainly hoped to make some of these issues more clear, bringing greater consistency to his at times wildly divergent positions and resolving some of the more difficult philosophical quandaries raised by the existence and characterizations of orcs.

There are a number of considerations involved in Tolkien's revisionary approach to orkish origins, but it seems that a key one was his increasing reluctance to imagine orcs as corrupted *elves*. As Fimi has put it, "the thought that the hideous and malicious Orcs were once Elves— the 'highest' beings of Middle-earth—became increasingly unbearable to Tolkien."[33] Such an attitude may be summed up emphatically by a marginal note Christopher found among his father's drafts from the late 1950s, which read, simply: "Alter this. Orcs are not Elvish."[34] The paragraph of the amanuensis typescript next to which this was note was scrawled contains information somewhat similar to that in *The Silmarillion* regarding the first appearance of the orcs. This section apparently replaced another handwritten interpolation of the typescript, which read in part:

> Melkor was on the watch, and his spies were many. And it is thought that lurking near his servants had led astray some of the Quendi that ventured afield, and they took them as captives to Utumno, and there enslaved them. Of these slaves it is held came the Orkor that were afterward chief foes of the Eldar.[35]

Tolkien's desire to distance his almost always "good people," the elves, from the "hideous race" of the orcs might be understandable, even if "corruption of the good" is very much the traditional view of "evil," after all, but in any event Tolkien began imagining alternative scenarios for the origins of orcs in the wake of the publication of *The Lord of the Rings*.

In a section in the *History of Middle-earth* titled "Myths Transformed," Christopher Tolkien includes a number of different theories of the origins of orcs that his father entertained and drafted in the 1950s and early 1960s. As Christopher observes, "these writings can be read as the record of prolonged interior debate."[36] The "thoughts" of the "Orcs" text suggest the logical problems Tolkien was grappling with. After citing the example of Aulë and the Dwarves, Tolkien reiterates that "only Eru could make creatures with independent wills, and with reasoning powers," but notes that "Orcs seem to have both: they can try to cheat Morgoth

2. Breeding Orcs 53

/ Sauron, rebel against him, or criticize him." From this Tolkien surmises (but adds a question-mark) that orcs "must be *corruptions* of something pre-existing." Thinking of the dwarvish-origin story again, Tolkien notes that Eru would not "sanction" the work of Melkor as he had done for Aulë, but adds parenthetically "[n]ot unless Orcs were ultimately remediable, or could be amended and 'saved'?" Tolkien then reasons that even if Melkor might be able to "utterly corrupt and ruin individuals," it would not be possible to pervert "a whole people, or group of peoples," all the more so if we were to imagine "*making that state heritable*," to which he amended a later note: "This latter must (if a fact) be an act of Eru." Tolkien concludes, "In that case Elves, as a source, are very unlikely. And are Orcs 'immortal,' in the Elvish sense?"[37] Such an idea seems unconscionable for Tolkien.

In the next section he proffers the notion that "talking beasts and birds with reasoning and speech […] have been rather lightly adopted from less 'serious' mythologies, but play a part which cannot now be excised," which indicates that Tolkien wanted to consider the possibility that orcs *were* simply beasts, enemy-animals like wolves or bats who thus would not be imagined as having souls or run the risk of being dehumanized. But Tolkien is obviously not comfortable with the idea that orcs are simply animals, for his "thoughts" then turn to the ways that some "spirits" had taken on the *form* of animals or "arrayed themselves" as such, as with Huan, a Maia in the shape of a hound (although Tolkien was not sure of that either, later affirming that Huan was merely a dog, albeit the greatest of them).[38] Since Melkor had corrupted many spirits to his own side, some great like Sauron and the balrogs, then perhaps the "least" such spirits "could have been primitive (and much more powerful and perilous) Orcs; but by practising when embodied procreation (cf. Melian) [become] more and more earthbound, unable to return to spirit-state (even demon-form), until release by death (killing), and they would dwindle in force."[39] If that is possible, Tolkien reasons that, when these spirits are released for their corporal or incarnate raiment—like Sauron after the destruction of the Ring—they would be "reduced to impotence, infinitely recessive," but then he parenthetically asks "or would not a very dwindled dead Orc-state be a poltergeist?"

Perhaps the word *Geist* nudges his mind in this direction, but in the following brief paragraph Tolkien revisits the problem of the "soul": "But again—would Eru provide *fëar* for such creatures? For the Eagles, etc. perhaps. But not for Orcs." The term *fëa* (plural *fëar*) refers to the spirit or "soul" of a being, whose physical manifestation or flesh is the *hröa*. Tolkien then observes that Melkor's "corrupting power" would always start "at a moral or theological level," such that the creature "became soon corrupted in all parts of its being, the *fëa* dragging down the *hröa* in its descent into Morgothism." (Curiously, in the next line, Tolkien mentions the putative but misunderstood "immortality" of the elves: "they in fact had enormously long lives, and were themselves physically 'wearing out,' and suffering a slow progressive weakening of their bodies.") Rather hastily, in my view, Tolkien sums up, "I think it must be assumed that 'talking' is not necessarily a sign of the possession of a 'rational soul' or *fëa*," before offering the following astonishing verdict:

> The Orcs were *beasts* of humanized shape (to mock Men and Elves) deliberately perverted / converted into a more close resemblance to Men. Their "talking" was really reeling off "records" set in them by Melkor. Even their rebellious critical words—he knew about them. Melkor taught them speech and as they bred they inherited this; and they had just as much independence as have, say, dogs or horses of their human masters. This talking was largely echoic [cf. parrots].[40]

The notion that the sort of conversations among orcs that readers of Tolkien's novels had witnessed could be the discourse of parrot-like "echoing" seems ridiculous, and it is hard to believe that Tolkien himself could have believed this. In fact, it is difficult to imagine how a theory of orcs as mere *beasts*—without souls, language, reason, willpower, and so on—would square with what Tolkien had already published in *The Hobbit* and *The Lord of the Rings*, and it would certainly require a great deal of imaginative effort to see the dialogue and actions of orcs in those books as being the equivalent of those found in parrots, dogs, or horses, or even more bizarrely, as being somehow prerecorded messages installed many millennia earlier by Melkor.

Tolkien seems to have bewildered himself slightly in his logic here, as he contradicts these ideas just afterwards, when observing that "it remains therefore terribly possible there was an Elvish strain in the Orcs. These may then have even been mated with beasts (sterile!)—and later Men."[41] Such an aetiology for orkishness is wildly fantastic and possibly a bit lurid as well, for it would involve picturing corrupted elves having sex with animals, somehow then producing offspring that would mate with men, which actions would in turn ultimately produce orcs who could then presumably reproduce sexually not only amongst themselves, but perhaps also with other elves, men, and beasts as well. The sheer weirdness of Tolkien's thinking here is a testament to the vexatious nature of the orc problem he had created!

In a related note written in pencil, the dating of whose composition Christopher does not hazard a guess, Tolkien wrote that,

> Since Melkor could not create an independent species, but had immense powers of corruption and distortion of those that came into his power, it is

probable that these *Orks* had a mixed origin. Most of them plainly (and biologically) were corruptions of Elves (and probably later also of Men). But always among them (as special servants and spies of Melkor, and as leaders) there must have been numerous corrupted minor spirits who assumed similar bodily shapes. [These would exhibit terrifying and demonic characters.]

There is even the suggestion that "the Elves would have classed the creatures called 'trolls' (in *The Hobbit* and *The Lord of the Rings*) as Orcs—in character and origin—but they were larger and slower," although Tolkien does not validate this surmise, adding, "[i]t would seem evident that they were corruptions of primitive human types."[42]

I think this line of thinking is important, partly because Tolkien here reminds us again that we are getting most of what we know about the orcs from a strongly biased, mostly ignorant, and certainly limited perspective, that of the elves themselves (or of those influenced by the elvish point of view). Perhaps then elves would be more likely to find that orcs are elf-like, only far worse in moral character, thus positing a racialist and racist theory without necessarily acknowledging it as such.[43] Such a perspective might also lead some to conclude that especially powerful orcs, ones too big, strong, or fierce to be "elvish" in origin, must seem like demons or some other such otherworldly force made incarnate. That elves and their allies could see many different possibilities for imagining, and demonizing, their enemies seems quite plausible.

In a more polished essay on the genesis of orcs, likely written a bit later than the thought-experiment discussed above (e.g., Christopher estimates that "it belongs to 1959–60"), Tolkien appears to have retreated from some of the more outlandish theories and adopted an origin story that would emphasize the more human, if still degraded, character of these creatures. Tolkien posits that, in the Elder Days (i.e., in the First Age, prior to the ultimate defeat of Morgoth), some "evil spirits" or Maiar "whose business it was to direct the Orcs often took Orkish shapes, though they were greater and more terrible," and those orcs we encounter later "were neither spirits nor phantoms, but living creatures, capable of speech and of some crafts and organization, or at least capable of learning such things from higher creatures or their Master." Perhaps to explain their numbers, Tolkien notes that "[t]hey bred and multiplied rapidly, whenever left undisturbed."[44] It is remarkable that here the orcs *themselves* breed and multiply, rather than being passively "bred" by dark powers; being "left undisturbed" undoubtedly helps in that process.

As for their origin, Tolkien acknowledges the problem of chronology, specifically wondering whether orcs could have existed before the emergence of either elves or men, which seems impossible, given his other thoughts on the matter.[45] Tolkien again mentions the scenario of the dwarves, pointing out that if Melkor had attempted "to make creatures of his own in imitation or mockery of the Incarnates, he would, like Aulë, only have succeeded in making puppets," adding somewhat definitively: "But the Orcs were not of this kind." For the most part, as Tolkien makes clear in this text, orcs were much like elves or men, "capable of acting on their own," continuing "to live and breed and to carry on their business," having "languages of their own" and speaking "in various tongues," needing "food and drink," and subject to death and disease. The orcs as described in this section appear almost entirely to be human, even if their cultures, norms, or personalities are considered odious.[46]

Tolkien takes this a step further by making "a cogent point, though horrible to relate." He asserts that "[i]t became clear in time that Men could under the domination of Morgoth or his agents in a few generations be reduced almost to the Orc-level of mind and habits; and then they would or could be made to mate with Orcs, producing new breeds, often larger and more cunning." Tolkien affirms that Saruman "rediscovered" this, "and in his lust for mastery committed this, his wickedest deed: the interbreeding of Orcs and Men, producing both Men-orcs large and cunning, and Orc-men treacherous and vile."[47] Leaving aside for the moment the spurious distinction between Men-orcs and Orc-men—perhaps this is supposed to be an indication of the race of the female or mother in this process?—and given the already stated position that orcs (and men) are perfectly capable of "breeding" on their own, without Melkor's or Saruman's instruction, this "wicked" deed seems little other than the more ordinary form of procreative sexual activity, calumnized as inappropriate miscegenation, but presumably carried out with the consent of the parties in question.

Needless to say, but the tendentious idea that race-mixing is somehow wicked is itself rather straightforwardly racist or bigoted. If orcs be imagined as a lesser "race" than men, but nevertheless remain capable of sexual reproduction together, then the objection to their "interbreeding" can only be rooted in racist beliefs. And, of course, considering Tolkien's own personal descriptions of the orc's appearance (i.e., the "least lovely Mongol type") and the multiple references to physiognomy and phenotypes in Tolkien's writings (viz. the "squint-eyed Southerner" who looks "more than half like a goblin" in *The Lord of the Rings*), the specter of race-mixing—perhaps especially the mixing of (northern) European and (eastern) Asian ethnicities—is invoked almost directly in Tolkien's legendarium. The implicit (or explicit) racial bigotry associated with this line of thinking does have a significant logical consequence, however. The very idea entertained by Tolkien in this passage from *Morgoth's Ring*, that is, that humans can become more orc-like and actively choose to marry and mate with orcs, emphatically affirms the view that orcs *are* humans.

The connection between orcs and men (as opposed to elves) is underscored later in the same essay, where it is mooted that, while Melkor came up with the idea for breeding orcs, mostly motivated by a desire to defile "the Children" and "blasphemously" mock the designs of Eru Ilúvatar, it was Sauron who saw to "the details of the accomplishment of this wickedness." Tolkien concludes that "the conception in mind of the Orcs may go back far into the night of Melkor's thought," but "the beginning of their actual breeding must await the awakening of Men." From this, Christopher concludes, that "this, then, as it may appear, was my father's final view of the question: Orcs were bred from Men."[48]

"The whole of 'Middle-earth' was Morgoth's Ring"

Beyond the question of whether orcs derived from elves, men, or some other form, there is a fascinating, more global argument that bears on these matters. In a document included in "Myths Transformed," most likely composed in the late 1950s, Tolkien sketches a revised portrait of Melkor (also known as Morgoth) that has some bearing on the nature of orcs. Tolkien writes that "Melkor must be made *far more powerful* in original nature," so much so that "he must *not* be able to be controlled or 'chained' by all the Valar combined." But in the process of exerting dominance over other creatures and throughout the world itself, Melkor becomes diminished in his "personal force," or as Tolkien puts it, "he is 'dispersed.'" As Tolkien further explains in a footnote: "One of the reasons for his self-weakening is that he has given to his 'creatures,' Orcs, Balrogs, etc. *power of recuperation and multiplication*. So that they will gather again without further specific orders. Part of his native creative power has gone out into making an independent evil growth out of his control."[49] Hence, presumably, as "the children of Melkor," orcs were imbued with some measure of Melkor's own power, what we might call his "life-force." Such a theory would also allow Tolkien to accept more readily the *inherent* "evil" in the orcs' natures, which essentially partake of the original diabolic power of this mythology's Satan figure.

Furthermore, it was not just that Melkor imbued his "creatures" with some of his own power, thus diminishing that which remained with his "person." In his lust to dominate the entirety of Arda, he effectively disseminated his power throughout the world. "But," as Tolkien writes, "in this way Morgoth lost (or exchanged, or transmuted) the greater part of his original 'angelic powers,' of mind and spirit, while gaining a terrible grip on the physical world." Indeed, this helps to explain why the Valar were reluctant to battle Morgoth directly, since they knew such a confrontation would inevitably entail the destruction of so much of the substance of the earth itself. To defeat Morgoth in open war would almost be tantamount to be destroying the planet, as the War of Wrath and its aftermath, an almost literally apocalyptic or Ragnarök-like end-of-the-world scenario, ultimately proved to be the case. As Tolkien put it, "Manwë's task and problem was much more difficult than Gandalf's. Sauron's, relatively smaller, power was *concentrated*; Morgoth's vast power was *disseminated*. The whole of 'Middle-earth' was Morgoth's Ring." Hence, whereas Sauron could be defeated through the destruction of a device into which he had concentrated so much of his own power, the eradication of Morgoth "required the complete disintegration of the 'matter' of Arda."[50]

As Tolkien explains further, "Sauron's power was not (for example) in gold as such, but in a particular form or shape made of a particular portion of total gold. Morgoth's power was disseminated throughout Gold, if nowhere absolute (for he did not create Gold) it was nowhere absent." Tolkien observes that "it was this Morgoth-element in matter" that allow subsequent "evils" like Sauron's manipulation of this matter through "magic" to occur, but then this is also to say that *everything* in Arda, all physical matter at least, which includes the incarnate forms of even spiritual beings, is "tainted" by Melkor. Orcs, being creatures of this world, are themselves therefore tainted by Melkor's diabolic life-force, but this must mean that, in some respects, they are no more tainted by such evil than any other terrestrial creatures.

Tolkien concludes this discussion of Melkor or Morgoth with a direct reference to orcs, although even here he seems to be questioning his own theories. Revisiting once more the idea that evil cannot create, only corrupt, Tolkien goes all the way back to the original creation of the world in imagining Melkor's "creative" powers or lack thereof. As he writes,

> Evil is fissiparous. But itself barren. Melkor could not "beget," or have any spouse (though he attempted to ravish Arien, this was to destroy and "distain" her, not to beget fiery offspring). Out of the *discords* of the Music—sc. not directly out of either of the themes, Eru's or Melkor's, but of their dissonance with regard one to another—evil things appeared in Arda, which did not descend from any direct plan or vision of Melkor: they were *not* "his children"; and therefore, since all evil hates, hated him too. The progeniture of things was corrupted. Hence *Orcs*? Part of the Elf-Man idea gone wrong. Though as for Orcs, the Eldar believed Morgoth had actually "bred" them by capturing Men (and Elves) early and increasing to the utmost any corrupt tendencies they possessed.[51]

By referring to the original Music of the Ainur, Tolkien suggests a fascinating variation on the orkish origin story. This example would suggest that, like *snow*, orcs were the result of the discordant music introduced by Melkor at the very beginning of Creation.

Snow? Yes. In the "Ainulindalë," Eru Ilúvatar reveals that the disruptions of Melkor's voice in the Music was ultimately part of the "plan" all along. For instance, far from destroying the marvelous waterworks that Ulmo's singing had brought into being, Melkor's injection of "bitter cold immoderate" had only helped to produce the beauty of "snow, and the cunning work of frost," not to mention Melkor's part in helping to produce "the height and glory of the clouds." This prompts Ulmo to declare: "Truly, Water is become now fairer than my heart imagined, neither had my secret thought conceived of the snowflake, nor in all my music was contained the falling of rain."[52] In other words, the seemingly "evil" purposes of Melkor prove, in the fullness of time and in light of what may well be some vaster "divine" plan (a.k.a. History), to have results that are not only less evil than anticipated, but that are positively "good." When added to Ulmo's seas, rivers, lakes, and fountains, Melkor's intense cold produced snow and his intense heat produced clouds, mists, and rainfall, all things that Ulmo and the others, not to mention Eru himself, acknowledge to be *good*. If orcs are simply the result of Melkor's discord affecting the musical formation or ideation of elves and men, then they too might be variations of those things that could be recognized as good. In any case, as Tolkien had stated in a 1954 letter, "by accepting or tolerating their making—necessary to their actual existence—even Orcs would become part of the World, which is God's and ultimately good."[53] So, perhaps, orcs are like snowflakes?

There are two problems with this model that arise at once, at least as far as Tolkien's legendarium goes. First, it would suggest that at the very outset of their existence orcs *cannot* be seen as evil or even merely bad, at least no more so than snow or rainfall. This would only complicate further the moral quandaries Tolkien and his readers might have felt about the orcs. To say that the "progeniture of things was corrupted" is to admit that any corruption happened prior to actual existence, which means it was "accepted" or "tolerated" by God in the first place, and thus could not be judged to be a bad thing. Second, there is a more technical matter: as many Tolkien fans would quickly point out, in the "Ainulindalë," Melkor was not involved in the third "theme" by which Ilúvatar figured forth the elves and men. Indeed, "the Children of Ilúvatar were conceived by him alone [...], and none of the Ainur had part in their making."[54] Therefore, Melkor's discordant music would not have affected them as it did when water turned to snow. If orcs are part of "the Elf-Man idea gone wrong," then it seems unlikely even in the transformed mythology that this would have occurred at the world's genesis. Presumably, elves and men had to come first, then be *made* to go wrong, which Tolkien alludes to in the final sentence of the paragraph quoted above.

That line is itself revealing, as it adds another element to the idea that orcs are "corruptions" of elves or men. Tolkien's decision to place the word *bred* within quotation marks indicates that he does not necessarily view the propagation of their species as a matter of animal husbandry, but rather sees this term as one that is possibly being misused or used only figuratively by the Eldar. Moreover, Tolkien suggests that what is imagined to be a form of "breeding" actually involves something quite different: taking men (or elves) and "increasing to the utmost any corrupt tendencies they possessed." In other words, Melkor, Sauron, or any other "Dark Lord" did not imbue these beings with some evil, corrupting their otherwise pure selves, but rather Morgoth apparently just "increased" the tendencies already existing in the humane beings. Orcs are thus not subhuman or inhuman, but rather—to use the Nietzschean expression once again—*all-too-human*. They are creatures whose "natural" corrupt tendencies have been increased to the utmost, which is to say that they are not unlike their fellow elves and men, except perhaps as a matter of degree. In many of their ways, Tolkien here puts forth, orcs may be "worse" than elves and men, but they are not distinct types of living beings, no more so than a "bad man" is less human than a "good man," at any rate.

In the same 1954 letter quoted above, Tolkien explains that he has represented the orcs "as pre-existing real beings on whom the Dark Lord has exerted his full power in remodelling and corrupting them, not making them." This is a crucial matter for Tolkien, and it suggests that Morgoth's (or Sauron's) "full power" does not involve any sort of *ex nihilo* creation but rather the enhancing or catalyzing of tendencies already present in the substance being "corrupted." As Tolkien writes in the next line, "[t]hat God would 'tolerate' that, seems no worse theology than the toleration of the calculated dehumanizing of Men by tyrants that goes on today."[55] We are well aware of the ways that powerful humans, governments, and societies can dehumanize people within their domains or spheres of influence, just as we are aware of the ways that, for example in wartime, even supposedly "good" people are capable of demonizing their enemies.[56] This awareness might serve as the basis for sympathy with, rather than for condemnation of, those so dehumanized or demonized, which in turn might spark some desire to aid in improving their condition.

From a strictly theological standpoint, within Christian belief at least, the idea that Middle-earth—the realm in which we live, our *oikumene*—is tainted by some original Satan figure makes sense. This is not only the Vale of Tears, after all, but it is to be contrasted with the Kingdom of Heaven. When the medieval theologian Hugh of Saint Victor in his

Didascalicon urged the faithful to move beyond seeing one's native land as sweet, then to move beyond feeling at home in all lands equally, so that they might eventually become "perfect" by viewing the entire world as a foreign land (*mundus totus exilium est*), he was emphasizing the need to free oneself from love of this worldly world. But, as Tolkien's contemporary and fellow philologist Erich Auerbach affirmed in his essay on "The Philology of World Literature," *mundus totus exilium est* is a good motto "for anyone who desires to secure a proper love *for* the world."[57] If orcs are fundamentally *of* this world, inhabitants of the planet that is itself "Morgoth's Ring," then so are we, and perhaps we need to recognize our fellowship as earthlings here. This is not Tolkien's view, of course, but it is clear that in his own philosophical musings on the mythology, he has made such a "worldly" perspective available to us.

CHAPTER 3

Great Goblins
Orcs in The Hobbit

Although Tolkien had for years included orcs in their vast, nameless and faceless hordes of enemy troops in his "Silmarillion" materials, the "History of the Gnomes" and other writings comprising his "private, beloved nonsense," the first appearance of orcs in his published work is made in *The Hobbit*, where they are for the most part referred to as *goblins*.[1] There, as elsewhere, orcs represent the implacable enemy of the "good" characters, but in *The Hobbit* there are references that offer more nuance and complexity to the characterization of this race. Indeed, one scene even provides a glimpse, albeit a very brief one, into the culture, history, worldview, and moral perspective of an orc community, while another moment indicates familial loyalty and honor, perhaps. There are even *named* orcs in *The Hobbit*, which means that readers are encouraged, if only momentarily, to see such orcs as individual persons rather than as indistinguishable or interchangeable components of the faceless masses.

The publication of *The Hobbit* transformed Tolkien's legendarium in ways that he was not always happy about. Tolkien was undoubtedly pleased with the success of the story itself, but was not initially interested in writing a sequel, telling his publisher, "I am a little perturbed. I cannot think of anything more to say about *hobbits*. [...] But I have only too much to say, and much already written, about the world into which the hobbit intruded."[2] This *intrusion* necessarily changed Tolkien's world, for now instead of unpublished notes and drafts that could be reworked, there was a public record of, along with a large audience for, the events, descriptions, and peoples of Middle-earth. As Dimitra Fimi has put it, "[w]ith *The Hobbit*, some elements of his legendarium became fixed because they were published and therefore available to the public as authoritative facts from the author." Fimi characterizes the results of this "real world" event as helping to instigate the movement "in his creative writing from a 'mythical' to a 'historical' mode."[3] This also means that the creatures inhabiting

Tolkien's universe become less legendary or mythical, and more historical in their own right. That makes it far more difficult to see orcs or goblins as fantastic demons or monsters, or as allegorical representations of "evil." Now they, like the elves, men, and dwarves, must have their own history, complete with all that entails: languages, cultures, communities, and so on. The early "Silmarillion" texts had rendered orcs as a mostly one-dimensional, homogeneous mass of devilish monsters, but with *The Hobbit*, orcs are definitively and colorfully depicted as people, if also as "bad" people.

"Goblins, hobgoblins, and orcs of the worst description"

The use of the word *goblin* in *The Hobbit*, especially after the publication of *The Lord of the Rings* with its far more common use of the term *orc*, has led to some confusion among Tolkien's readers. In this chapter, I use the terms *goblin* and *orc* somewhat interchangeably, but the word "orc"—which does appear a couple of times in *The Hobbit*—is effectively a synonym of "goblin," the term used throughout that novel to designate this kind of creature. This terminological choice has led some casual Tolkien fans to insist that goblins are a different race or species from orcs. Hence, a goblin might be imagined as being a distinct monster, nearly as different from an orc as an orc would be to a troll, for example. The popular Peter Jackson-directed film adaptations of these novels has helped to reinforce the idea that orcs and goblins, not to mention "Uruk-hai" and perhaps others, are entirely distinct and separate types, complete with radically different sizes, shapes, physiognomies, and so forth, as can be observed especially in their rather different appearances of the goblins of the Misty Mountains from the orcs elsewhere in *The Hobbit* trilogy or from the variety of those orc-like creatures on display in the earlier *Lord of the Rings* movies. As we have seen, in some of Tolkien's earliest writings, both within the legendarium and outside it (e.g., in *The Father Christmas Letters*), Tolkien did at times appear to distinguish among goblins, hobgoblins, and orcs, but by the time of *The Lord of the Rings* he had rejected that division or subdivision, making clear that these terms were effectively synonymous or better, that one word was merely the "translation" of the other.[4]

In the original version of *The Hobbit*, as published in 1937, the word *orc* appears only one time (not counting the six references to the sword named *Orcrist*, which is translated "Goblin-cleaver" and known to the goblins as *Biter*).[5] The word is used by Gandalf, who is explaining to Bilbo and the dwarves why they must journey through, rather than around, Mirkwood. Not only would a route around the forest to the north take them "two hundred miles or so out of your way," but even so, "there are no safe paths in this part of the world." Gandalf reminds them that they are "over the Edge of the Wild now," noting that, "[b]efore you could get round Mirkwood in the North you would be right among the slopes of the Grey Mountains, and they are simply stiff with goblins, hobgoblins, and orcs of the worst description" (138). This reference suggests that Gandalf simultaneously distinguishes and groups together the three creatures designated by those terms, which in turn confirms their fundamental identity as a "race" while also subdividing the race, perhaps by intra-racial ethnicity, or else by mere size, ferocity, or some other distinguishing characteristic.

However, despite some early inconsistency on the matter, Tolkien himself eventually affirmed that *goblins* and *orcs* are two terms that refer to the same creature, the *uruks* as they refer to themselves in *The Lord of the Rings*, with Tolkien's addition of the "Black Speech," purportedly developed by Sauron for the orcs.[6] With respect to the use of *goblin* in *The Hobbit* specifically, Tolkien added a note for the 1966 Ballentine edition in which he explains, "*Orc* is not an English word. It occurs in one or two places but is usually translated *goblin* (or *hobgoblin* for the larger kinds). *Orc* is the hobbits' form of the name given at that time to these creatures, and it is not connected at all with our *orc, ork*, applied to sea-animals of dolphin-kind."[7] Elsewhere, Tolkien expresses mild embarrassment at not recognizing that the prefix "hob denoted a diminution of the thing modified," and thus "the statement that hobgoblins were 'a larger kind' is the reverse of the original truth," but that is just to say that *goblins, hobgoblins*, and *orcs* all refer to the same creatures.[8]

In an oft-cited letter from 1954, Tolkien also explained that, while the word "actually derived from Old English *orc* 'demon,' but only because of its phonetic suitability," in their conception the orcs "owe, I suppose, a great deal to the goblin tradition (*goblin* is used as a translation in *The Hobbit*, where *orc* only occurs once, I think), especially as it appears in the world of George MacDonald." In another letter, written a few months later, Tolkien suggests that the "preference of *goblins* to *orcs*" is "a matter of taste," before adding, "Personally, I prefer Orcs." The Professor's word seems most authoritative in the matter: while *orcs* is preferable, *goblins, hobgoblins*, and *orcs*—like the terminology found within Middle-earth, whereby "the name has the form *orch* (pl. *yrch*) in Sindarin and *uruk* in the Black Speech"—are simply different words used to refer to the same type of being.[9]

Furthermore, perhaps less obviously but ultimately also true, the creatures so named were themselves fundamentally "human" or "humane" beings, which in turn suggests that much of their distinction from other human beings in Tolkien's legendarium is a matter of race or racism, or else (as discussed in Chapter 1) more of a moral distinction between those *men* who value beauty and kindness, say, versus those who do not. Needless to say, such orkish people can be found throughout the world: "I have met them [the Uruk-hai], or thought so, in England's green and pleasant land."[10] Most likely, it is a combination of both racial and more cultural or moral differences, which themselves owe a great deal to one's point of view. Whereas the elves, most but not all dwarves, the hobbits, Gandalf, Beorn, and others imagine and treat orcs as irredeemably evil and unworthy of existence itself, the goblins of the Misty Mountains, among others, do not see themselves as immoral, and with some good reason they recognize elves and elf-friends as cruel, hard-hearted, and murderous. Goblins are not so simple as it would seem, even in what was ostensibly an adventure tale for children. Indeed, as a careful reading of their representations in *The Hobbit* reveals, the orcs are a complex and fascinating people.

The Golfimbul Paragraph: Establishing Orcs in Middle-earth

The first reference to orcs in *The Hobbit*, which is also to say the first time they are mentioned in Tolkien's published tales, comes much earlier than the scene in which they are encountered by Thorin and his companions in the Misty Mountains. In fact, goblins are referred to several times in the first chapter, thus establishing their collective role in the history of Middle-earth, a history which comes to impinge very much on the present for Bilbo once Gandalf and the dwarves unexpectedly disturb his piece.[11] At first, the word appears among other legendary or fantastic creatures who inhabit stories, as Bilbo Baggins at last recognizes his visitor as Gandalf, "the fellow who used to tell such wonderful tales at parties, about dragons and goblins and giants and the rescue of princesses and the unexpected luck of widows' sons" (5). A few pages later, goblins are mentioned again, in a way that makes Bilbo far more anxious, as he begins to realize that these creatures of legend may have more bearing on the "real world" than he had imagined, for the dwarves "talked about mines and gold and troubles with the goblins, and the depredations of dragons, and lots of other things which he did not understand, and did not want to, for they sounded much too adventurous" (9). The third mention of goblins in *The Hobbit* establishes their place in the history and reality of life in Middle-earth, even for the relatively parochial hobbits who had hoped that the Shire provided a peaceful enclave insulated from the turbulence of the world at large.

Here we also find the first named orc in *The Hobbit*, Golfimbul, whose relative tiny and even humorous part in the history of Middle-earth offers one of those tantalizing glimpses into the "endless untold stories" that make Tolkien's work so very rich. In a letter written to Christopher during World War II, as he was working on *The Lord of the Rings*, Tolkien acknowledges his son's interest in Celebrimbor, the elven smith who crafts the "three rings" among others, but about whom quite little else had been written. He then says: "A story must be told or there'll be no story, yet it is the untold stories that are most moving. I think you are moved by *Celebrimbor* because it conveys a sudden sense of endless *untold* stories: mountains seen far away, never to be climbed, distant trees (like Niggle's) never to be approached."[12] Similarly, in a 1963 later letter to an admirer of *The Lord of the Rings*, Tolkien explained,

> Part of the attraction of The L.R. is, I think, due to the glimpses of a large history in the background: an attraction like that of viewing far off an unvisited island, or seeing the towers of a distant city gleaming in a sunlit mist. To go there is to destroy the magic, unless new unattainable vistas are again revealed.[13]

In this sense, arguably, the "endless untold stories" about the orcs—their heroes, quests, communities, cultures, and lore, not to mention their own perspectives on the larger, multicultural history of Middle-earth—is a tantalizing prospect. Golfimbul, his history, and that of his people are undoubtedly among those many unknown stories that make the *known* stories of *The Hobbit* and *The Lord of the Rings* so richly realized and enchanting.

Curiously, Golfimbul appears in an almost parenthetical aside, a short paragraph in which the narrator mentions one of Bilbo's ancestors, who is arguably the boldest, bravest, and most militarily accomplished hobbit in the history of that people. However, the reference is a way of indicating that hobbits, not even that one heroic one, are not especially "fierce." In context, Bilbo is listening to Thorin's summary of the mission they plan to undertake, and upon hearing and contemplating the words *may never return* the "excitable" hobbit shrieks, falls to the floor, and calls out "struck by lightning, struck by lightning!" Gandalf attempts to reassure the skeptical dwarves that, notwithstanding this alarming display, his chosen burglar is "one of the best, one of the best—as fierce as a dragon in a pinch" (17). The narrative voice then intervenes, effectively undercutting the wizard's comment while offering a brief history lesson. The paragraph is worth quoting in its entirety:

> If you have ever seen a dragon in a pinch, you will realize that this was only poetical exaggeration applied to any hobbit, even to Old Took's great-grand-

uncle Bullroarer, who was so huge (for a hobbit) that he could ride a horse. He charged the ranks of the goblins of Mount Gram in the Battle of the Green Fields, and knocked their king Golfimbul's head clean off with a wooden club. It sailed a hundred yards through the air and went down a rabbit-hole, and in this way the battle was won and the game of Golf invented at the same moment [17–18].

As "Bullroarer's gentler descendent was reviving in the drawing-room," the dwarves continue to discuss their plans to journey to the Lonely Mountain, defeat the dragon Smaug, and reclaim the kingdom, matters that will introduce Bilbo (and the reader) to the vast history and geography of Tolkien's world throughout the course of the rest of the novel.

As with so many of Tolkien's endless, untold stories, the Golfimbul paragraph tantalizes the reader with what might surely be a full novel's worth of narrative about the orc invasion of the Shire, heroics of Bullroarer Took in the Battle of the Green Fields, and the unlikely origins of a widely popular pastime. From my own orc-centered perspective, I find the rudimentary lineaments of this moment in orc history fascinating.

For one thing, Golfimbul is *named*, which implies at the very least that his name and personage is worthy of placing in the historical record. As discussed in Chapter 2, no named orcs appear in *The Silmarillion*, for example, a practice that facilitates the overall dehumanization of the race and thus contributes to the genocidal attitude toward them in the texts themselves.[14] It is true, Golfimbul's name seems to have been chosen in part merely to facilitate the joke about the origins of golf, but it still registers him as a distinctive person, an antagonist worthy of the challenge from the greatest hobbit "warrior" in Bilbo's family tree.

Shockingly, perhaps, Tolkien's original name for this goblin was Fingolfin, which as John Rateliff points would does preserve "the key 'golf' element necessary for the joke," but which readers of *The Silmarillion* would recognize as the High King of the Noldor, certainly one of the most noble of Tolkien's great and noble "high" elves.[15] At the earliest stage of writing *The Hobbit*, Tolkien was clearly borrowing from his "Silmarillion" materials, and he experimented with many names at the time: *Gandalf*, for example, was used for the character we know as Thorin, whereas the wizard was called "Bladorthrin" in the early drafts. Of course, other elements of Tolkien's as yet unpublished legendarium would find their way into *The Hobbit* in its finalized forms as well, notably the tale of Gondolin and the allusion to Sauron as the Necromancer, but in general the tale of Bilbo Baggins and his adventure "there and back again" lie largely outside of the larger mythology. Bullroarer Took, Golfimbul, and the Battle of the Green Fields are thus elements of a more deeply historical context within Bilbo's own world, which like the geographical context will become enlarged throughout the novel, and then further extended and integrated as *The Lord of the Rings* unfolds.

In addition to having a name, Golfimbul is identified as a king, which is significant. Contrary to later, frankly dubious visions of orcs as being mere slaves to the will of their evil lords (namely Melkor, Sauron, and perhaps Saurman), Tolkien here already imagines orc kingdoms in which the populations have their own rulers, just as the elves, men, and dwarves have their kings. Elsewhere Tolkien seems reluctant to identify orcs leaders as kings, perhaps because of the associations of good government, rule, and order that comes with a well-organized, hierarchical social structure of the sort pictured in Tolkien's many elven, human, and dwarvish kingdoms. If orcs are inherently disorderly, that is, then how could they maintain governments of this sort? Yet, again and again in Tolkien's writings, whenever orcs are depicted in any detail—as opposed to the more common portrayal as a collective mass of inhuman beings comprising indistinct hordes—they are shown to have complex social organizations, ranks, and regiments. Indeed, the very idea that orcs could constitute a military threat to others indicates that they are well organized enough to fight in orderly battalions and to be effective when doing so.[16] It also points to the existence of a large, complex society in which the production of weapons, armor, and clothing, along with the provision of food, drink, housing, and so on, not to mention the broader bureaucratic infrastructure of governors, managers, educators, and the like, was fostered. Presumably the orc king Golfimbul ruled over such a dynamic political economy in peacetime, while also preparing his people's military forces and leading its troops in battle.

In addition to establishing a clear sense of orkish social organization and naming a king of one such society, this "Golfimbul paragraph" (as I am calling it) specifies a place, potentially a homeland but certainly a defined geographical locale to which these goblins appear to *belong*. "Mount Gram" is a curious toponym for a number of different reasons, but perhaps mostly because it is a *named place* to begin with. That is, Tolkien could have easily omitted the name of the realm where the "goblins" fighting in the Battle of the Green Fields had come from, or else he could have referred simply to "the orcs of the mountains," without identifying a particular site of origin, and presumably the effects would have been the same.

By naming Mount Gram, he puts this place "on the map," as it were, although it is noteworthy that Mount Gram does not actually appear on any of Tolkien's maps. In fact, there is a great deal of speculation as to the exact location of Mount Gram among Tolkien scholars. In *The Atlas of Middle-earth*, which continues to be one of the most important studies

3. Great Goblins
69

of the geography of Tolkien's world, Karen Wynn Fonstad locates Mount Gram in the Ettenmoors, also known as the Troll-fells, a ridge of mountains or foothills north of Rivendell (and hence, not far from where Bilbo, Thorin, and company will encounter the trolls, Bert, William, and Tom).[17] Others have speculated that Mount Gram is one peak of the Misty Mountains, which suggests that Golfimbul's kingdom could have been the same as the one ruled over by the Great Goblin and encountered by Bilbo just a few chapters later. Else it could be another nearby kingdom or a predecessor realm, since Tolkien often seems to suggest that orc populations, after losing battles, are reduced to near nonexistence, their communities thus having to be repopulated thereafter. In the earliest version of the paragraph, Mount Gram was referred to as Gram Hill, which might suggest a slightly less grand and more proximate locale, but considering that the Bagginses were themselves longtime residents of The Hill, "as all the people for many miles round called it" (1), any Gram Hill must have existed well outside the Shire. Rateliff, in *The History of The Hobbit*, suggests that Mount Gram "may merely be another name for" for the great mountain Gundabad at the far northern end of the Misty Mountains, where the goblin "capital" is located.[18] In that case, Golfimbul might well have ruled in the same place at that from which Bolg's troops will issue forth in the Battle of Five Armies later in the novel. Regardless of its exact geographical coordinates, however, Mount Gram designates a part of the geography of Middle-earth that seems well understood to be territory belonging to orcs, a "kingdom" ruled by an acknowledged goblin-king, which is a rather different vision from the notion that orcs are inherently nomadic, placeless raiders of other countries.[19]

Another remarkable thing about the naming of Mount Gram is that distinctively proper names, as opposed to merely descriptive labels, are quite rare in *The Hobbit*. Whereas *The Lord of the Rings* will later inundate readers with multilingual toponyms, sometimes giving the particular name of a place in elvish, dwarvish, human, and occasionally even orkish tongues (e.g., Mount Doom = Amon Amarth, Orodruin, or Weathertop = Amon Sul, Hill of Wind, etc.), in *The Hobbit* most places are given names that register their description only. As Tom Shippey has observed, "[m]ost natural features have names which are just common names and adjectives with capital letters, like The Hill, The Water, Dale, the Long Lake, the River Running, the Lonely Mountain, Ravenhill and indeed the Carrock."[20] Thus also, Hobbiton is a town of hobbits, the Misty Mountains are misty, Mirkwood is a murky forest, Rivendell is a dell within a cleft, Lake-town is a city on a lake, and Goblin-town is an organized community of goblins. To name Mount Gram, as with Gundabad, is to specify a particular location that extends beyond a description, although

Rateliff notes that *Gram* "is a Norse name (famous as the name of Sigurd's sword forged or reforged by Regin) and thus would seem to belong to the area north and east of Bilbo's home."[21] In Old English, as the philologist Tolkien would have known all too well, the root *gram* suggested "angry" or "hostile," thus befitting his imagined home of the orcs in this story of Bullroarer Took's victory over Golfimbul and his legions, so perhaps Mount Gram is indirectly more descriptive a toponym than it first appears.

Finally, the connection between Golfimbul's name and fate with the game of golf deserves a word. Clearly, it is intended as a little joke, and I do not want to make too much of it. But the fact that such an act of violence, however legitimately performed in the course of military combat, could become the basis for a joke told largely *en passant* reaffirms the degree to which goblins or orcs can not only be dehumanized, but dehumanized with apparent glee, both by the original perpetrators and by storytellers in the years to come. That Golfimbul's gruesome demise, being decapitated with a wooden club, could be seen viewed as a form of sport is thus a precursor to the horribly sadistic "enemy-killing" competition between Legolas and Gimli in *The Lord of the Rings*, but then the idea of "hunting" orcs had already been well established prior to even that "game."[22] So demonized are the obviously human-like orcs that people who might otherwise be offended by displays of violence and murder taken lightly as forms for sport nevertheless cheer, much like Tolkien had imagined the "orc-crowd" hooting at the execution of vanquished enemies.[23] In Tolkien's aborted attempt to thoroughly revise *The Hobbit* again in 1960, which he wisely abandoned once he realized that would require rewriting the novel entirely, Tolkien removed the reference to golf. This likely had to do with his desire to eliminate the more egregious anachronisms and to render the tone of the narration more consistent with that of *The Lord of the Rings*. He even changed the spelling of Golfimbul to *Gulfimbul*, "either because of the further evolution of Tolkien's languages," as Rateliff reasons, "or because Tolkien had now dropped the 'golf' joke and so no longer needed (or wanted) the *-golf-* element to appear in the goblin-king's name."[24]

The "Golfimbul paragraph" is obviously a minor part of the substance of *The Hobbit*, even for orc sympathizers like me, but it hints at a deeper history of the orcs, their cultures and societies, and their relationship with others in Middle-earth. As such, even in its almost parenthetical presentation within this first chapter of the novel, the story of Goldfimbul remains a key site for exploring the representation of the orc in *The Hobbit*. This moment also sets the stage for the encounters with orcs to come.

"Down, down to Goblin Town": The King Under the Misty Mountains

Not that one needs to cite every instance in which the word "goblin" appears in *The Hobbit*, but following the "Golfimbul paragraph" the first chapter's next reference to orcs introduces another key moment in Middle-earth's history. Speaking to Thorin directly, Gandalf says: "Your grandfather Thror was killed, you remember, in the mines of Moria by Azog the Goblin" (25). That event and its aftermath will be prove to be crucial to the story that follows, even if this history is left so far in the background as to constitute another of the "endless *untold* tales," enriching the historical verisimilitude of Tolkien's world. (The battle in question will be discussed by Tolkien in Appendix A of *The Lord of the Rings*, in fact.) Azog's name will be mentioned again toward the end of *The Hobbit*, during the Battle of Five Armies, which itself is thus revealed to be merely another link in the chain of events that includes Azog's activities in Moria and that extends into the historical record much earlier.

Gandalf then explains how he had encountered Thorin's father Thrain in the dungeons of the Necromancer, which leads Thorin to assert, "We have long ago paid the goblins of Moria," adding, "we must give some thought to the Necromancer" (26). Gandalf quickly disabuses the dwarf of this latter notion—"He is an enemy far beyond the powers of all the dwarves put together, if they could all be collected from the four corners of the world"—but the reference to having *paid* the orcs of Moria back for their past crimes is meaningful, as reinforces the sense of this long history of antagonisms between the dwarves and the orcs, while also setting the stage for the later conflicts to come.

Some of this deeper history emerges over the course of Thorin and company's journey eastward, perhaps most notably in the reference to Gondolin and "the Goblin Wars" during their stay in Rivendell, as Elrond identifies the swords found among the trolls' hoard as weapons made by the High Elves in that place and time. As readers of *The Lord of the Rings* and *The Silmarillion* will discover, the fall of Gondolin was one of major events at the culmination of the First Age, a climactic moment in the *Quenta Silmarillion* that would have occurred many thousands of years earlier, so this reference helps to extend the orkish histories much farther back in time than the Battle of the Green Fields or those conflicts in and around Moria. Elrond's presence in the text illuminates this history further, for he is both a lore-master, steeped in the knowledge of this history, and also a "half-elven" but still immortal person who actually experienced some of these historical events himself.

But almost certainly the most memorable depiction of orcs in *The*

Hobbit comes in Chapter 4, when Bilbo, Thorin, and the other dwarves are captured by "goblins" in the Misty Mountains and taken to see their leader, the Great Goblin. Here we meet orcs in the flesh, as it were, seeing them as living beings very much of the current world, not just legendary monsters or historical villains. Although the encounter is quite brief, here orcs are also shown to be rational beings, with their own communities, customs, and cultures. "Goblin-town," as the orcs refer to it in their marching song, is yet another critical site in the geopolitical and cultural map of Middle-earth. And the fact that Tolkien uses the term "goblin-cities" elsewhere in *The Hobbit* (172), later mentioning "their capital" at Mount Gundabad, is ample evidence of a network of organized social forms among orcs throughout this world system.

The circumstances of the capture of Bilbo and the others is itself remarkable. By virtually any understanding of the term, the company is *trespassing* on lands belonging to the orcs, or at least belonging to this community of orcs in this part of the Misty Mountains. The way that this scene parallels the later one depicting the capture of the dwarves by the elves of Mirkwood is quite telling. In both, Thorin and company are caught in decidedly foreign lands, and however innocent their own motives in traversing such lands may be, they are doing so without leave of the people who live there. As the Elvenking angrily informs Balin, "It is a crime to wander in my realm without leave" (175). Indeed, as I discuss below, the elf-king's interrogation of Thorin and other dwarves is, in tone and manner, almost exactly the same as the Great Goblin's earlier questioning of the arrested dwarves. Indeed, up until the very moment of the outbreak of hostilities in what would become the Battle of Five Armies—as I discuss below, that fight actually begins *before* the arrival of the orcs—the elves are just as great an enemy of the dwarves and an obstacle to the success of their mission as are the orcs. Only anti-orkish prejudice would lead one to assume that the goblins had less right to their territorial sovereignty than do the elves in Mirkwood, yet as we have seen, the orcs are often depicted as being paradoxically ubiquitous and placeless, thus all the more susceptible to the genocidal view that they do not belong in *any* place and therefore can be exterminated as a means of removing them from *all* places.

Just before the appearance of the goblins in person, the narrator through indirect discourse supplies us with Gandalf's misgivings about the mountain crossing itself, for "he knew how evil and danger had thriven in the Wild," and that "the goblins had spread in secret after the battle of the Mines of Moria" (56). As the company seeks shelter amidst a terrible thunderstorm that also seems to feature stone-giants "hurling rocks at one another for a game,"[25] they are taken into custody by a large group of orcs: "Out jumped the goblins, big goblins, great ugly-looking goblins, lots of goblins, before you could say *rocks and blocks*. There were six to each dwarf, at least, and two even for Bilbo" (59–60). The large number, some eighty or more orcs to thirteen dwarves and one hobbit, is presumably needed to demonstrate the hopelessness of the heroes' cause in hoping to evade capture, and it is consistent with the treatment of orcs as a massive, overwhelming, and far more numerous force than their enemies throughout Tolkien's writing; such a policy at once renders the orcs as threats without granting them the honor of being especially skilled in battle (i.e., they can win not by being better fighters but by simply having greater numbers), while also ensuring that all elven, dwarfen, or human victories over orcs are all the more heroic, à la King Henry at the Battle of Agincourt or so many other improbable tales of heroic triumph. The paradox is that for a victory to be worthy of heroic treatment or remembrance, the enemy defeated must be formidable, so if the orcs are not going to be recognized for their martial skills—lest that render them almost heroic for readers who value martial skills—they must be cast as fierce, cruel, and above all plentiful, which maintains the additional advantage of making the mass killing of them a matter of course.

As the readers of *The Hobbit* discover in this chapter, these orcs are not an anarchic band of outlaws or a collection of slavering beasts enslaved to the will of some *diabolus* elsewhere.[26] That this is a well-organized community, a social form much like a town or even kingdom, seems beyond dispute. Tolkien's language actually emphasizes this, as when he notes that the "goblins that have taken to living in the heart of the mountains can see through" the "deep, deep dark" there, adding: "The passages there were crossed and tangled in all directions, but the goblins knew their way, as well as you do to the nearest post-office" (60). Indeed, if the analogy involving a post office were not "homey" enough, the goblins refer to the cave in which the dwarves were discovered as their "Front Porch" (62). As in their song, these orcs would seem to view "Goblin-town," a place where "Goblins quaff, and Goblins laugh" (60–61), as a real town, much as hobbits would think of Hobbiton or the men dwelling in that enclave upon the Long Lake would think of Lake-town as their hometown.

Arriving in what might count as the main square or perhaps throne room of this town, a space described as "a big cavern [...] lit by a great red fire in the middle, and by torches long the walls" which itself suggests that the supposedly nocturnal or night-seeing orcs nevertheless favor well lighted rooms, Bilbo and the dwarves catch their first sight of the Great Goblin. He was "a tremendous goblin with a huge head, and armed goblins were standing round him carrying axes and the bent swords they use" (61–62). The text does not directly make the connection, of course, but this Great Goblin might well be a distant successor to Golfimbul, at least in the sense that he is now a king of the orcs who dwell in this part of the Misty Mountains. In the original 1937 edition of *The Hobbit*, for instance, the "great goblin"—not capitalized, and elsewhere called "a very big goblin" or "the big goblin"—is referred to as "the King" of the goblins.[27] Given the widespread use of capitalization of even common nouns, it is not entirely clear that Tolkien intended the "Great Goblin" to serve as a proper name, rather than as a merely descriptive title (e.g., the chieftain of this community who happens to also be very large), but the decision to remove the title of "King" is likely strategic, for to name the Great Goblin as a *king* is to acknowledge that this orc community is indeed part of a *kingdom*, hence implying sovereignty, territorial boundaries, and a broader sense of belonging to a particular place.[28]

Along similar lines, readers can imagine that the place in question might well be Mount Gram or somewhere nearby. As noted in the previous section, the precise location of Mount Gram is never identified, but a reasonable surmise might place it in the Misty Mountains, and it is certainly possible that the "Goblin-town" referred to here lies within that self-same Mount Gram. There are several individually named mountains in the Misty Mountain chain, after all, such as Gundabad to the north or Caradhras (in *The Lord of the Rings*), and distinct settlements are also mentioned, as when Tolkien says that the orcs' "capital" city lay beneath Gundabad. Although the earlier reference in Gandalf's thoughts may have suggested that these orcs are refugees from the battles of Moria or their descendants, it is possible that the Great Goblin and his people are of the same "nation" as Golfimbul and his goblins, in which case the Great Goblin might bear a grudge against Bilbo—the great, great grand-nephew of Golfimbul's slayer—as he does against Thorin and his clan. In any event, the descriptions of Goblin-town, its geography, its society, and its place in the wider world-system are enough to show that these orcs also have a long history in this place.

Whether or not this Goblin-town is itself, or is part of, the same political and geographical entity as Golfimbul's kingdom at Mount Gram or Bolg's at Gundabad, Tolkien makes clear that these orcs have been here in the Misty Mountains for many years, centuries in fact. In *The Hobbit*, Gandalf himself points out that the orcs had made the eastern gate from which he and the dwarves escape "ages ago," and Tolkien had earlier referred to a "main gate" on the western side, distinct from this "new entrance at the top of the pass the dwarves had taken" (95–96). Speaking of the "new entrance," Gandalf says, "I must see if I can't find a more or less decent giant to block it up again" (95), which implies that even giants—that is, most likely, mountain trolls—are thought to be more worthy of respect and cooperation than these orcs, notwithstanding the dire escape of Thorin and company from a trio of trolls shortly beforehand. As to the history of *this* orc community, Gandalf's comments suggest that it has existed, continuously and as a self-governing society, for a very long time. "The Tale of Years" (i.e., Appendix B of *The Lord of the Rings*) records that orcs had begun to make "secret strongholds in the Misty Mountains" around 2480 of the Third Age, the same year that "Sauron begins to people Moria with his creatures" (whatever that means).[29] That is already 267 years *before* "Bandobras Took defeats an Orc-band in the Northfarthing" in 2747, which specifies the year of the death of Golfimbul and which is itself 23 years before the dragon Smaug descends upon the Lonely Mountain, conquering the kingdom that Thorin and company set out to reclaim. The events of *The Hobbit* take place mostly in 2941, nearly 200 years later than that. Thus, by the time Bilbo, Thorin, and the others encounter the Great Goblin in person, it seems, these orcs have been dwelling in that place for nearly five centuries: 461 years, to be exact, which at the time of this writing greater than the temporal span between the founding of the Jamestown Colony, the earliest permanent English settlement in the Americas, and the present (a mere 417 years).[30] Needless to say, perhaps, but the Great Goblin and his people appear to have been well established in this part of the world, and thus they had some reasonable expectation that their territorial borders would not be transgressed without notice or leave.

Culturally, the goblins are about as "advanced" as any other race, at least in terms of their social order, their technology, and their economy. Of course, Tolkien personally would find many of these "advanced" forms all the more regrettable in most cases, so the use of ironic "scare-quotes" is warranted. In fact, in *The Hobbit* he uses the convention itself, noting that "in those days and in those parts they had not 'advanced' (as it is called) so far," when it came to the development of complex machinery or engines. After declaring that goblins are "cruel, wicked, and hard-hearted," Tolkien elaborates upon their customs and practices:

> They make no beautiful things, but they make many clever ones. They can tunnel and mine as well as any but the most skilled dwarves, when they take the trouble, though they are usually untidy and dirty. Hammers, axes, swords, daggers, pickaxes, tongs, and also instruments of torture, they make very well, or get other people to make to their design, prisoners and slaves that have to work till they die for want of air and light [62].

Presumably, the capturing and enslaving of others is a major part of the orkish economy,[31] at least from this perspective, but given the fact that no other dwarves, not to mention elves, humans, or hobbits, are ever directly seen laboring in bondage among the orcs anywhere in Tolkien's legendarium, even in those rare scenes where, like here, we see orcs in their own element, reasonable readers might at least imagine this reference to slavery to be questionable, all the more so considering its value and use as anti-orkish propaganda. We frequently see orcs engaged in work, but never see orcs at leisure, enjoying the labors of others whilst they "quaff" and "laugh."[32] In any event, Tolkien establishes that orcs are remarkably skilled in mining, smelting, ironwork, tool- and weapon-making, and so on. As Robert Stuart has pointed out, the very clothing of orcs suggests an entire economy's worth of talented artisans, which must include armorers, leatherworkers, spinners, tailors, cobblers, not to mention the many who must labor to keep the fundamental infrastructures of the society in place, such as those involved in procuring food, fuel, building materials, and so on.[33] Hence, even in *The Hobbit*'s far less detailed descriptions of the social structures and cultures of Middle-earth, relative to those to be found in *The Lord of the Rings*, orcs (goblins) are understood to live in quite complex, dynamic, and "advanced" societies.

All too "advanced," perhaps. As Tolkien continues his discussion of the goblins' skills and crafts, he speculates that "it is not unlikely that they invented some of the machines that have since troubled the world, especially ingenious devices for killing large numbers of people at once" (62). Be that as it may, I would point out that the only times in *The Hobbit* when readers will actually *see* significant numbers of people killed "at once" is when Gandalf kills "several" goblins in the Misty Mountains, first in a cave, leaving behind "a smell like gunpowder" (60), then later setting fire to goblins and wargs in great numbers, while also personally killing their apparently unarmed leader, the Great Goblin, with his sword Glamdring. In *The Lord of the Rings*, as I discuss in Chapter 5, reference appears to be made to the development of military technology in the form of a bomb, which blasts open a whole in the fortifications of Helm's Deep, but even there it is Saruman, Gandalf's coeval being and fellow member of his "order" of the Istari, who is responsible. Although goblins are held responsible for the developments of these sorts of weapons in the future, there are already more powerful beings actually wielding similarly deadly ordnance in Middle-earth in the times of Bilbo and Frodo Baggins.

In his famous letter to Milton Waldman, Tolkien explained his view that what we think of as technology ("the Machine") and "Magic" are effectively the same thing, insofar as they involve "the desire for Power, for making the will more quickly effective," and on those grounds he endeavored to distinguish "Art" from both magical and machinic activities. Presumably Saruman is exemplary of this turn from the legitimate "development of the inherent inner powers or talents" to the "use of these talents" and "use of external plans or devices (apparatus)," with "the corrupted motive of dominating."[34] It is a difficult distinction to maintain, particularly as weapon-making is itself seen as an art, albeit one that will have the killing if not dominating of others as its ultimate "motive." Ethicists might debate whether murdering someone with a blade or bow is less morally objectionable than doing so with artillery or bombs. In any event, when it comes to destroying large numbers of lives in a single blow, in *The Hobbit* or in *The Lord of the Rings*, the "good" Gandalf is more likely than the "evil" orcs to exert such power.

Tolkien's brief description of the ways of the orcs continues, and in what some might find an astonishing admission, we learn that orcs—these particular orcs or perhaps all orcs, it is not made clear—were actively allied with dwarves, albeit "wicked" ones. Tolkien writes of the goblins, "[t]hey did not hate dwarves especially, no more than they hated everybody and everything, and particularly the orderly and the prosperous; in some parts wicked dwarves had even made alliances with them" (62). The wickedness of such dwarves is likely apparent in the mere fact that they would ally themselves with orcs, but it is noteworthy that others, including communities made up entirely of other races, envision orkish societies or cultures as allies. Not only does that underscore the degree to which orcs are essentially communities of fellow "people," ones with whom agreements can be made and hence neither bestial monsters or mindless automatons, but it establishes orcs as being core constituents of an existing geopolitical system, and therefore widely recognized as *belonging* to that world (i.e., not as alien or external threats to the system). It is true, disturbingly so, that in Tolkien's legendarium the treatment of so-called "petty dwarves" may be as genocidally racist as the treatment of orcs,[35] but the fact remains that Tolkien declares orcs to be a race of beings that works alongside or in concert with others, others who do not object to the very existence of orcs.

Having observed that orcs and *some* dwarves are allies, Tolkien then notes that Thorin's people are not among them. Although these orcs "did not hate dwarves especially," Tolkien writes, "they had a special grudge against Thorin's people, because of the war you have heard mentioned," that is, the troubles with Azog and the goblins of Moria (62). Presumably, then, the trespassing by dwarves in this region near Goblin-town would seem all the more suspicious to the Great Goblin. How likely is it that one's own enemy forces would just so happen to be innocently sheltering on your Front Porch, hundreds of miles away from their own countries? And how likely would it be to have the enemy king himself actually be among the "innocent" trespassers? From the perspective of the orcs, at least, it frankly beggars belief to suggest that Thorin and company could be innocently passing through this realm, given their long history of violence and hatred toward this people. The Great Goblin recognizes Thorin right away, identifying him by name, "Thorin Oakenshield," adding, "I know too much about your people already" (63). Little wonder that the Great Goblin is skeptical of Thorin's "innocent" motives!

In his questioning of Thorin, the Great Goblin somewhat humorously makes a number of surmises, but it is fairly remarkable how accurate these surmises are. Informed that these intruders were found on the goblins' Front Porch, the Great Goblin asks Thorin: "What do you mean by it? [...] Up to no good, I'll warrant! Spying on the private business of my people, I guess! Thieves, I shouldn't be surprised to learn! Murderers and friends of Elves, not unlikely!" (63). Responding with what the narrator calls "a polite nothing," Thorin objects, using speech that is obviously disingenuous, but politically calculating and diplomatic. Writing of this scene, Stuart observes that "Thorin, attempting to cozen the Great Goblin in his cavern, obviously believes that he is negotiating with a rational, if repulsive, equal."[36] And while it is "true enough," as Tolkien puts it, that Thorin and company had not intended on "inconveniencing goblins in any way whatever" when they sought shelter from the storm, the Great Goblin's suspicion that these were murderers and friend of elves is well warranted, in the reader's mind at least, by the fact that Thorin and company were outfitted with equipment provided by Elrond in Rivendell, and Thorin himself carries a sword named *Orcrist*, a name translated as "the Goblin-cleaver." Indeed, once Elrond identified that sword for him, Thorin immediately declared, "May it soon cleave goblins once again!" Elrond responds, "A wish that is likely to be granted soon enough in the mountains!" (52). Thus, Thorin not only proved himself to be ready, willing, and able to murder goblins, even looking forward to the prospect of doing so with a weapon that was apparently designed for that task and legendary for its effectiveness in accomplishing it, but also was alerted to the opportunity to "cleave goblins" by his (half-)elven friend Elrond in the elven enclave of Rivendell. By any reasonably standard, the Great Goblin is both correct and prudent to be worried about these trespassers and their presence in his domain.

The sword Orcrist gives Thorin's purpose away, in fact, for the Great Goblin actually recognizes it, as do the other orcs in the room! According to Tolkien, "[t]hey knew the sword at once. It had killed hundreds of goblins in its time, when the fair elves of Gondolin hunted them in the hills or did battle before their walls. They had called it Orcrist, Goblin-cleaver, but the goblins called it simply Biter. They hated it and hated worse anyone who carried it" (63–64).[37] At this point, the Great Goblin shouts "Murderers and elf-friends!" and, in his rage, "jumped off his seat and himself rushed at Thorin" (64), before what turns out to be a magical attack by Gandalf—using a weapon capable of "killing large numbers of people at once," apparently in a most painful and inhumane way—defuses the immediate threat. At that point Gandalf himself slays the Great Goblin with his own elven-forged sword, "Glamdring the Foe-hammer," which "was bright as blue flame for delight in the killing of the great lord of the cave" (65). Yes, the sword itself "delights" in killing orcs, showing that even inanimate objects might revel in murderous anti-orkishness. As far at the text indicates, the Great Goblin was unarmed at the time of his death; although he was in the presence of armed guards, there is no mention of himself having a weapon, nor is it mentioned that the guards engage in battle with the dwarves. This may explain why the Great Goblin was so "dumbfounded in the middle of his rage" when the sword went "right through him," at which point "[h]e fell dead, and the goblin soldiers fled before the sword shrieking in the darkness" (64).

Thus ends a scene in which thirteen dwarves and one hobbit are discovered by orcs to be occupying territory within their realm, captured, taken alive and largely unharmed (e.g., rough treatment in the form of "pinching" is mentioned, as are whips, but no injuries of any kind are reported), questioned, and—then when the questioning reveals evidence of malice aforethought and potentially murderous scheming by what turns out to be a famous ruler of the orcs' longtime enemies—menaced with an incipient assault (i.e., undoubtedly Thorin was in danger of being personally attacked by the Great Goblin before Gandalf intervened), only to then escape without casualties or deaths. As the reader discovers, many goblins are wounded and killed in this scene, not to mention the "several" killed by Gandalf in the cave originally, and others are killed during the dwarves flight from "Goblin-town." Thorin and company ultimately emerge from this ordeal relatively unscathed, much as they had with their encounter with the trolls earlier. The orcs, like those trolls, are not so fortunate, needless to say.

In their flight from the orcs of the Misty Mountains, the Gandalf and the dwarves are separated from Bilbo, who goes on to find a magic ring, meet a creature called Gollum, play his riddle-game, and eventually, with the help of his newfound ring, escape and make his way back to his companions. The adventure continues, and with it the world of Middle-earth continues to unfold in its diversity and complexity before the reader's eyes, as new creatures and communities are discovered along the way. The brief episode within the Misty Mountain offers perhaps the most detailed view of orkish life, behavior, and culture to be found in *The Hobbit*, but it reveals only a small part of the perspectives on orcs made available throughout the narrative.

Beorn's Captives; or, the Quality of Mercy

After emerging from the tunnels beneath the Misty Mountains, the heroes of *The Hobbit* are still in grave danger. The next chapter's title, "Out of the Frying-Pan Into the Fire," suggests the adventure to come, for Tolkien notes that Bilbo's exclamation "Escaping goblins to be caught by wolves!" became a proverb later (99). Indeed, goblins who survived Gandalf's attack pursue Thorin and company into the woods east of the mountains, and they are joined by wargs (i.e., wolves). These creatures are themselves apparently sentient, for Gandalf understood their "dreadful language" (101), and listening to their conversation, the wizard learns that the wargs had planned to meet the goblins there in order to participate in a coordinated raid, which with the death of the Great Goblin was now to be cancelled. Thorin's company is forced to climb into the trees, but Gandalf rains down upon his enemies "a most horrible and uncanny fire," one that was not easily extinguished, thus causing the wolves to run madly about in terrific pain whilst burning to death (103). The orcs arrive and taunt Thorin and company, still trapped in the trees. In Gandalf's retort, he calls them "little boys," adding, "naughty little boys that play with fire get punished," which indicates that, even if speaking metaphorically, Gandalf has to perceive orcs as "people." (He does not refers to the wolves as "boys," that is for sure.) From this terrible predicament, the Lord of the Eagles and his companions rescue the company, a *deus ex machina* moment in the novel, liberating the heroes from the dual threat of the goblins and the wargs.[38] These latter enemies are attacked by other eagles: "the dark rush of their beating wings smote them to the floor or drove them far away; their talons tore at goblin faces" (107). Whisked away to safety in the eyries of these saviors, Bilbo and the others once more escape the orcs, and as the narrator relates, "[s]o ended the adventures of the Misty Mountains" (111).

The only other reference to orcs in *The Hobbit* prior to the climactic Battle of Five Armies is quite brief, but rather telling. It involves on one of the most remarkable moments in the entirety of Tolkien's legendarium: the capture of a live orc. As it turns out, this will be the *only* instance of an orc being captured, rather than hunted down or summarily killed, in all of Tolkien's writings. But, perhaps not surprisingly, this does not go well for the orc.

The eagles deposit Bilbo and the others at the Carrock, a spot along the Great River (a.k.a. the Anduin) east of Mirkwood, where they will shelter briefly in the home of Beorn, a unique character. Beorn, it turns out, is a "skin-changer," a human man who can take the form of a great bear, and who seems to maintain somewhat ursine characteristics at all times, for better or worse. After they spend two nights in the home of this werebear, a "most jolly" Beorn "in a splendidly good humor" reveals to them that he had "caught a Warg and a goblin wandering in the woods" and received "news" from them (130–131). Beorn learns that the goblins were "fiercely angry because of the deaths of the Great Goblin," not to mention the "death from the wizard's fire" of many of the chief wolf's folks. The captives provided this information to Beorn only "when he forced them." As he tells this story to Bilbo, Gandalf, and the dwarves, Beorn "set them all laughing," and he "chuckled fiercely to himself" as he acknowledges that they had "[k]illed the Great Goblin, killed the Great Goblin!" (130–131). His initial skepticism concerning the unexpected and not entirely welcome arrival of the dwarves and all at his home is thus thoroughly allayed—indeed, it evanesces entirely—once he discovers that they had killed the Great Goblin and attacked the orcs. At that moment, Bilbo asks "What did you do with the goblin and the Warg?" Beorn answers, "Come and see!" Leading the party to the other side of the house, Beorn shows them: "A goblin's head was stuck outside the gate and a warg-skin was nailed to the tree just beyond" (131). Thus, the only orc in Tolkien's entire legendarium to be taken into custody while still living was "forced" to provide information before being summarily executed, decapitated by Beorn.[39]

As a bear-like man, Beorn is understood to be "fierce," a term that is used frequently in reference to his character, but the *jouissance* he experiences in the death and pain of orcs is shared by Gandalf himself in *The Hobbit*. Gandalf positively delights in his torture and slaying of orcs, and even laughs about it when reminiscing upon such sadistic acts. Furthermore, Beorn's relatively blunt approach to orc-killing is probably a good deal less cruel than that of the wizard, for Gandalf's magically weaponized forms of fire "scattered piercing white sparks among all the goblins," resulting in the following scene:

> The yells and yammering, croaking, jibbering and jabbering; howls, growls and curses; shrieking and skriking, that followed were beyond description. Several hundred wild cats and wolves being roasted slowly alive together would not have compared with it. The sparks were burning holes in the goblins, and the smoke that now fell from the roof made the air too thick for even their eyes to see through. Soon they were falling over one another and rolling in heaps on the floor, biting and kicking and fighting as if they had all gone mad [64].

As if witnessing the agony and torment of orcs' being "slowly roasted alive" were not enough, Gandalf "laughs" as he reflects on his fireworks. "All the others laughed too. After all," Tolkien writes, "they had killed the Great Goblin and a great many others besides" (96). Celebrating the escape from an enemy captor, the dwarves seem to express joy even more than relief. Gandalf and Beorn, never having been captives, seem to express delight in the very fact of having been able to torture and kill orcs.

Within the context of the narrative itself, there is some irony to all of this. The climactic Battle of Five Armies would not have happened as it did without the episode involving the assassination of the Great Goblin, the mass killing of the orcs in that community, and its immediate consequences. Orcs, or goblins, do not appear as obstacles or threats to Thorin and company again until the start of that battle. In the meantime, the terrible dangers of Mirkwood itself, including but not limited to its giant spiders, threaten to end their quest in horrid ways; then the elves of Mirkwood prove far more of an hindrance to the dwarves than even the orcs of the Misty Mountains had, for the immortal elves would happily imprison them for an indefinite period, one exceeding all of their natural lifetimes. The Elvenking himself initially suggests "a hundred years" as a possibility, in fact. Later the human people of Lake-town, a dragon, would-be population of a restored Dale, and (again) the elves of Mirkwood offer further resistance to Thorin's plans, but in the end, the battle will come down to orcs once more. That would not have been the case without the assassination of the Great Goblin earlier, for we later learn that the orcs armies are mustered, in large part, to avenge this attack on Goblin-town.

"This is how it fell out": Orcs in Council and at War

Following the episode with Beorn, there is little mention of orcs again in *The Hobbit* until the Battle of Five Armies, apart from a few references in which their behavior is contrasted with that of the Wood Elves.[40] Hence, Tolkien himself highlights for the readers the rough parallel between the dwarves' detention by the Elvenking and that much briefer one by the Great Goblin. The first mention of actual orkish activity following Beorn's decapitation of an orc comes seven full chapters (or 120 pages) later, in a paragraph describing how far and wide, and how quickly, the reports of Smaug's death had traveled, as we learn that "[t]he Elvenking had received news from his own messengers and from the birds that loved his folk," and "[e]ven before the Elvenking rode forth the news had passed west right to the pinewoods of the Misty Mountains; Beorn had heard it in his wooden house, and the goblins were in council in their caves" (255). This passing mention of the goblins is itself fairly significant, insofar as places them in the company of the various "players" in the drama—the men of Lake-town and Dale, the elves of Mirkwood, and Beorn, plus Bilbo and the dwarves, of course—while also reminding readers of the fundamentally human sentience, organization, and prudence of the orcs. For even without their leader, who was killed by Gandalf, they are obviously able to meet in council to plan military and political strategy. Once again, these *people* cannot legitimately be confused with mindless vermin, soulless automata, or bloodthirsty ghouls, not by any attentive reader, at least.

The orcs will eventually constitute one of the five armies that gives the Battle of the Five Armies its name. The armies, as it happens, are organized by "race," not by sovereign countries, allegiances, or even regions; they are identified as the goblins and the wolves on the one side, and the elves, men, and dwarves on the other, with the eagles arriving later as a potential sixth army, and one might call Beorn "an army of one" (to cite an old U.S. Army marketing slogan). The battle itself is a direct consequence of the death of Smaug and its geopolitical ramifications, which is one of the more brilliant—and *realistic*—aspects of Tolkien's novel. In some adventure tales, perhaps, the slaying of the dragon would be the climatic end of the narrative, but Tolkien is worldly enough to recognize that such a moment could only lead to greater and more complex forms of strife in its aftermath.[41] The removal of a theretofore presumed indomitable threat would certainly create not only a perceived power vacuum but a grand opportunity for looting, which may not be the term Tolkien wants to associate with the elves but which is clearly part of the Elvenking's plans, "for he too had not forgotten the legend of the wealth of Thrór" (255), not to mention that he "had a weakness" for treasure "and though his hoard was rich, he was ever eager for more" (168). If anything, therefore, the orcs are somewhat late to the party when it comes to invading the Lonely Mountain and laying claim to its riches, behind the men of Lake-town or Dale and the elves of Mirkwood. At any rate, there was going to be trouble once Smaug was vanquished.

The reappearance of the orcs comes quite unexpectedly, even for Gandalf. The "battle" which will become a fight between orcs and their enemies was actually going to happen entirely without them, as the army led by Dain of the Iron Hills and comprising "at least five hundred grim dwarves," of whom "a good many […] have had experience in the dreadful dwarf and goblin wars," had come to fight for Thorin against the elves of Mirkwood and the men of Dale and Lake-town (272). Hence a battle of three armies, presumably all made up of "good" races and characters, was about to erupt just before the orcs arrived. Indeed, the warfare did *in fact* begin, with dwarves instigating the hostilities. In what might be a telling detail about Tolkien's view of the dwarves, whereby even "good" or "decent enough" dwarves are still both morally and ontologically "lesser" beings than the real Children of Ilúvatar (i.e., elves and men), the dwarves here strike the first blows against such Children, not against the orcs. While Bard urges that the men and elves act quickly and while Elvenking counsels patience, the dwarves "resolved to strike while they debated. Suddenly without a signal they sprang silently forward to attack. Bows twanged and arrows whistled" (280–281). Thus the dwarves did attack their enemies, which in this instance does not include any orcs, but without answer; it is not clear whether any arrows hit their mark, but presumably the dwarves did at least *try* to kill elves and men in this moment, a detail never revisited thereafter. Just as "battle was about to be joined" by the elves and men, Gandalf, "who appeared suddenly," intervenes, crying, "Halt!" in "a voice like thunder" with his staff blazing "with a flash like lightning" (281).

The moment is memorable, not only for turning the course of events aside and immediately transforming hostile adversaries into cooperative allies, but also for introducing a new character. Gandalf declares: "Dread has come upon you all! Alas! it has come more swiftly than I guessed. The Goblins are upon you! Bolg of the North is coming, O Dain! whose father you slew in Moria" (281). By naming Bolg and citing this history, Gandalf both announces the arrival of a formidable foe, presumably, and also indicates why these orcs would be attacking. Vengeance and familial honor provide at least one motive for the assault. Furthermore, the attack by the goblins of Gundabad, a "capital" of their civilization that is located far to the north of "Goblin-town" in the Misty Mountains—it is located in the Grey Mountains, in fact—was further motivated by the need to answer the killing of the Great Goblin. The motives of the orcs who fight in the novel's climactic battle may not be especially virtuous, but it is not clear that the motives of the others (i.e., the elves of Mirkwood, the dwarves of the Iron Hills, or even the men of Dale) are particularly virtuous either.[42] Avenging a father's death, after all, looms large in Thorin's own family history (e.g., Azog had killed his grandfather), and the orcs' desire to pay the dwarves back for the killing of the Great Goblin is understandable, if not entirely noble.

As we have seen, *The Hobbit* had featured several references to Moria and to the strife between the goblins and the dwarves, but this history would be fleshed out further in *The Lord of the Rings*, especially in the Appendix A thereto, where reader learns that Dain Ironfoot slays Azog almost immediately after Azog kills his own father, Nain. Hence, even that encounter involved revenge and filial piety, so the presence of Bolg in a battle against Dain is evidence of the continuation of that longer tale that extends back to a time long before Bilbo Baggins receives his unexpected visitors. In other words, the Battle of Five Armies is revealed to be yet another event in a much vaster historical and geographical conflict between these particular orcs and dwarves, as well as the complex and dynamic political system of which that conflict is itself only a small part.

After Gandalf's announcement that Bolg and his army were descending upon the dwarves of Erebor, the narrator explains, "[t]his is how it fell out," providing a glimpse into the orcs' deliberate, well-organized, and calculated plan:

> Ever since the fall of the Great Goblin of the Misty Mountains the hatred of their race for the dwarves had been rekindled to fury. Messengers had passed to and fro between all their cities, colonies and strongholds; for they resolved now to win the dominion of the North. Tidings they had gathered in secret ways; and in all the mountains there was a forging and an arming. Then they marched and gathered by hill and valley, going ever by tunnel or under dark, until around and beneath the great mountain Gundabad of the North, where was their capital, a vast host was assembled ready to sweep down in time of storm unawares upon the South. Then they learned of the death of Smaug, and joy was in their hearts; and they hastened night after night through the mountains, and came thus at last on a sudden from the North hard on the heels of Dain. Not even the ravens knew of their coming until they came out in the broken lands which divided the Lonely Mountain from the hills behind. How much Gandalf knew cannot be said, but it is plain that he had not expected this sudden assault [281–282].

As with other hints and statements elsewhere, this paragraph establishes the orcs as an extraordinarily well ordered society or even as cooperative members of different societies, fully able to coordinate efforts across multiple cities and regions. Moreover, they were able to do so with such tactical secrecy, confidentiality, and stealth in their operations that not even Gandalf, with his preternatural prescience and ability to "find things out" (26), was aware of it until the charge was imminent.

The language here even suggests that the orcs' resolve "to win the dominion of the North" was not made out of lust for power or territory, but rooted in a strategy for military and political defense, as a result of an unforeseen invasion of and assault upon a key city within their current realm that had resulted in the deaths of many, including one of their leaders. The death of the Great Goblin demonstrated the need for the orcs to secure their borders against future attacks. And the death of Smaug, with the sudden power-vacuum it created and the subsequent threat of even more powerful enemies of the orcs gaining control of wealth and lands nearby, practically demanded that the orcs do something about their now obviously compromised position. To do nothing was arguably out of the question, and all of these considerations militated in favor of martial action against those enemies, who had proven throughout their history to be merciless and uncompromising in their dealings with orcs. Indeed, from the perspective of *Realpolitik* as well as that of moral compunction, the orcs had far more reason to besiege Erebor and to go to war with the dwarves than did either the elves of Mirkwood or even the men of Lake-town.

In the battle itself, it seems, the combined forces of the goblins and the wargs did not initially have the upper hand. Even before the eagles and Beorn arrive, the elves' and the dwarves' assaults on the orcs seemed like they might rout the orcs, for "[t]he rocks were stained black with goblin blood" and "[v]ictory seemed at hand" (284). At that moment, orc reinforcements arrive, including "the bodyguard of Bolg, goblins of huge size with scimitars of steel," not to mention a "host of Wargs" and "great bats" that "swirled about the heads and ears of elves and men, or fastened vampire-like upon the stricken" (284). As noted above, for the battle to be truly heroic, the enemy must be formidable, and in the case of the orcs, that means they must offer an overwhelming numbers. Bolg, who is imagined as a dangerous individual, a leader who is also *known* to some of his combatants, may serve as an example of a skilled warrior among the orcs; he and his "bodyguard" prove impenetrable to even Thorin's offensive, whose "numbers were too few" (285). But ultimately the sheer numbers of the orcs prove to be the real threat, which in turn would seem to justify the decision to reduce those numbers even after the battle is over and even after the orcs have stopped fighting completely.

Once the tide of battle turns, however, the orcs of quickly vanquished. The already once employed *deus ex machina* arrival of the eagles return, and they "come speeding down in the nick of time." The eagles "dislodged the goblins from the mountain-slopes, casting them over precipices, or driving them down shrieking and bewildered among their foes" (291). The orcs' military leader, Bolg, is "crushed" by Beorn "in bear's shape," who "seemed to have grown almost to giant-size in his wrath" and "tossed wolves and goblins from his path like straws and feathers," and indeed "nothing could withstand him, and no weapon could bite him" (291). The eagles and Beorn are not counted among the "five armies," but their attacks on the orcs and wolves make possible the victory of the elves, men, and dwarves.

Although the orcs are likely not at this moment "leaderless"—that is, although Tolkien rarely takes note of it, the organizational structure of such a formidable force as the orcs would seem to require the sorts of regimentation and order that would include something like ranks and a chain-of-command—the orcs are soon defeated once Bolg and his bodyguard have fallen. With Bolg's death, Tolkien writes, "dismay fell on the Goblins and they fled in all directions" (291). If we are to take this seriously, then we can see that *the battle is over*, for all intents and purposes, since one (or perhaps two) of the five armies, those representing one entire side of the conflict, have *stopped fighting*. Indeed, not only have they ended their offensive, effectively enacting a "cease-fire," but they are actively retreating and abandoning combat altogether. That is to say, they are not even adopting a defensive stance; rather, the orcs are fleeing for their lives. The elves, men, and dwarves, along with Beorn and the eagles, can most certainly declare victory at this point, knowing that their battle is won and that their enemies are no longer a threat.

Of course, this is not what happens. Once the goblins flee in all directions, "weariness left their enemies with the coming of new hope, and they pursued them closely, and prevented them from escaping where they could" (291). The meaning is crystal clear, notwithstanding Tolkien's uncharacteristically promiscuous use of the third-person plural pronouns: when goblins stop fighting entirely and even attempt to "escape" from the field of battle, when they thus no longer represent a direct threat, and when they are not in fact even military combatants or adversaries at all, *their* enemies—the elves, men, and dwarves—actively hunt them down and kill them. Needless to say, these elven, human, and dwarven forces are not pursuing their quarry in order to arrest them, make them prisoners of war, or prosecute them for their putative war crimes. Instead,

> They drove many of them into the Running River, and such as fled south or west they hunted into the marshes about the Forest River; and there the greater part of the last fugitives perished, while those that came hardly to the Wood-elves' realm were there slain, or drawn in to die deep in the trackless dark of Mirkwood [291–292].

Nothing in these lines suggests that the forces that were *pursuing* or *driving* or *hunting* the orcs as they fled were engaged in *fighting*. On the contrary, the language used here indicates that armies led by the Elvenking, Bard, and Dain, the purported "good guys" in *The Hobbit*, were no longer involved in anything like combat, but rather had taken up the role of ethnic cleansers. These are not soldiers at war, but exterminators of what they take to be vermin. Even the eagles seem to realize that this war had ended, for Gandalf mentions that some of the eagles are "in the hunt [...] but most have gone back to their eyries" (292). The next line of the paragraph is all the more chilling in this context, as it seems to refer less to the Battle of Five Armies itself than to this genocidal attempt to annihilate the remaining orcs: "Songs have said that three parts of the goblin warriors of the North perished on that day" (292).[43] From the perspective of the Elvenking, Bard, Dain, and perhaps Gandalf too, it seems, the goal of this battle once Bolg's forces joined it was not so much to defeat the orcs as to eliminate them entirely.

The orcs' opponents had their own casualties, and indeed, the deaths of Fili and Kili are mentioned directly. Thorin apparently dies of his wounds, not before repenting his ill treatment of Bilbo and, to a certain extent, his own values more generally. Presumably part of his disavowal would have to do with the petulance and "dragon sickness" that led to the bellicose situation to begin with. For the battle between the dwarven army and that of the men (and elves, perhaps) had begun prior to the arrival of orcs (or wolves), and one can only imagine the casualties that may have been suffered on all sides even without the participation of Bolg's forces. The solidarity of these erstwhile adversaries against their common enemy, the orcs, makes the Battle of Five Armies seem a triumph of "good" and "decent enough" people against those "cruel, wicked and hard-hearted" people, even where Tolkien emphasizes the degree to which good intentions and ethical choices were not significant considerations. The dwarves are depicted as greedy and stubborn, after all, and the Elvenking appears as a rapacious if otherwise noble coveter of treasure. Bard's people seem to have some reasonable claim, given their hospitality, their losses, and their role in defeating the dragon, but even so, they have no more legal claim to the riches of Erebor than the orcs or wolves do. This is not to say that these people are "as bad as" the orcs, of course, but Tolkien provides enough information to make one question the inherent righteousness of the anti-orc position. Thorin's deathbed admission of his own folly suggests that the entire quest, which along the way had led to the killing of a great many orcs, was not necessarily justified. In any event, many casualties might have been avoided.

After the line about how "three parts of the goblins of the North perished that day," there are just a few other references to orcs in the remainder of *The Hobbit*. One potentially notable one comes on the return journey, when Gandalf and Bilbo decline the Elvenking's offer of hospitality, instead opting to go the long way around Mirkwood. "They intended to go along the edge of the forest, and round its northern end in the waste that lay between it and the beginning of the Grey Mountains. It was a long and cheerless road, *but now that the goblins were crushed*, it seemed safer to them than the dreadful pathways under the trees" (294, emphasis supplied). That is, so certain are they that, between the deaths on the battlefield itself and the hunting down and slaughter of fugitives, the orcs are effectively if not totally eliminated, they are willing to walk through what they still acknowledge to be orc territory on the way home. Even so, Tolkien says that Bilbo "had many hardships and adventures before he got back. The Wild was still the Wild, and there were many other things in those days besides goblins," but then Bilbo was well guarded and thus "he was never in great danger again" (295). The remaining orcs in Goblin-town, if any, pose no threat, as we learn that "[t]he goblins of the Misty Mountains were now few and terrified, and hidden in the deepest holes they could find." Notwithstanding their now relative harmlessness, however, the same paragraph ends by noting that, in the years to come when Beorn's kingdom (i.e., "he ruled a wide land between the mountains and the wood") flourished, "the last goblins were hunted from the Misty Mountains and a new peace came over the edge of the Wild" (295–296). Thus, and not surprisingly perhaps, one of the last appearances of the word *goblins* in the novel is found in the phrase "the last goblins were hunted." Even in peacetime, orcs are not permitted to live.

The Orphaned Bolg

Some years ago the fantasist George R.R. Martin caused a stir when he suggested that, much as he admired and was influenced by Tolkien's work, *The Hobbit* and *The Lord of the Rings* lacked a certain *Realpolitik*. That is, for all its vivid worldbuilding, Tolkien's universe was missing the sort of realistic political and economic considerations that made the complex intrigues and nebulous morality of the world of *A Song of Ice and Fire* so striking. Specifically noting that "[r]uling is hard" and that "Tolkien did not ask the question[s]," Martin muses,

> What was Aragorn's tax policy? Did he maintain a standing army? What did he do in times of flood and famine? And what about all these orcs? By the end of the war, Sauron is gone but all of the orcs aren't gone—they're in the mountains. Did Aragorn pursue a policy of systematic genocide and kill them? Even the little baby orcs, in their little orc cradles?[44]

The disposition of the orcs in the Fourth Age of Middle-earth—that is, after the events of *The Lord of the Rings*—is an interesting question in its own right, as there is little in Tolkien's writings about them. However, given what Tolkien does say about orcs, the existence of "little baby orcs, in their little orc cradles," after the defeat of Sauron or long before, is a distinct possibility.

As it happens, Bolg is the only named "son" of an orc (Azog), thus presumably at one time a child or a baby and hence clearly a person with a family, along with all that entails. Tolkien in *The Silmarillion* avers that "Orcs had life and multiplied after the manner of the Children of Ilúvatar," hence, sexually.[45] As we have seen, orcs are not very likely to be parthenogenic, nor are they made of stone and mud, and they are not merely reanimated or demon-infused corpses or zombies. Biologically, not to mention culturally, they appear to be human. That Bolg is also the son of Azog, a slain warrior from a previous battle between the orcs and the dwarves, provides additional, perhaps personal motivation. He certainly must have viewed Dain in particular and the dwarves more generally as subjects of a vendetta. (True, from the dwarves' perspective, Azog's cruel murder of

Thrór [Thorin's grandfather] and the desecration of his body was reason enough to go to war, but from Azog's point of view, Thrór's invasion of Moria was itself an act of trespass and aggression.) Dain slew Azog during the War of the Dwarves and the Orcs, and presumably, even after that war ended, the memories of it among the orcs did not. Why mention Bolg's filial relationship to Azog at all, if not to underscore that family—for orcs no less than for dwarves, elves, men, and of course hobbits—was significant? From the perspective of the orcs, a major motivation of their fighting appears to have been to avenge their family and people's honor, as well as more pragmatic and potentially baser motives.

Admittedly we do not see a lot of orc families in Tolkien's writings, although one could point out that readers see very little of the families of other races either. Virtually no dwarf women and children appear in the legendarium—only one female dwarf is named, in fact, and she only in the appendices to *The Lord of the Rings*—and few from other races appear. Apart from genealogical histories references, along with those titular formalisms whereby someone "son of" someone else is a key way of naming individual persons, certainly, there are few depictions of family life, especially of mothers and children, present in any of the texts. Orcs in this sense are not really outliers when it comes to the representations of family life in Tolkien's work.

As Tolkien himself explained in a 1963 letter: "There must have been orc-women. But in stories that seldom if ever see the Orcs except as soldiers of armies in the service of the evil lords we naturally would not learn much about their lives. Not much was known."[46] Here Tolkien tacitly invokes the putative "author" of these tales, which is really Bilbo Baggins himself, later Frodo, and Sam (and eventually Sam's daughter Elanor), inscribing these histories in The Red Book of Westmarch. To such writers, and even to the elves and men whose accounts they drew upon, knowledge of and even concern for orkish psychology, culture, and society would have been rather limited. We might also chalk this up to another instance of those "endless *untold* stories," of course, which further enrich the world and its many narratives. However, when it comes to "humane" beings who are actively dehumanized throughout these histories, who are treated as inhuman and in ways that facilitate an almost gleefully genocidal attitude toward their very existence as a people, the lack of acknowledgment or concern for their families or children seems both ideological and strategic.

Who knows how long an orphaned Bolg wept for his father, defeated and beheaded outside the gates of their own home? According to The Tale of Years, 142 years passed between Azog's death and the Battle of Five Armies. A dutiful son, Bolg appears to have fought bravely in leading his people against those who had attacked them in the Misty Mountains and in avenging his own father's death. As we know, it took a fierce Beorn, "in bear's shape; and [...] giant-size in his wrath," to "crush" Bolg. His troops were then mercilessly hunted down as they fled. Small wonder, then, that orc children grow up in fear and loathing of elves and elf-friends. The orkish race's history is written in blood, after all, most of it their own, and hence their legacy cannot but be one of trauma.

In the unexpected sequel to *The Hobbit*, as we shall see in the subsequent chapters, the orcs—along with the rest of the races, communities, cultures, languages, histories, and geography of Middle-earth—become far more complex, with further detail provided as to their backgrounds, societies, personalities, and values. Orcs remain in *The Lord of the Rings* essentially what Shippey calls "a continual supply of enemies over whom one need feel no compunction," of course, but the readers of that extensive novel gets a much enlarged sense of the orcs as a people.[47] The abundance of orcs there, like the enchanting overflow of details about so many aspects of Middle-earth in *The Lord of the Rings*, is part of the grandeur of that work. But even as early as in *The Hobbit*, Tolkien provides ample evidence of the basic humanity of these creatures, inviting the critical reader to question the facile assumptions about their being inherently evil and thus deserving of genocidal extermination. Golfimbul, the Great Goblin, Bolg, and the rest are depicted in such a way that orcs in general, although they may not often be particularly "good," can at times be great, and in any event most remain, like hobbits in fact, somewhat ordinary people throughout.

Chapter 4

They Are Coming

The Resurgence of Orcs in The Fellowship of the Ring

At the end of *The Hobbit*, as we have seen, it is suggested that the orcs as a people were almost completely wiped out. Whether they had been blown up, burned, stabbed, beheaded, defeated in battle, slain as they fled, or later tracked down and killed their own homelands, "the goblins were crushed," those who remained were "few and terrified," and in the coming years "the last goblins were hunted from the Misty Mountains" entirely. Nevertheless, unsurprisingly, orcs would play an important role in the sequel, *The Lord of the Rings*. It is a similar role, to be sure, inasmuch as the orcs remain essentially the foot-soldiers of the purportedly "evil" forces; hence, orcs are necessary in order to provide a steady supply of enemies to menace, fight with, and be defeated by the various heroes.[1] However, as with almost everything else in J.R.R. Tolkien's vastly expanded narrative and world, orcs as a race and as individuals will prove to be far more complicated and interesting. Indeed, from what had been the relatively slight archive of cultural, linguistic, geographical, and historical knowledge to be found in *The Hobbit*, everywhere in *The Lord of the Rings* one discovers an abundance. This is true with respect to orcs as well.

In this chapter I examine the resurgence of orcs in the first volume of *The Lord of the Rings*, that is, *The Fellowship of the Ring*. As we know, the decision to divide the novel into three volumes was, from a literary perspective, not just arbitrary but somewhat damaging to the over continuity of the story. Tolkien himself was not happy about it, and he insisted that this was not in any way a "trilogy," but he understood the non-literary, pragmatic, and business-related reasons for the decision. For my part, I follow this artificial division for mostly practical reasons as well, to help divide the long narrative into reasonable segments for analysis. However, just as Tolkien worried that the narrative itself would seem unbalanced by these artificial divisions, I recognize that any analysis of the orcs following along those lines will seem a bit disproportionate across the novel. *The Fellowship of the Ring* contains relatively little material that directly features orcs. In fact, orcs appear in only a few scenes, and mostly just while the protagonists are in Moria. By contrast, in *The Two Towers* and to a slightly lesser extent in *The Return of the King*, orcs feature prominently in many chapters. Nevertheless, as I argue, the relative absence of orcs in the first "part" of *The Lord of the Rings* is significant, for it indicates the degree to which orcs within the world of Middle-earth also seemed to have evanesced, only to resurge mightily, hence their greater presence near the end of the novel. The resurgence of the orcs in the aftermath of the Battle of Five Armies is a fundamental feature of the novel's world-system.

Hence, I will begin by examining the degree to which orcs are almost considered legendary creatures at the beginning of *The Fellowship of the Ring*, notwithstanding the fact that dealings with them had occurred within the living memories of some (Bilbo, for instance). Later, the introduction of a "squint-eyed Southerner" in the relatively cosmopolitan town of Bree suggests a wider world in which orkishness, in a racial as well as perhaps cultural sense, persists. Then, in Moria, orcs are at last encountered in the flesh, although even there they are a mass of faceless enemies, less fearsome than the much more terrible monsters to be found in that place, such as the Watcher in the Water and Durin's Bane. Finally, I examine those few moments in which orcs appear after the fellowship's escape from Moria, where the elvish cry *"yrch!"* signals linguistically as well as geographically the vaster world of orcs into which the heroes have ventured. In the "wild" lands west of the Misty Mountains, the various members of the broken fellowship—not to mention the readers of *The Lord of the Rings*—will gain greater experience of the orcs and the world they, and we, live in.

"The old bogey-stories":
An Abundance of Monsters

Not counting a passing reference to one of Gandalf's "superb" fireworks—"a generous distribution of squibs, crackers, backarappers, sparklers, torches, dwarf-candles, elf-fountains, goblin-barkers and thunderclaps"—the first mention of orcs or goblins in *The Lord of the Rings* comes in the form of a mere rumor (I.i.27).[2] Many years after this fireworks display, and about seventy-seven years after the Quest for Erebor and related events depicted in *The Hobbit*, we discover that "[t]here were rumors of strange things happening in the world outside" the Shire, and "some spoke in whispers of the Enemy and of the Land of Mordor":

> That name the hobbits only knew in legends of the dark past, like a shadow in the background of their memories; but it was ominous and disquieting. It seemed that the evil power in Mirkwood had been driven out by the White Council only to reappear in greater strength in the old strongholds of Mordor. The Dark Tower had been rebuilt, it was said. From there the power was spreading far and wide, and away far east and south there were wars and growing fear. Orcs were multiplying again in the mountains. Trolls were abroad, no longer dull-witted, but cunning and armed with dreadful weapons. And there were murmured hints of creatures more terrible than all these, but they had no name [I.ii.43–44].

The mention of orcs in this paragraph suggests that, for the inhabitants of the Shire at least, the orcs had theretofore been imagined as almost a thing of the past, and for people in the present orcs were the stuff of legends, much like dragons, in fact. This indicates the degree to which many assumed that the orcs had been, or had largely been, destroyed long ago, hence their worries about the potential resurgence of orc populations elsewhere.

The "rumors" of orcs "multiplying again in the mountains" appears to be the first indication of the very existence of orcs in this time, a surmise possibly reinforced by the references to goblins as being mere "bogey-stories" by Meriadoc Brandybuck later. In that scene, Merry is speaking of the many folktales and legends surrounding the Old Forest, just outside the Shire on the borders of Buckland. Fredegar ("Fatty") Bolger, saying his goodbyes to the company, had warned them of the dangers of the forest, which leads Pippin to ask: "Are the stories about it true?" Merry responds, "If you mean the old bogey-stories Fatty's nurses used to tell him, about goblins and wolves and things of that sort, I should say no. At any rate I don't believe them. But the Forest *is* queer" (I.vi.110). This moment foreshadows the general malevolence of the trees, the attack by Old Man Willow, and the introduction of Tom Bombadil, but the inclusion of "goblins" among the various "bogey-stories" that Merry does not believe suggests that he too find orcs to be more folkloric than real. Undoubtedly, he believed Bilbo's stories of his adventures to the East and back again, so it must be the case that Merry imagined that the entire race of orcs disappeared in the aftermath of those events. At the very least, Merry does not see orcs as a threat to be encountered anywhere near the Old Forest. Merry is only thirty-six years old at this point, which may indicate that "goblins" really had receded into the study of children's "bogey-stories" in the years following the Battle of Five Armies, an event that took place more than forty years prior to Merry's birth. This also suggests the degree to which the goblins or orcs were pervasive features of the world in the minds of those who had never encountered them, except in legends or folk tales.

But still, could their near annihilation of the orcs in the wake of that Battle have been so complete as to make the entire race seem like material for old wives' tales?

Merry's speech about the Old Forest hints at many things that are similarly legendary, apparently, and yet all too real, as the hobbits discover for themselves. The general menace of the trees foreshadows the Huorns and perhaps also the Ents at war later in the novel, and the specific attack by Old Man Willow provides a death-defying adventure within the forest, which then leads to the introduction of an equally legendary if not at all monstrous Tom Bombadil, along with this wife Goldberry. This scene lies between two other exciting and terrifying encounters: first, the escape from the Black Riders as the hobbits make their way to Buckland and ultimate out of the Shire; then, the horrific scene on the Barrow-downs, with one of Tolkien's most eldritch terrors, the Barrow-wight, from whom Tom Bombadil again saves the hobbits. These *real* monsters tend to make the "bogey-stories" all the more significant, for if these tales can be true, then scary tales of goblins and wolves certainly can be as well. The abundance of monstrous and otherwise preternatural creatures in early chapters of *The Lord of the Rings* figures forth the monstrous threats to come, including those of the orcs.

I use the word *abundance* advisedly, but it seems appropriate for Tolkien's grand project in *The Lord of the Rings*, "a tale that grew in the telling," as he put it in his Foreword to the Second Edition (xviii). Although his publisher Allen & Unwin almost certainly had wished for a sequel with plot and characters quite similar to *The Hobbit*—indeed, I am fairly sure *The Hobbit II: The Hobbiting* would have been most welcome!—Tolkien could not find it in himself to write a simple tale of Bilbo's next adventure or something like that. In fact, Tolkien was not interested in writing a sequel at all, explaining that he had said all he wanted to say about hobbits and that Bilbo's own story was quite complete. He offered Stanley Unwin materials from his "Silmarillion" writings to that point in 1937, but Unwin declined, not surprisingly, if for no other reason than that those tales had nothing whatsoever to do with hobbits and featured not even a single hobbit character. Tolkien suggested the idea of a story focusing on Tom Bombadil, about whom he had recently published a poem, which if nothing else demonstrates Tolkien's desire to build upon his previous work in any potential sequel to *The Hobbit*. Build upon it he did, in fact, but perhaps not in the ways he had originally intended. The world that was limned in the delightful adventures of Bilbo Baggins would practically overflow with detail, drawing from vast histories and legends, thus making the world of *The Lord of the Rings* so deep, wide, rich, and "real." The word *abundance*, etymologically at least, suggests "overflow," as the Latin prefix *ab-* (from) and noun *unda* (wave) figures forth the sense of the "overwhelming"; as such, *abundance* refers not only to ideas of the much and the many, *a lot* as opposed to *a little*, but really to a surfeit, almost *too much*, if one wants to put it that way. Certainly, from the publisher's perspective, a nearly 500,000-word novel, comprising six "books" and 62 chapters (*not* counting the Prologue, a Note, and all the Appendices), intended as the sequel to a popular, 95,000-word work of children's literature, must have seemed rather overwhelming indeed.³

The world in *The Lord of the Rings* is certainly abundant. Take, for example, the very name of one of its key characters. In *The Hobbit*, we had come to know a wizard named Gandalf, and perhaps the more philologically inclined reader, like Tom Shippey, would note that even this name is really little more than a description, for *gand-* suggests "staff" or "wand" and *alf-* is a form of "elf"; hence a wizard *is* essentially a "wand-elf" or a "staff-elf," at least from the perspective of humans who do not know better.⁴ The name Gandalf, like the names of the Misty Mountains, Mirkwood, or the Long Lake, could thus even be imagined as a description as much as a "proper name." But the Gandalf who appears in *The Lord of the Rings* has many names, partly owing to Tolkien's fastidiousness about displaying the many languages spoken in Middle-earth (and therefore, some of the names are also mostly descriptive, but in the respective tongue). As the character himself puts it, as quoted by Faramir in *The Lord of the Rings*: "Many are my names in many countries [...] *Mithrandir among the Elves, Tharkûn to the Dwarves; Olórin I was in my youth in the West that is forgotten, in the South Incánus, in the North Gandalf; to the East I go not*" (IV.v.670, italics in original). Add to this the various epithets used to identify him, such as The Grey Pilgrim, The White Rider, or the more insulting Stormcrow or Láthspell, and there are a lot of ways to name Gandalf. Perhaps it goes without saying that many other people, places, and events also have many names. In fact, Tolkien even provides us with examples of "the Black Speech" used by orcs, at times, which is yet another way in which he indicates the fundamentally "humane" or human character of these creatures. It is perhaps understandable that some readers can feel a bit overwhelmed by the abundance of the world as presented in *The Lord of the Rings*, but for so many readers, that is the great strength of the novel.

Given this abundance, my discussion of the representation of the orcs in *The Lord of the Rings* extends over the next several chapters. In this chapter, I will limit my discussion to *The Fellowship of the Ring*, which is admittedly a perverse thing to do, considering that *The Lord of the Rings* is a single novel, which Tolkien objected to dividing and never viewed as a trilogy. Tolkien was concerned about the results of this artificial division, noting, for one thing, there is "too much 'hobbitry'" in the first volume, which bears on my argument as well.[5] For *The Fellowship of the Ring* does not feature orcs extensively, whereas the subsequent volume *The Two Towers* has perhaps the most significant, orc-related chapters to be found in Tolkien's entirely legendarium, and *The Return of the King* also includes some key scenes featuring orcs.

The Squint-Eyed Southerner: Bree, Cosmopolitanism, and Xenophobia

By the time that Frodo, Sam, Merry, and Pippin reach the village of Bree, they had already had many adventures worthy of a sequel to *The Hobbit*. Intriguing to leave the Shire in secrecy, these conspirators had escaped from the Black Riders, had survived the Old Forest, had been rescued from attacks by the arboreal murderousness of Old Man Willow and the eldritch horror that was the Barrow-wight, and of course had met and spent time with their mysterious rescuer, Tom Bombadil, and his wife, the River-daughter Goldberry. Arriving in Bree, where they expected to meet Gandalf, they enjoy what would seem to be a welcome respite from the dangers behind them, as well as a fortifying rest before facing those to come. The episode in Bree turns out to be more of the adventure, but it is also an interesting moment in the consideration of orcs in *The Lord of the Rings*. Although no actual orcs will appear until the fellowship members travel through Moria, the indication of orcs and orkishness in the world system more generally gets highlighted while the hobbits are in Bree.

Bree is itself rather noteworthy, and Tolkien suggests that it may in fact be a unique place in the known world of Middle-earth. Situated east of the Shire, along the Great Road connecting the Grey Havens to the west and Rivendell to the east, Bree is also located along the Greenway, north-south road that of old would have connected the northern kingdom of Arnor with the realms to the south, leading to the Gap of Rohan and eventually to Gondor. Hence, Bree lies upon a major crossroads of the western part of Middle-earth, and it is not surprising that it becomes the meeting place of travelers from nearly all parts of that world. In fact, as Tolkien reveals, it is perhaps the most cosmopolitan place to be found in the West, as least with respect to racial and cultural intercourse. A humorous indication of this comes when Sam later reveals that the expression *"news from Bree"* is used by the parochial hobbits he grew up with to mean fanciful, far-fetched, or unbelievable tales, the opposite of *"sure as Shire-talk,"* in fact (IV.iii.284). But there Sam is also insisting that the news of the wider world, its real wonders and not just legends, can be learned from those travelers one could encounter in Bree.

Moreover, we quickly learn that Bree is a town of "men," but that many hobbits also live there. "The Men of Bree," in Tolkien's words, "were more friendly and familiar with Hobbits, Dwarves, Elves, and other inhabitants of the world about them than was (or is) usual with Big People" (I.ix.149). These men of Bree were descended from humans who had settled that region long ago, in the "Elder Days" (i.e., the First Age), which makes this a rather ancient community, older than even Rivendell, Lothlorien, or Gondor, and of course much older than the Shire. Along those lines, "[t]here were also many families of hobbits in the Bree-land; and *they* claimed to be the oldest settlement of Hobbits in the world, one that was founded long before even the Brandywine was crossed and the Shire colonized" (149). This would make Bree a truly significant site, as it would appear to be the earliest continuous settlement of both humans and hobbits in "the West of the middle-world." Moreover, "[t]he Big Folk and the Little Folk (as they called one another) were on friendly terms, minding their own affairs in their own ways, but both rightly regarding themselves as necessary parts of the Bree-folk. Nowhere else in the world was this peculiar (but excellent) arrangement to be found" (149–150). Tolkien's addition of the albeit parenthetical *excellent* suggests that readers ought to approve of this arrangement.

As Robert Stuart has noted, this is not just the only reference to humans and hobbits living together in a single community, but the only reference to a community continuously inhabited by two different races,[6] although I would *hasten* to add that, if we are to view orcs and men as distinct races, then clearly Isengard, Mordor, and perhaps other countries are clearly multicultural and multiracial as well.[7] The racial homogeneity within Tolkien's various realms is striking. Although guests from other races are sometimes welcome, or, more often, merely grudgingly permitted, and even *that* seems to occur rather infrequently across Tolkien's various narratives, the communities themselves tend to be made up of the single "race," be it elves, dwarves, men, or hobbits. Even in areas where there is almost constant interaction or trade, such as the dwarven kingdom of Erebor and the mannish town of Dale, the two races do not live together in the same community. And it is perhaps noteworthy in this regard that, notwithstanding the "peculiar (but excellent) arrangement" that had allowed men and hobbits to live together in Bree, there is no indication whatsoever of any mixing of the races beyond day-to-day commerce, and certainly no suggestion of human-hobbit intermarriage or sexual relations. (A speculative reader might suggest otherwise, as Bree-men are said to be shorter than other men, and despite Tolkien's general reticence with respect to sexual activity, he frequently notes the ways that "intermingling" of what are taken to greater or lesser peoples within the more general category of being affects both the physical and moral stature of different ethnicities of men.) Tolkien seems to view racial mixing, at both the social and biological levels, to be a bad thing.

Perhaps that is why some of the communities in which orcs are to be found do often include other races, and even where some orcs may have their own orkish communities, we certainly see them working with humans. The orkish societies such as the Great Goblin's realm in the Misty Mountains, the "capital" city in Gundabad, or later the community in Moria seem to be mostly made up of orcs alone, but even in those examples, we find orcs allied with other beings (e.g., wargs, bats, trolls, and even some dwarves). Moreover, as I discuss in Chapter 5, humans and orcs make up the armies of Saruman and of Sauron, dwelling together and presumably cooperating throughout. Referring to those "in the service of the Dark Lord in Mordor," for example, Gandalf tells Frodo, "[t]here are orcs and trolls, there are wargs and werewolves; and there have been and still are many Men, warriors and kings, that walk alive under the Sun, and yet are under his sway. And their number is growing daily" (II.i.222). Mordor thus may well be the most multiracial, multicultural, and cosmopolitan country in Middle-earth.

Given the persistent rhetoric both of racial purity and xenophobia to be found throughout Tolkien's work, one might argue that a sign of orkish "evil" is their willingness to "mingle" with other races. In *The Hobbit*, we learn that "wicked dwarves" had sometimes made alliances with the goblins, but in *The Lord of the Rings*, it seems, there is a much closer connection between orcs and some humans, not only in that they could form alliances, fight alongside one another, and even live together, but also in the way that they might intermingle sexually. In Bree, the presence of a character referred to only as "the squint-eyed southerner" (I.ix.160) is taken as some indication of the interbreeding (or "miscegenation") of orcs and humans, which is itself merely further evidence of the fundamental humanity of orcs themselves, of course.

Although there is no direct evidence that the "squint-eyed southerner" in Bree is in fact a biracial character, the implication that he might be is made by Frodo, who observes, "[h]e looks more than half like a goblin" (I.xi.180). Merry and Aragorn will supply further evidence much later when they refer what they imagine to be "half-orcs" that reminded them of this person. As Merry puts it, after listing the ranks of both orcs and men marching from Isengard in Saruman's army, "there were some others that were horrible: man-high, but with goblin-faces, sallow, leering, squint-eyed. Do you know, they reminded me at once of that Southerner at Bree; only he was not so obviously orc-like as most of these were." Aragorn responds, "I thought of him too […] We had many of these half-orcs to deal with at Helm's Deep. It seems plain now that that Southerner was a spy of Saruman's" (III.ix.566). One of the distinguishing characteristics of the orkish race, with respect to physiognomy at least, is "slanted" or "squint" eyes, so even the very description of this Southerner in Bree offers a clear sign of his apparent orkishness. First mentioned as a "squint-eyed ill-favored" traveler from the South, the "squint-eyed Southerner" leaves the Inn of the Prancing Pony with human Bill Ferny, who is himself described as a "swarthy Bree-lander" (I.ix.160), and indeed, Tolkien refers to the Southerner as "Ferny's squint-eyed companion" (I.xi.180). He is later spotted through the window of Bill Ferny's house, "a sallow face with sly, slanting eyes" (180). Much later, near the end of *The Lord of the Rings*, the hobbits find similar-looking men on their return to the Shire: "they were disturbed to see half a dozen large ill-favoured Men lounging against the inn-wall; they were squint-eyed and sallowfaced. 'Like that friend of Bill Ferny's at Bree,' said Sam. 'Like many that I saw at Isengard,' muttered Merry" (VI.viii.1004).

As mentioned in Chapter 1 above, Tolkien in a letter provided his clearest sense of the physical appearance of the orcs using terms not unlike those use to characterize this Southerner's looks. Tolkien affirms that "Orcs are definitely stated to be corruptions of the 'human' form seen in Elves and Men. They are (or were) squat, broad, flat-nosed, sallow-skinned, with wide mouths and slant eyes: in fact degraded and repulsive versions of the (to Europeans) least lovely Mongol-type."[8] Referring to the "squint-eyed, ill-favored fellow," Stuart points out that "squinting is a sign of evil throughout *The Lord of the Rings*, and 'bad guys' are reliably ugly."[9] In the case of this particular Southerner and those others who are compared to him in their appearance, the "least lovely Mongol-type" seems to be what the author had in mind. Notably, however, these Southerners are imagined, *not* as orcs themselves, but as "more than half like a goblin," "half-orcs," or just reminiscent of orcs. Indeed, although they are sometimes compared to orcs, part of the point seems to be that they are not orcs—not "full-blooded orcs," at any rate—but rather orkish in other ways. The variously (if vaguely) described "half-orcs" or "goblin-men" are distinguished from orcs, after all, and no actual orcs encroach upon the territories of Bree or the Shire in *The Lord of the Rings*.

The obviously racialized depiction, along with the later accusations that Saruman has "blended the races of Orcs and Men" (III.iv.473) and that this Southerner is a spy in his service, suggests that sexual intermingling is occurring, but there is also the sense that the *becoming-orkish* of humans is part of the decline of civilization more generally. As more "foreigners" come into these lands, it seems, the quality of life for the residents there will diminish, or worse, the quality of the people themselves will diminish, thus contributing to a great ontological, metaphysical, and moral diminution. The threat is thus simultaneously racist and xenophobic, although one might infer that they two are connected, insofar as foreigners who settle in places that were previously inhabited by a racially and culturally homogeneous population would likely be perceived as contaminating such a territory not by their mere presence but by their influence over the changing nature of that population, which might well include intermarriage as well as more general intercourse.[10]

"Hybridity," whether cultural or racial, "in Middle-earth is treated negatively, to the extent that it can be most accurately termed miscegenation," as Helen Young has observed.[11] During his Council, Elrond points out that since the Last Alliance of Men and Elves, "the race of Númenor has decayed," "the Men of Westernesse were diminished," and "the blood of the Númenoreans became mingled with that of lesser men" (II.ii.244). Thankfully, it seems, Aragorn himself remains unsullied, for he is "of the race of the West unmingled" (VI.v.971). Elsewhere, Faramir explains his people's view of the matter: "For so we reckon Men in our lore, calling them the High, or Men of the West, which were Númenoreans; and the Middle Peoples, Men of the Twilight, such as are the Rohirrim and their kin that dwell still far in the North; and the Wild, the Men of Darkness" (IV.v.678–679). Virginia Luling has referred to this as "the Gondorian theory of anthropology," one that delineates the racially hierarchical "orders" of men, thus establishing categories by which "high" men could become diminished through intermingling with "lesser" men.[12] And this overall worldview in Tolkien applies with regard even to respected allies, such as "the hardy folk" of "fair Lebennin," who "were reckoned men of Gondor, yet their blood was mingled, and there were short and swarthy folk among them whose sires came more from the forgotten men who housed in the shadow of the hills in the Dark Years ere the coming of the kings" (V.i.750). Diminution in height and in "fairness"—that is, becoming shorter or more swarthy—is generally a sign of the diminishing nobility as well.[13] Thus, the mingling of peoples of different backgrounds or from different countries, even within the same race, is generally frowned upon in Tolkien's world.

This is the case even in Bree, which as a crucial nexus in the Middle-earth world system, situated as it is at the crossroads of two major highways, seems to be a place that would benefit mightily from the sort of multicultural intercourse that comes with cosmopolitan locales. The squint-eyed Southerner first appears, in fact, as an advocate for greater immigration, even if he does so in a way that makes the locals uneasy. The Bree-landers are wary of the numbers of people coming into their lands from the south, but the "squint-eyed ill-favored fellow" predicts more will come, proclaiming: "If room isn't found for them, they'll find it themselves. They've a right to live, same as other folk," and Tolkien writes, "[t]he local inhabitants did not look pleased at the prospect" (I.ix.155). There is, perhaps, some irony in the fact that the Bree-landers would fear and seek to limit the incursions of "Southerners" into their lands, since Tolkien informs us that "the Men of Bree" came from the same folks as the Dunlendings to the south, the very peoples who would later fight on Saruman's side in his war against the people of Rohan. As Tolkien writes in Appendix F of *The Lord of the Rings*, the Dunlendings "were a remnant of the peoples that had dwelt in the vales of the White Mountains in ages past. [...] But in the Dark Years others had removed to the southern dales of the Misty Mountains; and thence some had passed into the empty lands as far north as the Barrowdowns. From them came the Men of Bree" (1129–1130). This lineage might help to explain the physical forms of the Bree-men, who were "brown-haired and rather short" (I.ix.149), for Tolkien also explains that "*Dunland* and *Dunlending* are the names that the Rohirrim gave to them, because they were swarthy and dark-haired" (1130). The generally xenophobic character of the Bree-landers, not surprisingly and perhaps hypocritically, comports with a pervasive xenophobia to be found nearly everywhere in the realms of western Middle-earth, even as these regions are shown to have remarkably diverse and multicultural histories.

The squint-eyed Southerner is without question a very minor character in *The Lord of the Rings*, and he is clearly not thought to *be* an orc. Yet his presence in Bree, and in Tolkien's representation of that town and the events taking place there, reveals much about the overall sense of orkishness in Middle-earth. That this Southerner might be of mixed race, part human and part orc, figures forth the combined fears of the foreign, the demotic, and the "taint" of miscegenation. Although Bree is the only place in the world in which men live alongside hobbits, and it occupies a critical node in the circuits of travel and trade in its part of world, with travelers of all races passing through its city limits—thus representing a potentially unique site for cosmopolitanism within Middle-earth, not counting the lands of the "enemies"—this squint-eyed Southerner is identified, both by his appearance and his provenance, as a threat. This is presumably the threat of the orcs, "the wretched of Middle-earth," whose resurgence threatens to alter the social fabric of many realms.

Drums in the Deep: The Orcs of Moria

Orcs will not appear in person in *The Lord of the Rings* until the company finds themselves in Moria, but the inchoate sense of an orkish menace subtends the more generally anxious mood throughout most of *The Fellowship of the Ring*'s chapters. Apart from the vague rumors mentioned above, the first references to actual orcs are made by those guests in Rivendell who take part in the Council of Elrond. The dwarf Glóin, for example, reports that the Beornings control "their land between the Mountains and Mirkwood" where "neither orc nor wolf dared to go," thus making the passage between Dale and Rivendell accessible, even if "their tolls are high [...] and like Beorn of old they are not over fond of dwarves" (II.i.228). Legolas, the elf prince (son of *The Hobbit*'s Elvenking) recounts how the elves of Mirkwood lost the captive Gollum during an orc attack, the first direct reference to orcs in combat since the Battle of Five Armies, adding that "dark things that were driven out in the year of the Dragon's fall have returned in greater numbers" (II.ii.255). Perhaps most alarmingly, Gandalf then reveals the apparent treason of Saruman, pointing out that "[w]olves and orcs were housed in Isengard, for Saruman was mustering a great force on his own account, in rivalry of Sauron and not in his service" (260). These reports are enough to confirm that orcs have made a comeback from the nearly total defeat of their race in the battle seventy-eight years earlier.[14]

Even so, when the Fellowship come to consider the option of traveling through Moria, Gandalf himself is not sure that the orc populations have recovered from their near annihilation earlier. As he says, "[i]f there are Orcs there, it may prove ill for us, that is true. But most of the Orcs of the Misty Mountains were scattered or destroyed in the Battle of Five Armies. The Eagles report that Orcs are gathering again from afar; but there is a hope that Moria is still free" (II.iv.296). The unpopular decision to venture through the Mines of Moria is made, in part, due to the more immediate threat of wolves, whose not-so-distant howling punctuates the discussion. As Boromir puts it, "[t]he wolf that one hears is worse than the orc that one fears," to which Aragorn responds: "True! [...] But where the warg howls, there also the orc prowls" (298). Later, arriving at the Doors of Durin on the western wall of Moria, Gandalf wracks his brain in search of the password, declaring, "I once knew every spell in all the tongues of Elves or Men or Orcs, that was ever used for such a purpose" (306), which at the very least indicates that being able to speak in orkish tongues would be advantageous, even if few people seem to value the study of their languages.[15] Just when Gandalf manages to open the doors, the fellowship is attacked by the tentacular terror that is the Watcher in the Water, a mysterious monster dwelling in the lake (itself formed by a dammed river) outside the walls of Moria. Escaping inside, the company is trapped when the Watcher tears down the very stone of the mountains, sealing the gate behind them. In a line that can at that point be taken as understatement,

Gandalf declares: "There are older and fouler things than Orcs in the deep places of the world" (309).

That line also serves as foreshadowing, considering that the balrog is a far greater threat to Gandalf himself and to the company than even many ranks of orcs later found in Moria. The first indication of actual orcs, perhaps, comes when the company hears the ominous sounds of faint knocks ("*tap-tom, tom-tap, tap-tap, tom*"), apparently triggered in response to Pippin's ill-advised dropping of a stone into a well. In the Chamber of Mazarbul, the fellowship discovers the tomb of Balin, thus confirming that he had in fact returned to Moria, only to die there. There Gandalf reads from a broken, dusty book that records the doings on Balin's people, beginning with "*We drove out orcs from the great gate and guard*" (II.v.321), reporting on the victory and installation of Balin as "Lord of Moria," only to then tell of the orcs' eventually victorious counter-offensive. "It is grim reading," Gandalf says, adding:

> I fear their end was cruel. Listen! *We cannot get out. We cannot get out. They have taken the Bridge and second hall.* [...] Then there are four lines smeared so that I can only read *went 5 days ago*. The last lines run *the pool is up to the wall at Westgate. The Watcher in the Water took Óin. We cannot get out. The end comes*, and then *drums, drums in the deep*. I wonder what that means. The last thing written is in a trailing scrawl of elf-letters: *they are coming*. There is nothing more [322, italics in the original].

Just as the company is about to leave this room, a thunderous drumbeat and horn-blast indicate the arrival of orcs, the first to be seen "in person" in *The Lord of the Rings*. Legolas cries, "They are coming!" as Gimli says, "We cannot get out!"

Gandalf identifies these adversaries as "Orcs, very many of them," adding, "some are large and evil: black Uruks from Mordor" (324). Although Tolkien has made clear that the terms *goblins, orcs*, and *uruks* all refer to the same "race"—*uruk* being the orc's own word for "orc," and *goblin* being the modern (human) translation of "orc"—clearly Gandalf is making a distinction here, one that is likely based on ethnicity as well as region. Compared with regular "orcs," the "black Uruks of Mordor" are apparently larger and more "evil," though it is not clear how one's relative moral character could be ascertained upon such a brief glimpse. Presumably, with respect to creatures prejudged as "evil," simply being larger or perhaps "black" might be enough to render one more evil. In any event, the most knowledgeable member of the fellowship makes what the reader must take as an informed distinction among the various orcs found in Moria.

In the skirmish that follows, as in so many battles featuring orcs versus Tolkien's heroes, the orcs come in for the worst of it, notwithstanding their apparently evil natures and superior numbers. After the first advance, "thirteen had fallen and the rest fled shrieking, leaving the defenders unharmed, except Sam who had a scratch along his scalp" (325). Just then, "a huge orc-chieftain, almost man-high, clad in black mail from head to foot, leaped into the chamber; behind him his followers clustered in the doorway. His broad flat face was swart, his eyes were like coals, and his tongue was red; he wielded a great spear," which he manages to thrust at Frodo before falling, "with cloven head," at the hands of Aragorn (325).

As the company flees, Gandalf tries to hold the door with a "shutting spell," explaining afterward, "I could hear orc-voices on the other side: at any moment I thought they would burst it open. I could not hear what was said; they seemed to be talking in their own hideous language. All I caught was *ghâsh*: that is 'fire.' Then something came into the chamber—I felt it through the door, and the orcs themselves were afraid and fell silent" (327). It is, of course, the balrog, a "demon of might" who would be classified in the more general category of the Maia, hence coeval with Gandalf himself (i.e., a being who existed at the very creation of the world, participating in the Music of the Ainur). Although this is another "evil" creature, it is noteworthy that the orcs themselves are afraid; they do not seem to view the balrog as an ally, much less a leader, but as a terrifying "demon," just as the elves, dwarves, and men would. Shortly afterwards, the "hundreds of orcs" make way for the balrog, "as if they themselves were afraid" (329). The orcs continue to pursue, but pause, not interfering with the showdown between Gandalf and the balrog. As those combatants fall into the abyss, the remaining members of the fellowship escape Moria, with only a token resistance from their orkish enemies. While there was "a guard of orcs" by the eastern gate, "Aragorn smote to the ground the captain that stood in his path, and the rest fled in terror of his wrath" (331). The fading drum-beats in the distance is all that remains of the menace of the orcs at the end of this episode.

Yrch! *Orcs Abroad*

Unsurprisingly for a novel of such abundance as *The Lord of the Rings*, the escape from Moria is much more complex than the arguably parallel scene in *The Hobbit* in which Thorin and company escapes from Goblin-town, but in both cases the travelers come into the lands west of the Misty Mountains, known to some as the "Wilderland" (or *Rhovanion* in the Sindarin tongue). For the most part, orcs had been depicted either within their own underground enclaves or on the battlefield, although occasional raiding parties were mentioned, as in *The Hobbit*, when the wargs were to have met with their goblin allies. At the end of *The Fellowship of the Ring*, however, we see large numbers of orcs abroad, in regions well beyond the places generally recognized as their homes. Later, for example, Treebeard expresses his wonder that orcs would pursue hobbits "down all the leagues of Wilderland" (III.iv.472), an indication of both the surprising relevance of hobbits caught in this "great storm" and the abnormal conditions under which orcs would roam these lands. As readers will learn in *The Two Towers*, the situation is even more complicated than Treebeard imagines, but at this stage, it is enough to note that the presence of orcs in these regions is considered quite uncommon, albeit not nearly as uncommon as would be the presence of hobbits there.

Urging the company on as they flee Moria, Aragorn observes that "[t]he Orcs will not, maybe, come out till after dusk, but we must be far away before nightfall" (II.vi.334). This is one of several references to the essentially nocturnal nature of orcs, but contrary to some representations of them (e.g., in *The Lord of the Rings: The Rings of Power* television series), Tolkien never suggests that orcs cannot tolerate the sunlight. Unlike the trolls in *The Hobbit*, who turn to stone at dawn's first light, the orcs can function in sunlight, even if they would prefer not to. In *The Hobbit*, we learn that orcs "don't like the sun: it makes their legs wobble and their heads giddy,"[16] but presumably the orcs were able to continue fighting day or night during the Battle of Five Armies and elsewhere. As I discuss in Chapter 5, this relative tolerance for sunlight may well speak to either cultural differences or training regimens. In any event, Aragorn's surmise about his potential pursuers likely stands as a useful guideline for those dealing with orcs rather than a hard and fast rule with regard to this race. Given that so many of the orcs' enemies are wont to actively hunt them, day or night, it is perhaps not surprising that such people hope to operate most unseen.

In Lothlórien, the elf Haldir reports that "we saw a great troop of Orcs going north towards Moria, along the skirts of the mountains, many days ago" (II.vi.344). As they are to the south of Moria, these orcs are almost certainly not inhabitants of Moria, the ones recently encountered by the Fellowship in that location; rather, these were probably the motley assemblage of orcs who feature prominently in scenes to come, or else some combination of the two. As Frodo and the others rest in the trees for the night, another elf raises the alarm, whispering the elvish word "*Yrch!*" or "Orcs!" Haldir explains that a "strong company of Orcs has passed," but with the elvish reinforcements, "[n]one of the Orcs will ever return out of Lórien" (344–45). This is for the most part confirmed a few pages later, as "[t]he marauding orcs had been waylaid and almost all destroyed; the remnant had fled westward towards the mountains, and were being pursued" (349).

4. They Are Coming

The company spends nearly a month in Lothlórien, staying as guests of Galadriel and Celeborn. The next sighting of orcs comes as the company is attacked from the riverbank, far to the south, by what Tolkien calls "the archers of Mordor" (II.ix.386), which may indicate the provenance of the orcs in question, but perhaps here *Mordor* functions metonymically to implicate all of the Fellowship's enemies. If these orcs are the same as those who capture Merry and Pippin later, then we will see that their cohort contains orcs from multiple regions and with various allegiances. This encounter with the orcs along the river is brief, ending with Legolas's slaying of the winged beast, whereupon the voices of the orcs along with their bows fall silent (386–387). The Fellowship continues downriver unmolested.

The final chapter of *The Fellowship of the Ring*, memorably titled "The Breaking of the Fellowship," features another orc raid, but the gravest danger to Frodo's quest emerges from within his own company, as an increasingly despondent and desperate Boromir attempts to seize the One Ring from him by force. Already aware that orcs are nearby, Frodo retreats to Amon Hen, the Hill of Seeing, where—his vision further magnified by the power of the Ring—beholds distant and possibly future events:

> everywhere he looked he saw the signs of war. The Misty Mountains were crawling like anthills: orcs were issuing out of a thousand holes. Under the boughs of Mirkwood there was deadly strife of Elves and Men and fell beasts. The land of the Beornings was aflame; a cloud was over Moria; smoke rose on the borders of Lorien.
>
> Horsemen were galloping on the grass of Rohan; wolves poured from Isengard. From the havens of Harad ships of war put out to sea; and out of the East Men were moving endlessly: swordsmen, spearmen, bowmen upon horses, chariots of chieftains and laden wains. All the power of the Dark Lord was in motion [II.x.400–401].

Eventually, the hobbit's far-seeing gaze alights on Minas Tirith, Osgiliath, Minas Morgul, and Mount Doom—tantalizing glimpses of key sites to come in the narrative—before settling on Barad-dûr, the Dark Tower, at which point his gaze is met by another's. To play upon a well-known line from Nietzsche, Frodo had stared into the abyss, and the abyss stared back. At this point, arguably, orcs are the least of his worries.

Frodo's magically enhanced descrying of "orcs issuing out of a thousand holes," with due dehumanizing reference to the resemblance to "crawling" anthills, turns out to be the final mention of orcs in *The Fellowship of the Ring*. The anticipated attack by those orcs prowling the eastern shore the Great River will not appear until the next book. This vision offers a fitting end for our consideration of the volume's treatment of the orcs. At the beginning of the novel, it seems that orcs as a race had been so nearly annihilated in previous conflicts and in genocidal policies of their enemies as to have become almost legendary, the stuff of "bogey-stories" or at worst vague threats from a great distance, and later potential contaminants of ethnical or cultural purity. By the end of Book II, the ominous and foreboding image of an abundance of orcs, swarming like insects across the whole of Middle-earth, suggests the degree to which orcs become central to the history of the world in this era.

If this volume, containing Books I and II, contained far too much "hobbitry" in Tolkien's words, then its sequel might be said to feature a "rising tide of orquerie," to quote the professor again, this time completely out of context. As a sequel to *The Hobbit*, which ended with the apparently near-total annihilation of the orcs of Middle-earth (or, at least, of the northern and western regions thereof), *The Lord of the Rings* in its first part contains little in the way of orcs, perhaps not surprisingly. The rumors of a resurgence of that race is enough to cause disquiet amongst hobbits, and the arrival of foreigners who look "more than half like a goblin" into the western lands near the Shire is more disconcerting still. But Book I of the novel passes without a direct sighting of an actual orc, and prior to the scenes in Moria itself, the only eye-witness account of an orc in the novel comes from Legolas's report during the Council of Elrond of an orc raid in Mirkwood. The spear-wielding orc who attacks Frodo, along with the various arrow-firing orcs in the mines and along the riverside, are clearly *real* enough, but for most of *The Fellowship of the Ring*, orcs remain a vaguely ominous menace of the outside world's encroachment upon various hobbit, human, dwarvish, or elvish homelands. Not only are there no named orcs, such as had been the case with Golfimbul, the Great Goblin, Azog, or Bolg, but there is little elaboration of the orcs as people.

In *The Two Towers*, that changes dramatically, as orcs will not only continue to serve as enemies to be feared and loathed, but will also be presented as people, regular sorts of people, if also crude and violent ones (all too "regular" in our own world, surely). Orcs are shown to have their own motives, goals, dreams, loyalties, values, lives, communities, cultures, and languages, and at that point it becomes apparent beyond all doubt that orcs represent a people who belong to and in Middle-earth, and who have every right to remain part of that world system.

CHAPTER 5

The Fighting Uruk-Hai

Orcs, Geopolitics, and the Utopian Impulse in The Two Towers

For the first-time reader, moving from *The Fellowship of the Ring* to *The Two Towers*—or, rather, to put it properly, from to Book II to Book III of *The Lord of the Rings*, which is a single novel, not a trilogy, after all—must be quite disconcerting.[1] The novel up to that point had to do almost exclusively with the experiences of the hobbits, more especially those of Frodo himself, except the first chapter, where the focus was mostly on Bilbo. The third-person narrative allowed for distance from those characters, of course, but the narrative was *focalized* on the hobbits, as narratologists might put it.[2] Other tales were told by characters, as in the songs sung or the discussion during the Council of Elrond, but the "live action" as it were comes with the imaginary camera pointed predominantly at hobbits or guided by their point of view. With Book III, this changes, for the various characters in the story are separated. In the final scene of *The Fellowship of the Ring*, Frodo and Sam have gone off on their own, crossing the Anduin river and making for Emyn Muil to the northwest of Mordor. In the first chapter of *The Two Towers*, we discover that Merry and Pippin have been captured by the raiding party of orcs, who had slain Boromir, leaving Aragorn, Legolas, and Gimli on their own. The Frodo-and-Sam plotline will not be taken up until Book IV, and for most of Book III, the adventures of Merry-and-Pippin are separated from the story of Aragorn and company, with each party appearing in different chapters until reunited near the end of the Book. Frodo and Sam will not be reunited with Merry, Pippin, and the others until Chapter 4 of Book VI (i.e., in *The Return of the King*), some 640 pages after "The Breaking of the Fellowship."

Throughout all of this, orcs play a prominent role, far more so than in *The Fellowship of the Ring*. The first chapter of *The Two Towers* begins with Aragorn's discovery of the orc raid, before witnessing Boromir's death, learning of the capture by orcs of Merry and Pippin, and surmising that

Frodo and Sam had gone off on their own; that chapter ends with the decision by Aragorn, Legolas, and Gimli to hunt the retreating orcs and to try to rescue Merry and Pippin. *The Two Towers* ends in a cliffhanger with the capture of Frodo by orcs at the Tower of Cirith Ungol in Mordor, while Sam contemplates the best course of action. Orcs do not appear in all the chapters in between, of course, but the reader sees and learns far more of them in this volume of *The Lord of the Rings* than perhaps anywhere else in the whole of Tolkien's legendarium. In two chapters especially, "The Uruk-Hai" in Book III and "The Choices of Master Samwise" in Book IV, different orcs are featured, and we learn through overheard conversations and direct discourse of their quite different and altogether human personalities. These scenes also give greater insight into the geopolitical situation of Middle-earth, particularly with respect to the "enemies," who do not form anything like a united front, notwithstanding the common perception among many readers that orcs and their allies are homogeneously "evil." In *The Two Towers*, the orcs are shown to have distinctive views, differing loyalties, and even dreams of a better life to be had if there were no "big bosses" at all. Enemies of the putative "good guys" they remain, and for the most part these orcs are revealed to be rather horrid people, but more than almost anywhere else in Tolkien's writings, they are also definitely revealed to be *people*, not demons or monsters. As such, implicitly at least, they are people worthy of life, liberty, and the pursuit of happiness, "rights" certainly not accorded to them by any of the supposedly admirable characters in *The Lord of the Rings*.

"*Orcs travel fast*": Entrelacement and Political Geography

As Tom Shippey has discussed at length, Tolkien's narrative in *The Lord of the Rings* makes use of a technique employed in medieval romances and other works known as *entrelacement*. By "interlacing" the narrative threads, Tolkien allows the reader to follow certain characters and events for a time, before switching back to others. This allows one to see events taking place in disparate places at the same time in a complex array of geopolitical happenings. This lends the text a sort of "spatial form," as Joseph Frank would famously call it,[3] in which the reader must mentally map out a plot which, while narrated in a linearly temporal manner (e.g., beginning, middle, end), must also register the simultaneity of events through different chapters or "books" depicting them. Such spatial form is perhaps well suited to the "cartographic plot" of *The Lord of the Rings*, as Shippey has referred to it.[4] For all the memorability of Frodo and Sam, Aragorn,

Gandalf, and the other "main" characters, Tolkien's masterpiece is really about the "world" itself in which these people live. Tolkien "wisely started with a map," and the tale unfolds in various narrative streams across the lands depicted on the map.[5]

Indeed, for all the complexity and detail of Tolkien main narrative lines, which are divided into two, three, or four distinct narratives within the overall story, they are but a small part of the "story" taking place in Middle-earth during this time. As we will learn, almost implicitly at first and then more fully later (and in the Appendices), there are intrigues, battles, and other events happening throughout the known world—never mind in the countries and populations in territories located beyond the edges of the map that appears in *The Lord of the Rings*, which must themselves be vast and complex—that the reader never "sees," but which have immense significance to the geopolitical order during and after the War of the Ring. While in the company of orcs in Rohan, Pippin himself wishes "he had learned more in Rivendell, and looked more at maps and things" (III.iii.453), so vast and variegated is political geography of the world system.

Among those places with which readers of *The Hobbit* and *The Lord of the Rings* are familiar, for example, we later learn that dwarves of Erebor and the men of Dale fought battles in that region, while the elves of Mirkwood waged war beneath the trees there, and Galadriel's troops threw down Dol Guldur in southern Mirkwood, all "off-camera" as the main narrative follows the stories of the members of the "fellowship" along their various paths. Notably, for our purposes, almost all of these places and events, whether depicted in the text or not, feature orcs. Tolkien's various regions and kingdoms may be diverse, culturally, geographically, and otherwise, but his "enemy" forces remain the same: orcs who can be killed without the remotest inkling of sympathy or compassion.

The events depicted in each of the first three chapters of Book III take place at roughly the same time, such that, for example, when Aragon encounters Éomer in Chapter 2, some of the events witnessed at the end of Chapter 3 have already occurred. This will in some senses continue through the first nine chapters, until the parties including Aragon, Legolas, and Gimli, on the one hand, and Merry and Pippen on the other, are reunited in Chapter 10, only to break apart again at the end of Book III. Meanwhile, of course, the adventures of Frodo and Sam along the marches near Mordor, the material of Book IV, are also occurring, and the simultaneity of these events becomes crucial to the plot, as things happening far away can significantly affect what is going on more locally. The subtle moments in which the various narrative threads can be seen to intersect at such distances are rather delicious, particularly for readers returning to the text a second (or third, or one-hundredth) time. Tolkien occasionally draws the reader's attention to the coincidences more directly, as when Sam and Frodo while crossing the plains of Gorgoroth in Mordor notice a change in the wind, and the narrator then describes events taking place as "Theoden lay dying on the Pelannor Fields" far away (VI.ii.919). Usually, however, the coincidences are more subtly evoked, as when the reader might make a connection between something glimpsed in one storyline that related to an event in another. But more often the connections are even less overtly made, and the reader comes to see how something like fate, divine providence, or the ruses of History itself must have a hand in things.[6] The simultaneity of the adventures also highlights the diversity of the regions and cultures of Middle-earth, for each distinct party will travel across rather different lands, encounter different peoples, and discover the multiple facets of a larger geopolitical system that is whole in itself.

"Orcs travel fast." Such an observation might seem hardly worth saying, and as a passing comment, it would be rather unremarkable. But Aragorn makes this brief statement in the context of the dawning sense of the vast, complex system in which he and the others of his company operate, and the sense of urgency is all the more profound given just how quickly things can change. Speaking extradiagectically, we might note that "Orcs travel fast" also makes the interlacing narrative threads of *The Two Towers* all the more effective, as the fast-moving orcs set the pace for the action in the opening chapters. Aragorn's comment opens a vista onto the broader historical, geographical, and political realities of this part of Middle-earth, which in turn informs our understanding of the various personages and events revealed in the pages to come.

Living orcs do not appear "on camera" in the first two chapters of *The Two Towers*, but orcs nevertheless determine much of the substance. On the very first page, in fact, Aragorn hears "the harsh voices of Orcs," and rushing in that direction, discovers the dying Boromir, with "many" slain orcs "piled all about him and at his feet" (III.i.413–414). Before perishing, Boromir explains that the orcs have taken "the Halflings," and thus at first it seems that the orcs captured Frodo and Sam as well; Aragorn will read the clues and later guess aright that Frodo and Sam had taken a boat across the river at the time of this attack. Legolas and Gimli arrive, stating: "We have hunted and slain many Orcs in the woods" (414). As they are deciding upon a course of action, the heroes search the bodies of the fallen orcs, discovering that, as Aragorn puts it, "[h]ere lie many that are not folk of Mordor. Some are from the North, from the Misty Mountains, if I know anything of Orcs and their kinds. And here are others strange to me. Their gear is not after the manner of Orcs at all!" The narrator then explains,

> There were four goblin-soldiers of greater stature, swart, slanteyed, with thick legs and large hands. They were armed with short broad-bladed swords, not with the curved scimitars usual with Orcs; and they had bows of yew, in length and shape like the bows of Men. Upon their shields they bore a strange device: a small white hand in the centre of a black field; on the front of their iron helms was set an S-rune, wrought of some white metal [415].

Gimli assumes that the "S is for Sauron," but Aragorn notes that Sauron "does not use his right name [...] And he does not use white," surmising that this sigil must refer to Saruman, who he concludes must have received news of their journey and of Gandalf's fall. "Pursuers from Moria may have escaped the vigilance of Lórien, or they may have avoided that land and come to Isengard by other paths." Then he states, "Orcs travel fast," only to suggest that news might travel even faster to Saurman, who has many ways of keeping track of things.

Thus the presence of (dead) orcs here in the first pages of *The Two Towers* brings Isengard back into the picture, setting the stage for the events to come in Book III, which will involve the contest between Saruman's forces and those of our heroes, along with the people of Rohan, some of whom we soon meet in Book III, Chapter 2. Aragorn also discerned that there was a sort of multinational force of orcs involved in the raid, in which presumably some from Mordor worked together with others from Isengard and still others from the Misty Mountains to the north (as will be confirmed in Chapter 3). The various factions involved in the vaster War of the Ring thus multiply.

The chapter ends with a curious addition. Starting on his hunt for the orcs, Aragorn declares: "We will make such a chase as shall be accounted a marvel among the Three Kindreds: Elves, Dwarves, and Men. Forth the Three Hunters!" (420). I believe this is the *only* time that dwarves are referred to as kindred of elves and men, who are frequently seen as "the two kindred"—as Tolkien put it, "Elves and Men are in their incarnate forms kindred."[7] So, at a moment in which Aragorn recognizes the cultural or national diversity within the races of orcs, he also magnanimously expands his own racial kinship to the dwarves, who had usually been viewed by men and elves as "a race apart," as Tolkien puts it (*The Lord of the Rings*, Appendix F, 1488).

As the "three hunters" pursue their orkish quarry through the lands controlled by the kingdom of Rohan, they encounter Éomer and his cavalry, just after they had killed a company of orcs. During this meeting, Éomer informs them that Rohan has not allied itself with Mordor; the kingdom remains neutral, yet wary. Such neutrality does not seem to extend to orcs, even those directly in the service of Sauron, and the ease with which the Rohirrim can casually kill orcs who enter their lands suggests that the genocidal racism with respect to orcs actually trumps political alliances and wartime policies. Éomer tells Aragorn and the others that after Rohan declined Sauron's offer to purchase horses, Sauron "sent plundering Orcs" to take what they can, adding, "[f]or this reason our feud with the Orcs is bitter," without explaining why they have no feud with Sauron, the power behind any orc raids. A consistent policy of killing orcs, whether they represent an "enemy" or not, is never questioned.

Éomer then states that Rohan *is* at war with Saruman, who "has taken Orcs, and Wolf-riders, and Evil Men into his service" (III.ii.437), thus announcing the enemy as Saruman and pointing out that Saruman's forces include non-orcs. Throughout Tolkien's work, human "men" have always fought on "both sides," of course, and Tolkien asserts that even some few dwarves, though none of Durin's folk, fought for Sauron during the war of the Last Alliance at the end of the Second Age.[8] Nevertheless, the desire not only to kill orcs but to hunt them to the death remains a consistent aspect of the Rohirrim's worldview, no less than Aragorn's for that matter, even when military or political concerns, not to mention ethical ones, would seem to warrant other policies. In any case, Éomer does not hesitate to confess (or to brag) that his company "destroyed" all the orcs they found, lamenting only the loss of fifteen men and twelve horses. The exact number of orcs killed by the Rohirrim is not clear, but it must have greatly exceeded two hundred, not counting the "many" killed by Boromir, Legolas, and Gimli during the initial raid, or the five killed by the orcs amongst themselves. Tolkien mentions "four score at least" of Isengarders, a "few of the larger and bolder Northerners," and "couple of score" of orcs from Mordor (III.iii.451), and even after the riders of Rohan had begun their attack, "[m]any Orcs had fallen, but fully two hundred remained" (453). All of those will be killed, of course, within another page or two. Regardless of politics, it seems, Rohan—like so much of the world—is not a place where orcs are permitted to exist, much less travel through.

Along these lines, the racial demonization of the orcs extends, in the views of the heroes and the narrator, at least, to the natural world itself. Hunting the orcs across the fields of Rohan, Aragorn avers that "[t]he land must groan under their [i.e., the orcs'] hated feet," and earlier the narrator notes that as "the marching Orcs tramped," the "sweet grass of Rohan had been bruised and blackened as they passed" (III.ii.426, 424), which would seem to make the trail easier to follow, if true. (Hence, it is almost certainly not true in the literal sense, else Aragorn would have not expressed doubt about being able to track the orcs across Rohan.) This attitude is yet another way of justifying the wanton slaying of "rational, incarnate beings" who obviously "belong" to this Middle-earth in an ontological sense, but who are denied any right to live by those who encounter them, whether in orkish enclaves or in the open air.

The mysteries of Merry and Pippin's captivity, the orcs' fast-moving travel from Parth Galen toward Isengard, and the attack by the Rohirrim will be mostly resolved in Book III, Chapter Three, which also affords the most detailed view of orcs and their worldviews in Tolkien's legendarium. Featuring for the first time in *The Lord of the Rings* direct observation of orcs, with at least three distinct groups of orcs and several memorable, named individuals, these scenes evoke the highly complex and diverse social relations in orcdom.

The Common Speech: Orcs in Debate

"The Uruk-Hai," Chapter 3 of Book III of *The Lord of the Rings*, offers the most detailed representation of orcs to be found in Tolkien's entire legendarium, as the entirety of the chapter features "a great company of Orcs" (444). For the most part, the chapter is presented from the perspective of Pippin—focalized on him, as it were—as he awakes to find himself and Merry captives of these orcs. Much of the substance of the chapter comes from the overheard conversations of many different orcs, who themselves represent different political factions among the orkish forces of Middle-earth. As such, the chapter gives insight both into orkish behavior, culture, and values and into the geopolitical situation of the world in the latter part of the Third Age.

"The Uruk-Hai" begins with Pippin waking up, discovering that he and Merry are bound about the legs and feet, dimly recalling what had happened before (i.e., Boromir's battle with the orcs), and wondering to himself "if Merry is much hurt. What has happened to Boromir? Why didn't the Orcs kill us? Where are we, and where are we going?" (444). Pippin feebly struggles a bit, and "[o]ne of the Orcs sitting near laughed and said something to a companion in their abominable tongue. 'Rest while you can, little fool!' he said then to Pippin, in the Common Speech, which he made almost as hideous as his own language." That the orc speaks both his own native tongue and the "Common Speech" is significant, for if nothing else it shows this orc is far more worldly, multicultural, and cosmopolitan than the parochial, xenophobic hobbits or most men, in fact. We soon learn that all of these orcs are capable of speaking what Tolkien actually calls "ordinary language" (although that may be an indirect way of indicating that Pippin thinks only one tongue, his own, is the "ordinary" one). Few seem interested in learning the various "abominable" or "hideous" languages of the orcs, but thanks to orcs' willingness to learn other peoples' languages, communication between orcs and the men, elves, dwarves, and hobbits is always possible in Tolkien's writings. Presumably the *philologist* in Tolkien, literally a "lover of the word," would applaud the orkish tendency to learn foreign languages, even if their voices make those languages sound "harsh," but given Tolkien's abhorrence of the cosmopolitan, he may well have found fault with their apparent internationalism. In any case, we find here multiple "nations" of orcs working together in common cause (almost!).

After being told to rest while he can, Pippin is menaced by a second orc,[9] who laments the need to follow "orders" and more specifically curses "the Isengarders," before muttering maledictions in his own language (*Uglúk u bagronk sha pushdug Saruman-glob búbhosh skai*).[10] Pippin then listens to the debate being held amongst the various orcs nearby:

> There were many voices round about, and though orc-speech sounded at all times full of hate and anger, it seemed plain that something like a quarrel had begun, and was getting hotter.
>
> To Pippin's surprise he found that much of the talk was intelligible; many of the Orcs were using ordinary language. Apparently the members of two or three quite different tribes were present, and they could not understand one another's orc-speech. There was an angry debate concerning what they were to do now: which way they were to take and what should be done with the prisoners [III.iii.445].

The multilingual orcs from at least three different discernible communities, each presumably having its own language or dialects, are able to communicate by using the Common Speech, the "ordinary" language used by men in the north and west that Tolkien elsewhere calls "Westron."

The reference to "tribes" is, of course, itself a somewhat racially and culturally biased one, implicitly used to refer to "savages" rather than to civilizations. The people of Rohan, for instance, are not referred to as a "tribe," even when they are considered as a distinct and inferior race of men, as in Faramir's "Gondorian theory of anthropology."[11] Nor are the Woses, "the Wild Men of the Woods" in Drúadan Forest who use "poisoned arrows" and who have apparently also been hunted "like beasts" by the Rohirrim before (831, 833), referred to as a "tribe," even as Ghân-buri-Ghân, their leader, speaks in a broken English sadly reminiscent of Tonto from *The Lone Ranger*, as Robert Stuart has observed. In fact, the only times that the word "tribes" appears in *The Lord of the Rings* is in reference to orcs, here in "The Uruk-Hai" chapter and later in Appendix F, where Tolkien discusses "the Black Speech," a language apparently devised by Sauron to be used by orcs. There we learn that orcs had no languages themselves—another revoltingly dehumanizing gesture, of course—but they "took what they could of other tongues and perverted it to their liking," making "brutal jargons" that were "scarcely sufficient" except "for curses and abuse." Further, "these creatures, being filled with malice, hating even their own kind, quickly developed as many barbarous dialects as there were groups or settlements of their race, so that their Orkish speech was of little use to them in intercourse between different tribes." Tolkien's appended section on the language of orcs is intended, at least partly, to explain the discourse Pippin overhears, for Tolkien tells us that "in the Third Age Orcs used for communication between breed and breed the Westron tongue; and many indeed of the older tribes, such as those that still lingered in the North and in the Misty Mountains, had long used the Westron as their native language, though in such a fashion as to make it hardly less unlovely than Orkish" (App. F, 1131). Needless to say, perhaps, but Tolkien's reference to "breeds" of orcs only further dehumanizes the "barbarous" people he identifies as being members of groups, settlements, and *tribes*.

It becomes readily apparent to Pippin that the three groups of orcs comprising that company represented three distinct polities in the world of his putative "enemies," thus demonstrating both the diversity of the enemy forces and their more questionable abilities to cooperate and to coordinate their efforts. With respect to the latter, the very fact that Merry and Pippin were tracked down and captured proved that the three distinct groups, which also include hundreds of individual orcs, *can* coordinate their efforts to achieve a joint military operation. However, as this debate proves, the different representatives have rather different ideas about what should be done now, and this leads to violent disunity among the orcs.

One group, led by Uglúk, is based in Isengard and loyal to Saruman. Calling themselves the *Uruk-hai*, a term they seem to use to indicate a more elite status amongst the different types of *uruk* or orc.[12] Regardless of the terminology, Uglúk and his fellow Isengarders are in fact bigger, stronger, and potentially better fighters than many others in this company, and not surprisingly—employing a rhetorical strategy more suited to Thrasymachus than to Socrates—Uglúk's side prevails in this debate. The second, smaller faction is a group of orcs from Mordor, led by Grishnákh their "captain," who represents the interests of Sauron. Grishnákh reveals the degree to which Sauron already suspects that Saruman is not his ally, and hence Grishnákh opposes Uglúk and wants to take the hobbits eastward to the river, where a Nazgûl waits on the far bank. Each captain expressly states that he has received orders, from each's respective "boss," to return the captive hobbits to their respective leader "alive and as captured," without being searched or plundered (III.iii.445).

In response, the nameless speaker, one of the "earlier voices," urgently differentiates his own third group, crying, "[n]ot out orders! [...] We have come all the way from the Mines to kill, and avenge our folk. I wish to kill, and then go back north." Most likely, this third group would appear to be from the Mines of Moria, survivors of the clash with the Fellowship of the Ring and of the elven hunters in Lothlórien; the geography and the timing, as well as that context, suggests this provenance as being probable.[13] However, without a clear reference to a particular place—unlike Uglúk's to Isengard or Grishnákh's to Lugbúrz (also known as Barad-dûr, Sauron's stronghold in Mordor)—one can imagine that this third group of orcs could hail from even farther north, such as the Goblin-town of *The Hobbit* or even Mount Gundabad, which would raise the possibility that these orcs are the remnants or descendants of those who had fought in the Battle of Five Armies. The unnamed orc's reference to avenging their *kin* implies that these older grievances may be motives still, much as Bolg was presumably avenging the death of his father Azog in *The Hobbit*. And, in what may have been a moment of foreshadowing, in fact, Gimli while still just outside Moria had observed that "Orcs will often pursue foes for many leagues into the plain, if they have a fallen captain to avenge" (II.vi.337). Regardless of where these orcs were based, they are clearly wary of the orcs of both Mordor and Isengard: They fear that Grishnákh will "fly off with our prisoners, and get all the pay and praise from Lugbúrz, and leave us to foot it as best we can through the Horse-country," but they also disdain the Uglúk and his fellows as "the muck-rakers of a dirty little wizard" (446). Indeed, "the Northerners" not only refuse to take sides between the rival bands of orcs of those two countries, but they expressly reject being a part of Sauron's or Saruman's wars with Gondor, Rohan, or the elves or men of "the West" at all. The desire "to kill" and to "avenge our kin" has little to do with the politics or international relations of Middle-earth. It is far more "personal," one might say.

This has all been merely overheard by Pippin, but when he turns around to see what is happening "he saw a large black Orc, probably Uglúk, standing facing Grishnákh, a short crook-legged creature, very broad and with long arms that hung almost to the ground. Round them were many smaller goblins. Pippin supposed that these were the ones from the North. They had drawn their knives and swords, but hesitated to attack Uglúk" (446–47). The goblins' apprehension is warranted, for Uglúk springs forth and kills two with two strokes of his sword, while a third—the one who had threatened Pippin and cursed the Isengarders earlier, as it happens—is killed by one of Uglúk's fellow soldiers. Grishnákh himself runs away, while "the Northerners" are soon quelled (not before two more were slain), then agreeing to follow Uglúk's orders to march to Isengard. At least for now, the debate is ended, and Uglúk provides a relatively detailed plan to "go straight west from here, and down the stair. From there straight to the downs, then along the river to the forest. And we march day and night" (447).

This brief debate is revealing. Grishnákh's comments in particular indicate that Saruman is not on the same "side" as Sauron, thus further complicating the already untenable view of the War of the Ring as pitting "good" versus "evil" armies. Notwithstanding his suggestion to Gandalf (as reported by the latter during the Council of Elrond) that they "join" with Sauron, it is clear that this was a ruse, and Sauron himself—not just Gandalf and the White Council—was being betrayed by Saruman of Many Colors.[14] Grishnákh already knows this, and presumably the main reason he and his company of orcs from Mordor are on this expedition in the first place is to prevent Saruman from getting whatever it is he seeks (i.e., the One Ring). That a "winged Nazgul" is also part of the mission, albeit stationed on the other side of the river, is a sign of the urgency of this mission from Sauron's perspective, as well as a sign that he thinks Saruman has already betrayed him. In a later scene, the Mouth of Sauron—a man, not an orc—will confirm that Sauron knew Saruman was not "worthy of trust" (V.x.890), so the presence of Grishnákh's company of orcs from Mordor in this mission is evidence not so much of an alliance between Orthanc and Barad-dûr as of an already existing antagonism between them, here expressed through suspicion and mistrust.

In fact, Uglúk's disagreement with Grishnákh is political, not just strategic. Speaking to the "Northerners" who apparently have no interest in the politics involved in the debate, Uglúk declares: "We are the fighting Uruk-hai! We slew the great warrior. We took the prisoners. We are the servants of Saruman the Wise, the White Hand [...]. We came out of Isengard, and led you here, and we shall lead you back by the way we choose." Upon hearing this, Grishnákh retorts:

> I wonder how they would like it in Lugbúrz. They might think that Uglúk's shoulders needed relieving of a swollen head. They might ask where his strange ideas came from. Did they come from Saruman, perhaps? Who does *he* think he is, setting up on his own with his filthy white badges? They might agree with me, with Grishnákh their trusted messenger; and I Grishnákh say this: Saruman is a fool, and a dirty treacherous fool. But the Great Eye is on him [III.iii.446].

The fact that Saruman is not on Sauron's "side" does not make him less treacherous, of course, but it does indicate the degree to which the "enemy" is not a homogeneous bloc of "evil" beings. Saruman wishes to gain control of the One Ring in order to defeat Sauron, something that both Gandalf and Galadriel express their own desire or temptation to do as well. Sauron "failed the test" that Galadriel and Gandalf managed to pass, but he is not, and never was, a servant or even an ally of Sauron.[15]

The brief debate between the different factions in the first few pages of "The Uruk-Hai" discloses a great deal about the geopolitical order in the contemporary world system of Middle-earth, particularly with respect to the different cultures, communities, goals, and to values on display even among orcs, never mind many others that make up the "enemy" forces in *The Lord of the Rings*. As the chapter continues, these various orcs who represent three distinct groups are more-or-less united by the need to flee from their own common enemies, enemies who do not recognize subtle differences, who offer no mercy, and who will kill them on sight. Far from being the terrifying monsters that Pippin and Merry might have imagined, and notwithstanding their crudeness and violence, these orcs will prove to be prudent, cautious, and ultimately terrified refugees, desperately attempting to avoid annihilation at the hands of "the Whiteskins."

"The Whiteskins will catch you and eat you": Orcs in Flight

The Northern orc's comment about having to "leg it out as best we can through the Horse-country" is enough to show he knows his political geography, for he adds that "[t]hese lands are dangerous: full of foul rebels and brigands" (III.iii.445). From the reader's perspective, it cannot be known what rebellions or brigandry this orc is referring to, and most likely these are just terms of opprobrium used to tar the reputations of one's adversaries. It is perhaps noteworthy that orcs are not in favor of rebels and brigands, but that they seem to share the exact same moral values of their putative enemies, even if they do not always follow their own moral guidelines. (In that, of course, they prove themselves to be very *human* indeed!) As Shippey has observed, orcs "have a clear idea of what is admirable and what is contemptable behavior, which is exactly the same as ours. [...] They are moral beings, who talk freely and repeatedly of what is 'good,' meaning by that more or less what we do."[16] Moreover, the orcs' fear of the men of this land seems altogether rational and justified, given their later treatment by Éomer's cavalry, which kills all of them summarily and without even bothering to capture or question any of them. Even Uglúk seems to have thought that the captives would be "rescued" by the Rohirrim (453–454), but he need not have concerned himself about that. So total is their annihilation of the orcs, in fact, that Éomer assumes his men must have killed Aragon's hobbit friends as well, since they left no one alive at all. This is enough to show that the "rebels and brigands" in question would kill strangers without regard to "innocents" among them, which does seem rather "foul." Understandably, then, as Uglúk tries to lead his company through these lands on the way to Isengard, he and his fellow orcs are worried.

Light as the burden of three-foot-tall hobbits must be, the orcs recognize the need to move quickly, so Uglúk frees Merry and Pippin of their bonds, allowing them to be able to run on their own. Pippin is in no shape to run, and Uglúk forces him to drink a potion that turns out to be wholly beneficial. "Uglúk thrust a flask between his teeth and poured some burning liquid down his throat: he felt a hot fierce glow flow through him. The pain in his legs and ankles vanished. He could stand" (448). Uglúk then gives the potion to Merry, while also tending to Merry's headwound: "he smeared some dark stuff out of a small wooden box," and clearly this salve was effective. Uglúk "was healing Merry in orc-fashion; and his treatment worked swiftly. [...] The gash in his forehead gave him no more trouble, but he bore a brown scar to the end of his days" (448). Needless to say, Uglúk was not doing this out of the kindness of his heart, but owing to the need to travel with speed and to see than his prisoners were delivered intact. However, perhaps also needless to say, there is never any scene in which wounded orcs are provided with restorative medicine or have their injuries treated. Regardless of intent, in other words, this scene further humanizes the orcs, showing them not only to be formidable warriors, but also capable medics with competence in first aid. The potion itself seems to be a direct analog of the *miruvor* with which Elrond had provided the fellowship for their journey, and which Gandalf prudently administered when the members of that company were flagging in body or spirit. It is quite telling that the orcs maintain a similarly restorative cordial, particularly since—at this point in their imaginative development—orcs are thought have been created from elves. Hence, they seem to have been able to share some of the medicinal magic or technology of their distant, supposedly non-corrupted kin. In any case, Pippin and Merry are now capable of running where before they could not even stand; they are restored to full (physical) health, for the time being at least, by Uglúk of all people.[17]

Uglúk emphasizes the urgency of the orcs' situation throughout their flight. When some of the Northerners suggest that they cannot run in the sunlight, Uglúk asks: "What do you think? Sit on the grass and wait for the Whiteskins to join the picnic?"[18] (If nothing else, this indicates that the practice of picnicking is not foreign to the Uruk-hai.) Uglúk complains that these "mountain-maggots" were useless, "only half-trained," thus showing his own willingness to dehumanize but also demonstrating that his criticism has as much if not more to do with preparation (training) than with ethnicity or "tribe." After a time, many of the Northern orcs, alarmed by what they perceive as threats from the south and the east—these threats turn out to be the riders of Rohan and Grishnákh's forces from Mordor, respectively—break off from the company and flee on their own. As Tolkien writes, "[t]he hobbits were left with the Isengarders: a grim dark band, four score at least of large, swart, slant-eyed Orcs with great bows and short broad-bladed swords. A few of the larger and bolder Northerners remained with them" (451). Grishnákh then arrives with "a couple of score of others like him," and he resumes his argument in favor to taking the captives to Mordor. When Uglúk taunts him, particularly making light of the legendary prowess of the Nazgûl, Grishnákh rebukes him sharply, calling him an "Ape." Uglúk, who had himself already made reference to "the apes of Lugbúrz," is unfazed, but complains that "the Uruk-hai of Isengard" must do the "dirty work." He questions Grishnákh's own motivations, but ultimately accepts him and his troops back into their company as they flee toward Fangorn Forest.

The "quicker and hardier" Isengarders soon overtake the Northern orcs who had fled, and they jeer at them: "You're cooked. The Whiteskins will catch you and eat you. They are coming!" In the next line, we learn this is not a "mere jest," as "Horsemen, riding very swiftly, had indeed been sighted: still far behind but gaining on the Orcs, gaining on them like a tide over the flats on folk straying in a quicksand" (452). The murderously efficient brutality of the Rohirrim is widely recognized, but it is not very likely that they "eat" orcs. However, it is also not likely that orcs "eat" other people. When Uglúk had claimed that Saruman "gives us man-flesh to eat," a Northern orc immediately disputes it, mockingly averring, "[i]t's orc-flesh they eat, I'll warrant" (446). Obviously, at no point in Tolkien's vast writings do we find orcs raising "humane" beings (i.e., elves, men, dwarves, or other orcs) as livestock, nor are they depicted as hunting humans for food like deer or rabbits. (Gollum is said to have eaten orcs, and threatens to eat Bilbo in *The Hobbit*, of course, but at no point in *The Lord of the Rings* is even Gollum imagined as literally cannibalistic.) It is possible that the orcs of Isengard have been led to *believe* that the men of Rohan will eat the orcs that they capture and kill, but there seems little reason for the reader to trust that it true. Likewise, there seems little reason, apart from a prejudicial interpretative framework that would extend orkishness to outlandish extremes of taboo, for readers to imagine that orcs would eat the people of Rohan either. Still, for the orcs, the threat of the "Whiteskins" is real.

With only some two hundred troops left alive, Uglúk remains canny enough not to try to launch an ill-advised attack. Overhearing his own men questioning his judgement, he complains that they are "as bad as the other rabble: the maggots and the apes of Lugbúrz," pointing out with the wisdom of a seasoned military leader that "there are more than enough of these filthy horse-boys to mop up our lot on the flat" (454). But escape proves impossible once the Rohirrim themselves launch their attack. As it happens, this last stand is a relatively anti-climactic one, as the riders of Rohan win victory with relative ease, losing only fifteen men (and twelve horses) while killing hundreds of orcs, with Éomer himself eventually slaying Uglúk in single combat. And, as we know is quite typical of all encounters between bellicose enemies and orcs who attempt to flee for their lives, "over the wide fields Riders hunted down the few Orcs that had escaped and still had strength to fly" (459).

Grishnákh, who had attempted to kidnap Merry and Pippin in order to take them to Mordor, was among those slain by the riders of Rohan. Pippin had bought time by imitating the *gollum* sound and thus suggesting that he knew about the Ring, but even then Grishnákh appeared to remain loyal to his cause, unwilling to be bribed or swayed from his purpose by the implied offer. The orc says, "everything you have, and everything you know, will be got out of you in due time: everything! You'll wish there was more that you could tell to satisfy the Questioner, indeed you will: quite soon" (456), only to be killed by an arrow shortly thereafter.[19] Uglúk and Grishnákh, opponents of one another but also captains loyal to their own political parties right to the end, represent the figure of orc as miliary leader, with all the attributes one might expect in such a figure (e.g., tactical, intelligent, canny, imperious, and violent). As with other orcs whom we do not get to know quite as well, they are also utterly human.

Helm's Deep, Isengard, and Ithilien: Orcs (and Men) in Battle

Among the more memorable scenes in *The Two Towers* are those depicting battle, particularly the Battle of Helm's Deep, a chapter-long, detailed representation of warfare in Tolkien's Middle-earth, as the men of Rohan are besieged and attacked by an army of soldiers loyal to Saruman, an army made up of both orcs and men. Sometimes forgotten amid the bloodlust some readers seem to share with Legolas and Gimli, who gleefully engage in a friendly competition to see which one could kill the most "enemies," the orcs depicted in scenes of battle in Middle-earth *frequently* fight alongside humans. Notably, those humans are fully capable of cooperating with orcs, showing no indication of racial animus, revulsion, or hatred toward their orkish comrades in arms. In Isengard and in Mordor, orcs clearly live and work among "men," even when not engaged in battle, so the murderously anti-orc perspective of the men of Gondor or Rohan is obviously not universal. Dunlendings, Easterlings, Haradrim, and others find themselves in the company of orcs, and only their treatment by the various "heroes" among their opponents would suggest that orcs are somehow inferior or less worthy of life than they. Indeed, as I maintain, orcs really *are* humans, albeit ones whom the elite elves and elf-friends of Middle-earth consistently distinguish from other humans on racial, cultural, and moral grounds, dubious as those grounds may ultimately be. The scenes of battle and of its aftermath reinforce this sense.

Following their escape from the Uruk-hai and Grishnákh, Merry and Pippin encounter the Treebeard, the ent, who declares, "if I had seen you before I heard you, I should have just trodden on you, taking you for little Orcs, and found out my mistake afterwards" (III.iv.464). This meeting will help to precipitate the attack by the ents on Isengard and the defeat of Saruman, but it is notable that Treebeard himself admits that he would have had no trouble killing "little Orcs" (orc children, no doubt!) without the slightest provocation, somewhat like the attitude of the Rohirrim in killing all the orcs they encountered without bothering to see whether any, or even any non-orcs among them, might be spared. Lucky for Merry and Pippin that Treebeard is not so *hasty*!

Having never seen hobbits, Treebeard tries to place them on the list of "Living Creatures" he does know, starting with what he names "the free peoples," which turn out to be elves, dwarves, ents, and men (perhaps in the chronological order of their "awakening" or coming into being in Arda). Pippin suggests a new line to add hobbits: "Put us in amongst the four, next to Man (Big People), and you've got it" (465–465), thus asserting his race's place squarely among the "free peoples," only minutes after having met this strange and seemingly inhuman creature. Treebeard's next reference to orcs is prefaced with the word *burárum*, "a deep rumbling noise like a discord on a great organ" (466), which Tolkien elsewhere explains is an "Entish word of disgust."[20] Treebeard says that while he takes no "sides" in "the Great Wars" that "mostly concern Elves and Men," he is decidedly *not* on the side of "'*burárum*' (he again made a deep rumble of disgust)—'these Orcs'" (472), and later in *The Lord of the Rings* mentions "those, *burárum*, those evileyed-blackhanded-bowlegged-flinthearted-clawfingered-foulbellied-bloodthirsty, *morimaite-sincahonda, hoom*, well, since you are hasty folk and their full name is as long as years of torment, those vermin of orcs" (VI.vi.979).[21] Treebeard's believes that orcs were "made by the Enemy in the Great Darkness" in "mockery" of the elves (III.iv.486), and hence the orcs are clearly on Treebeard's list, but they are not in his view worthy of mention as "living creatures."

Treebeard's and his fellow ents' loathing of orcs animates their actions later, and it is all the more remarkable that they hold even the mere servants of the offending parties, in this case Saruman, to higher and deadlier account than the actual culprit who gave the orders. Indeed, although he was tasked with watching over the perfidious Saruman, Treebeard confesses to letting him go, telling Gandalf, "You should know that above all I hate the caging of live things, and I will not keep even such creatures as these caged beyond great need" (VI.vi.980). Treebeard's decision has baleful consequences, as the hobbits discover thereafter. Earlier, in describing the ents' successful assault on Isengard, Pippin says that "[t]he Ents let the Men go, after they had questioned them," but that he did not think "many orc-folk, of any size, escaped" (III.ix.567–568). This is confirmed, when Treebeard happily declares that there are "[n]o more Orcs in Isengard" (572). Saruman's Isengard appears to have been a community of orcs and men, but Treebeard and the ents, along with the tree-like Huorns, carefully distinguish amongst these enemy "races" and determine that one of them is worthy on continued existence and the other only of total annihilation.

Unlike the Goblin-town of *The Hobbit* or even Moria in *The Lord of the Rings*, Isengard under Saruman's rule appears to be a multicultural and multiracial city. Within the city, "[t]housands could dwell there, workers, servants, slaves, and warriors with great store of arms; wolves were fed and stabled in deep dens beneath," and "Saruman had treasuries, store-houses, armouries, smithies, and great furnaces" (III.viii.554). Outside the walls, there are "acres tilled by the slaves of Saruman" (553), as Tolkien puts it, which presumably helped to provision his armies, but there was also obviously a great deal of trade with other communities, including the introduction of hobbit-grown tobacco (pipe-weed) from the Shire into these southern regions. When Gimli and the others arrive there after the Battle of Helm's Deep, Merry explains that "there were many other folk in Isengard," not just orcs, including "Men to guard his gates: some of his most faithful servants, I suppose" (III.ix.560). In Merry's description of Saruman's army departing for Helm's Deep, he notes the variety of "races" present:

> He emptied Isengard. I saw the enemy go: endless lines of marching Orcs; and troops of them mounted on great wolves. And there were battalions of Men, too. Many of them carried torches, and in the flare I could see their faces. Most of them were ordinary men, rather tall and dark-haired, and grim but not particularly evil-looking. But there were some others that were horrible: man-high, but with goblin-faces, sallow, leering, squint-eyed [III.ix.566].

These last, Aragorn recognizes as the "half-orcs" he had encountered at Helm's Deep earlier. Treebeard had proclaimed the blending of "the races of Orcs and Men" a "black evil" (III.iv.479), and Gamling of Rohan had mentioned that "the foul-craft of Saruman has bred" these supposedly miscegenated people (III.vii.536), but a more rational explanation would of this phenomenon would hold that "men" and orcs were living amongst each other, working alongside one another, and yes, perhaps, "intermingling" sexually while also dwelling in the same city. Tolkien's own "realism," with respect to historical accuracy and ordinary probability, not to mention his meticulous attention to cultural and linguistic details, suggests that neither forced "breeding" nor dark magic has anything to do with the existence of hybrid races and cultures. In a metropolitan city like Isengard, the "mixing" of races was probably normal in day-to-day life, and intermarriage among persons from different backgrounds hardly seems odd. In any case, the fact of Isengard's mixed population suggests a cosmopolitan or international character that is wholly consistent with the emergence of new ways of thinking and being.

Given the proximity of orcs and men among the enemy forces, not to mention these who seem to include both races in their own person, one wonders how capable the "good guys" are in distinguishing between them. Before the Battle of Helm's Deep, a scout reports to Théoden that "Wormtongue was seen earlier, going northward with a company of Orcs" (III.vii.529), for example; Gríma is quite recognizable, of course, but his being a human with a company of orcs is not altogether remarkable.[22] Looking out from the Deeping Wall at the approach enemy army, for example, Legolas and Gimli "saw all the space between them and the Dike lit with white light: it was boiling and crawling with black shapes, some squat and broad, some tall and grim, with high helms and sable shields. Hundreds and hundreds more were pouring over the Dike and through the breach" (III.vii.532). A moment before, some Westfolders state that "[w]e loosed every arrow that we had, and filled the Dike with Orcs," but it is not made clear how they were able to distinguish orcs from men among those they were shooting at, particularly since Gimli had explicitly observed that it was "too dark for archery," in fact. In battle, of course, the enemy soldier is just a soldier, and presumably both orcs and men would be slain by sword, axe, arrow, or spear, regardless of which "race" is on the receiving end of such weaponry, but if a powerfully moral distinction is to be drawn between orcs and men, one that mandates that the former have less right to life than the latter, then one hopes that the military would be paying attention.

During the battle itself, the narrator explicitly mentions the orcs and men in Saruman's army at times, distinguishing them here and there, while often reverting to depicting seemingly all enemy combatants as orcs only elsewhere. For example, as the assault on Helm's Deep begins, "the hugest Orcs were mustered, and the wild men of the Dunland fells. A moment they hesitated and then on they came. The lightning flashed, and blazoned upon *every* helm and shield the ghastly hand of Isengard was seen" (III.vii.533, emphasis supplied). Aragorn leads the rush against this vanguard, as "a great press of Orcs and Men were gathering again beyond the stream," while a group of orcs who had been cunningly "playing dead" amidst the bodies of the fallen sprang up to attack Éomer. Out of the shadows, Gimli emerges, beheading two orcs with his axe and sending the rest fleeing. Gimli, at least, does distinguish between the "races" of his enemies, for he explains: "I looked on the hillmen and they seemed over large for me, so I sat beside a stone to see your sword-play […] But I am content. Till now I have hewn naught but wood since I left Moria" (536–537). This moment nicely resolves his prior comment—"my axe is restless in my hand. Give me a row of orc-necks and room to swing and all weariness will fall from me!" (532)—but one suspects, or hopes, that Gimli would willing to swing also at the "over large" necks of the hillmen in order to save Éomer's life.

As the battle continues, the orcs and men of Saruman's forces continue to fight alongside one another, but the dehumanizing language of the narrative is mostly reserved for the "demonized" race of orcs, not surprisingly. Thus, "the hosts of Isengard roared like a sea. Orcs and hillmen swarmed about its feet from end to end," and "Orcs sprang up them [i.e., ladders] like apes in the dark forests of the South" while "the dead and broken were piled like shingle in a storm; ever higher rose the hideous mounds, and still the enemy came on" (535). Meanwhile, "Orcs had crept like rats through the culvert" and into the Deep, prompting Gimli to shout: "Come, Legolas! There are enough for us both" (535). At the end of this rush, the dwarf and elf compare "scores," with Gimli claiming twenty-one to Legolas' two dozen, totals reflecting only orc lives, presumably, but there is certainly no reason to assume they would refuse to engage with the soldiery of other "races" in the course of their battles.

During the lull that follows, Gamling of Rohan notes the presence of "half-orcs and goblin-men," as well as "the wild men of the hills," whose voices he can hear in the distance. When Éomer, chauvinistically and disdainfully, says that he hears them, but that "they are only the screeching of birds and the bellowing of beasts to my ears," Gamling states that "the Dunland tongue" is "an ancient speech of men, and once was spoken in many western valleys of the Mark," adding:

> Hark! They hate us, and they are glad; for our doom seems certain to them. "The king, the king!" they cry. "We will take their king. Death to the Forgoil! Death to the Strawheads! Death to the robbers of the North!" Such names they have for us. Not in half a thousand years have they forgotten their grievance that the lords of Gondor gave the Mark to Eorl the Young and made alliance with him. That old hatred Saruman has inflamed. They are fierce folk when

roused. They will not give way now for dusk or dawn, until Théoden is taken, or they themselves are slain [536–537].

While not exactly sympathetic with the Dunlanders, Gamling at least recognizes that they have a legitimate "grievance" underscoring their "hatred" of the *Forgoil* ("Strawheads" or blond people, that is, the Rohirrim), who had taken their lands with the aid of foreign imperialists and who continued to dominate the region to this day. Éomer's ignorance and denigration of the native tongue spoken in his own kingdom is itself significant. He is the beneficiary of his ancestors' ancient collusion with invading Númenóreans, after all, and finds no value whatsoever in the languages or cultures of the people who were indigenous to those lands. From the perspective of the "wild" men, however, Saruman may well have seemed a far better ally and neighbor than their longtime foes, those who continue to oppress them.

Oddly, when the enemy forces next call "Bring out your king!" it is the Uruk-hai, not the Dunlendings, that make the request. The orcs are not attacking, but engaged in parley, if also a raucous one in which they "yell and jeer." When Aragorn tells them, "Get you gone," the orcs cried, "This is no parley. You have nothing to say," and Aragorn responds: "Depart, or not one of you will be spared. Not one will be left alive to take back tidings to the North" (539–540). For the orcs, at least, his prediction proves accurate, but it turns out that the "wild men" were in the audience as well, as they are explicitly mentioned as being part of that group. Aragorn's threat applies to all races in Saruman's army, but as we shall see, only those labeled *orcs* will be subject to the genocidal extermination to come, which is enough to show that race, not "enemy" status, is what determines such a policy by Aragorn, the Rohirrim, the ents and Huorns, or any other anti-orkish forces in *The Lord of the Rings*.

At this point, things go badly for Saruman's army, as several things happen nearly at once. Heralded by a blasts of the horn, Théoden and his guard ride out to face the enemy at one front ("Neither orc nor man withstood them"), and, on the other, the forest itself has mysteriously entered the battlefield from the north; these are the Huorns, which are something like treeish ents or entish trees. The Huorns will destroy all remaining orcs but, it seems, let all the remaining "men" live: "There now cowered the proud hosts of Saruman, in terror of the king and in terror of the trees" (541). At that point, Gandalf returns with Erkenbrand's legion to rout the now quailing forces, and being now surrounded by foes, "[t]he hosts of Isengard roared, swaying this way and that, turning from fear to fear" (541). The "terror" of Gandalf's coming "filled the enemy with madness," and the chapter ends with these lines: "The wild men fell on their faces before him. The Orcs reeled and screamed and cast aside both sword and spear. Like a black smoke driven by a mounting wind they fled. Wailing they passed under the waiting shadow of the trees; and from that shadow none ever came again" (542). Having cast aside "both sword and spear," therefore, the orcs are expressly said to be unarmed when they are slain, but then the extermination of orcs in Tolkien's world has little to do with any actual or imminent threat posed by them. Thus ends the Battle of Helm's Deep.

In the aftermath of the battle, it is discovered that "[n]o orcs remained alive; their bodies were uncounted," while "a great many of the hillman had given themselves up; and they were afraid, and cried for mercy" (III.viii.545). The Dunlendings are disarmed, forced into labor to help with the clean-up, and—so long as they swear an oath never to take up arms against Rohan again—freed. "The men of Dunland were amazed; for Saruman had told them that the men of Rohan were cruel and burned their captives alive" (545). Such propaganda undoubtedly serves the cause, but one cannot help but note the proximity of this line to those detailing the conscience-free killing of *all* orcs. The Rohirrim do not burn their captives alive, but nor do they take orcs captive at all. In Tolkien's writings, orcs never sue for peace, it is true, but considering the ways they are dealt with when merely making an appearance, it is difficult to imagine why any orc should dare hope for mercy. "The Whiteskins will catch you and eat you" may also be Saruman-concocted propaganda, but it seems as reasonable a surmise as any, once one considers the facts of the life of an orc in Middle-earth.

As for the lurid competition, Gimli claims forty-two lives, lamenting only the "notch" on his axe, for the "forty-second had an iron collar on his neck"; Legolas killed forty-one, but "I do not grudge you the game, so happy am I to see you" (III.viii.543). Readers may assume, but are not told directly, that all of Gimli's and Legolas's "kills" were orcs, but it is nevertheless well known that many of the forces of Isengard who were slain during the battle were also humans, not to mention these "half-orcs" or "goblin-men," whose disposition along the spectrum from merciful treatment to summary execution is not elaborated within the text. Great funeral mounds are raised for the dead, one for the soldiers of Rohan, while "the men of Dunland were set apart in a mound below the Dike." However, "[t]he Orcs were piled in great heaps, away from the mounds of Men" (545). We later learn that the bodies of the orcs mysteriously disappear, replaced with pit covered in stones that thereafter was called the Death Downs, and thus "the strange trees […] were revenged upon the Orcs" (553). Even in death, it seems, orcs cannot be accorded humane treatment.

Orcs do not appear so prominently in Book IV of *The Lord of the Rings*, which relates Frodo and Sam's difficult trek through the eastern lands around, and ultimately into, Mordor. Mostly, they are trying to avoid the "enemy," orcs and men alike, while dealing with Gollum as their "tamed" guide. However, before reaching Mordor there is a remarkable scene of battle in which the hobbits witness warfare "between men and men." Sméagol (Gollum) had already pointed out that "[v]ery dreadful things live" near Mordor, "Orcs, yes always Orcs; but worse things, worse things live there too" (IV.iii.642). He observes "[m]ore Men going into Mordor," and elaborates,

> Dark faces. We have not seen Men like these before, no, Sméagol has not. They are fierce. They have black eyes, and long black hair, and gold rings in their ears; yes, lots of beautiful gold. And some have red paint on their cheeks, and red cloaks; and their flags are red, and the tips of their spears; and they have round shields, yellow and black with big spikes. Not nice; very cruel wicked Men they look. Almost as bad as Orcs, and much bigger. Sméagol thinks they have come out of the South beyond the Great River's end: they came up that road. They have passed on to the Black Gate; but more may follow. Always more people coming to Mordor [646].

Sméagol's description of these "foreign" humans with their distinctive (and racially coded) features sets the stage for the scene to come, in which Sam witnesses his "first view of a battle of Men against Men" (IV.iv.661).

Regarding that brief skirmish, Sam "did not like it much," for he witnessed a Southron soldier killed in battle, "green arrow-feathers sticking from his neck below a golden collar"; his "black plaits of hair braided with gold were drenched with blood," while his "brown hand still clutched the hilt of a broken sword" (660–661). At this point, Sam "wondered what the man's name was and where he came from; and if he was really evil of heart, or what lies or threats had led him on the long march from his home; and if he would not really rather have stayed there in peace" (661). It probably goes without saying that Sam never wonders "what lies or threats had led him on the long march from" his *own* home in the Shire, well over a thousand miles away, although the he and his fellow hobbits often wish they could have remained at home in peace. Moreover, Sam's momentary sympathy for the fallen Southron offers another indication of the degree to which orcs, even those who fight alongside their "human" comrades, are never accorded sympathy, mercy, or some other sort of fellow-feeling by Sam or any of the other "heroes" in *The Lord of the Rings*. Yet Sam himself will discover that orcs have human, all-too-human feelings—complaints, worries, aspirations, desires, and so forth—when he encounters two distinctive orcs shortly thereafter, not that he sympathizes with them, of course. For Tolkien's heroes, even (or especially) the innocent, empathic, and hopeful Sam, the only good orc is a dead orc, after all.

"No big bosses": Orcs in Conversation

The final chapter of *The Two Towers* (i.e., of Book IV of *The Lord of the Rings*), "The Choices of Master Samwise," features the terrifying battle between Sam and Shelob, the monstrous spider-like being that haunts the tunnels above Minas Morgul, a fortress on the edge of Mordor. Frodo had been stung by the venomous Shelob, and as far as Sam can tell, he is dead. Sam makes the decision to take Ring and try to complete the quest on his own. Just then, a group of orcs arrive—two groups, in fact, comprising soldiers descending from the Tower of Cirith Ungol and others coming up from Minas Morgul below. Sam estimated their numbers: "Thirty or forty from the tower at least, and a lot more than that from down below" (IV.x.735). Sam then overhears the conversation between the respective captains, Shagrat and Gorbag, and learns that Frodo is only paralyzed, not killed, but has now been captured by the orcs. (This is yet another example of orcs taking an enemy, a "spy" in this case, alive, and we later learn that, although he was not treated very kindly, Frodo was unharmed, even cared for and fed by his captors.) During the conversation, readers learn more about these particular orcs, gaining insight into their motives and concerns, and by extension, learning more about the cultures of orcs more generally. In their worries about the state of the world and the war, along with their memories of a preferable past and dreams of a better future, Shagrat and Gorbag indicate a sort of utopian impulse in the orcs: a world without "Big Bosses."

When the orcs approach, Sam puts on the Ring, rendering him invisible to them, but also enhancing his ability to hear, it seems. He even understands the language spoken by the orcs, but unlike in "The Uruk-Hai" chapter, where it is explained that the multilingual orcs had chosen to use the Common Speech, here Tolkien suggests that the Ring itself offers the power of understanding otherwise foreign tongues: "He heard them both clearly, and he understood what they said. Perhaps the Ring gave understanding of tongues, or simply understanding, especially of the servants of Sauron its maker, so that if he gave heed, he understood and translated the thought to himself" (734).[23] The first words Sam hears are, "Hola, Gorbag!"—that is, Shagrat's greeting or hailing of his Minas Morgul counterpart—which has prompted some perplexed readers to wonder if orcs speak Spanish; more likely, *hola* is just a variation of "hullo" or perhaps "whoa," but in any case, Sam's preternatural ability to "translate" the speech of these orcs into his own idiom does not extend to such interjections, which thus come across as mere *sounds* as opposed to *words*. A bit later, we find that the group of orcs "gabbled and yammered after the fashion of their kind," but while "Sam heard the noise of their harsh voices, flat and hard in the dead air," "he could distinguish two voices from among all the rest." These belong to Shagrat and Gorbag, whose conversation he attends to carefully.

The initial, brief meeting of the two captains in the tunnel indicates immediately their respective stations with regard to current events. As Frodo, Sam, and Gollum had witnessed, the armies within Minas Morgul had issued forth to march to war, and so Shagrat questions (or taunts) Gorbag about not being with those troops: "What are you doing up here? Had enough of war already?" Gorbag responds by calling Shagrat a "lubber," explaining that he was given "orders," before asking, "what are you doing, Shagrat? Tired of lurking up there? Thinking of coming down to fight?" Shagrat counters, "Orders to you. I'm in command of this pass. So speak civil. What's your report?" Gorbag says, "Nothing." Already in the few lines the reader perceive the rivalry among different "camps" within the same army, one stationed at a high pass in the mountains over "the Dead City," the other garrisoned in the city itself, and neither is particularly happy with his post, as we will see. The apparent antagonism between Shagrat and Gorbag here also betrays a strong sense of fellow-feeling, not quite sympathy perhaps, but a clear understanding of what it means to be a leader who must also follow orders, a condition admittedly freighted with great responsibility and thus anxiety. At this point their conversation is interrupted. There is a commotion among their respective troops, as the orcs discover Frodo's body, but the captains will resume their discussion as they make their way up to the Tower, while Sam listens.

As the now mixed company of orcs venture through the tunnels, Gorbag asks (or, rather, *grunts*, as Tolkien puts it), "Can't you stop your rabble making such a racket, Shagrat? [...] We don't want Shelob on us." Shagrat responds, "Go on, Gorbag! Yours are making more than half the noise," adding, "But let the lads play!" The use of the word *lads* is notable here, and it is used several times by these orc captains. It is, of course, a term for young men or boys, often used affectionately. In idiomatic British, in fact, a *lad* can be thought of as a friend as well as a youngster. Shagrat's use of the term, in response to Gorbag's reference to the "rabble," is something of a rebuke, while also indicating a sense that *both* of their companies comprise "lads" who ought to be allowed to express high spirits. For Shagrat then explains that Shelob had clearly been wounded and thus would not be troubling them. "So let 'em laugh!" This is the expression of a caring leader of men, even if it does come from a rather uncouth and even violent person (which, as Tolkien himself notes, is not uncommon in the ranks of British officers in his own "real" world, as I discussed in Chapter 1). Shagrat's concern for his "lads" and their right to "play" is a sign of his almost paternal and certainly amiable leadership qualities, which no doubt explains how he came to become a captain of a key regiment in Mordor in the first place.

Shagrat next says, "we've struck a bit of luck at last: got something the Lugbúrz wants." *Lugbúrz* is another name for Barad-dûr, Sauron's great tower and redoubt, and hence stands here metonymically as the locus of Mordor's power itself (much as a U.S. soldier might say that "the White House" wants something). Intrigued by this reference to Frodo, Gorbag responds, "Lugbúrz wants it, eh? What is it, d'you think? Elvish it looked to me, but undersized. What's the danger in a thing like that?" Shagrat says he does not know, and Gorbag exclaims: "Oho! So they haven't told you what to expect? They don't tell us all they know, do they? Not by half. But they can make mistakes, even the Top Ones can." A circumspect Shagrat shushes Gorbag, answering in a whisper, "They may, but they've got eyes and ears everywhere; some among my lot, as like as not. But there's no doubt about it, they're troubled about something. The Nazgûl down below are, by your account; and Lugbúrz is too. Something nearly slipped." Gorbag questions the "nearly" in that comment, and Shagrat urges them to wait until they can find a safer place to talk (737).

Already, in this brief exchange, the reader witnesses a very *human* interaction, a shared sense of cautious celebration ("luck at last") with grave worry ("Something nearly slipped"), combined with the all-too-human and wholly sensible mistrust of the powers that reign over their lives, political and miliary leaders who "don't tell us all they know" and who "can make mistakes," even those at the very top of the power structure. The fear of being unable to speak openly about one's views is part of this vexed condition, one that Tolkien knew all too well.

As a veteran of the British army in the Great War and as the father of a soldier serving in the Royal Air Force in the Second World War, Tolkien could not help but sympathize with the feelings of these orkish soldiers, if only unconsciously, and I would suggest that his inclusion of the conversation between Shagrat and Gorbag thus does far more than merely fill in some plot details. Tolkien uses these orcs to show what the life of the common soldier is like, one haunted by constant threats from both their enemies and their fellow soldiery (i.e., potential spies among them), military superiors, and political overlords. Tolkien may have imagined the orc captains as opportunities to express sympathy for England's own enemies, the common German, Japanese, or Italian infantrymen, along with Russian and American troops. In Shagrat and Gorbag, we can see Tolkien's sense of remaining "a patriotic Roman citizen, while preferring a free Gaul and seeing good in Carthaginians," as he had put it in a wartime letter to Christopher.[24] Whether he intended this or not, Tolkien's depiction of these orcs indicates a sympathy toward them that none of his "heroes" in the novel ever feel or display.

The manner of speech and the language used is also noteworthy. Verlyn Flieger, observing the quite "familiar," somewhat lower-class diction, phrasing, and delivery of orcs when speaking, has suggested that this feature of their being, ironically, helps to estrange orcs all the more, since their very speech does not appear to "fit" in the more epic setting of Middle-earth and the elevated speech to be found among many of its peoples. When orcs use "language that is at once familiar and out of place," Flieger says,

> alterity doubles back upon itself and the result is radical estrangement through the incongruity of unexpected familiarities. Recognizable speech patterns and diction conventionally associated with familiar, even stereotypical character types (lower-class, uneducated) fall strangely on the ear when put in the mouths of equally stereotypical monsters, and we realize with surprise that Orcs actually talk as much or more like real people than do the rest of the species that inhabit Middle-earth.[25]

Interesting as this insight is, it relies on imagining that orcs are not "real people," that they remain "stereotypical monsters," which does not strike me as an accurate characterization of the orcs that appear in *The Lord of the Rings*. As we have seen, orcs are mostly depicted as vile "men," even when being demonized or dehumanized, and readers undoubtedly encounter their speech as one might that of "an apparent orc on a motor bike" in the present "real" world, as Tolkien mentioned.[26] Given how realistically demotic the orcs are shown to be, as fundamentally members of the *hoi polloi* if not the *les damnés de la terre du milieu*, it is more likely the absurdly improbable references to their fangs and claws that are intended to *estrange* the orcs' being from our own humankind.

Many readers, including Flieger here, have noted that the orcs' speech is intended to represent a lower-class or working-class manner. The orcs are often ruder or cruder that these others, but they mostly speak in ways that are similar to such working-class hobbits or humans as Sam, the Gaffer, Nob or Bill Ferny from Bree, or even Ioreth, the loquacious nurse in Minas Tirith. These characters, like Shagrat and Gorbag, speak in a more modern, everyday idiom and manner than even such villainous enemies as the Lord of the Nazgûl or the Mouth of Sauron, who like Aragorn or Gandalf represent "higher" classes. However, as Brian Rosebury has pointed out, Tolkien seems to employ "at least three different dialogue-types for Orcs," adding that "[n]one of them, incidentally, is 'working-class.'"

The "comparatively cerebral Grishnákh, for example, talks like a melodrama villain," saying such phrases as "My dear tender little fools," and "We shan't hurry the enquiry. Oh dear no!" Uglúk, by slight contrast, represents the mode of speech to be found in warriors, full of declarations and boasts ("We are the fighting Uruk-hai!"), whereas Shagrat speaks more like a desperate and put-upon middle-class manager ("The Black Pits take that filthy rebel," and "I gave him better than I got").[27] What remains clear in all these ways of speaking is the degree to which these orcs, sometimes representing different ranks or cultures, consistently speak like regular human beings.

In a tale featuring non-heroic, ordinary small folk (hobbits) caught up in a grand, world-historical drama, the lives of everyday soldiers "on the other side" in some ways parallel that of our heroes. These orcs, much like the hobbits of the Shire, are thoroughly subordinated to the great powers of the geopolitical order of Middle-earth, including Sauron on the one side, Galadriel, Elrond, Gandalf, along with Aragorn and Denethor on the other, plus Saruman representing a "side" to himself, not to mention the many kingdoms and enclaves that have more or less to do with the "great events" of the era (such as the remaining orcs of the Misty Mountains, the elves of Mirkwood, the dwarves of the Iron Hills or Erebor, the men of Dale or of Dunland, along with Easterlings, Southrons, and so on). And yet, as with Merry, Pippin, Sam, and Frodo, the orcs are caught up in it. As with those others, we learn, they also wish that things could be different.

When Shagrat and Gorbag find a quiet corner in which to have their conversation, these very human emotions come to the fore. The next voice Sam overhears is that of Gorbag, confessing that he also does not know what exactly is going on:

> The messages go through quicker than anything could fly, as a rule. But I don't enquire how it's done. Safest not to. Grr! Those Nazgûl give me the creeps. And they skin the body off you as soon as look at you, and leave you all cold in the dark on the other side. But He likes 'em; they're His favourites nowadays, so it's no use grumbling [IV.x.737].

The reference to the Nazgûl being favorites of Sauron recalls Grishnákh's similar remark, admonishing Uglúk for doubting the power of the Ringwraiths: "*Nazgûl!* Ah! [...] You ought to know that they're the apple of the Great Eye" (III.iii.452). This is enough to show that even the orcs working for, alongside, or underneath the Nazgûl are awestruck and often afraid of them. Not surprisingly, then, Gorbag adds, "I tell you, it's no game serving down in the city" (IV.x.737).

Not to be outdone, Shagrat observes that his own situation is far from enviable. "You should try being up here with Shelob for company," he says, to which his counterpart responds, "I'd like to try somewhere where there's none of 'em" (739). In this simple declaration, Gorbag sums up a most profound impulse toward freedom. It is an expression of the desire for individual and collective autonomy, without monstrous and despotic authorities threatening one's life, liberty, and the pursuit of happiness. Perhaps it is because of the utopian spark behind this quite reasonable comment, but Gorbag—who in the few pages in which we get to know him is normally rather pessimistic, with Shagrat even stating that "you always did take a gloomy view" (739)—then allows himself a brief moment to dream of a better life, even including his erstwhile rival in his hopes for what that may be. Pointing out that they cannot do much about their present, undesirable situations whilst the war continues, Gorbag expresses hope that things will improve once the war is over. When Shagrat tells him, "It's going well, they say," Gorbag skeptically responds, "They would. [...] We'll see," thus reiterating his mistrust of the propaganda of their leaders. But then he adds, "if it does go well, there should be a lot more room. What d'you say?—if we get a chance, you and me'll slip off and set up somewhere on our own with a few trusty lads, somewhere where there's good loot nice and handy, and no big bosses." "Ah," Shagrat answers, almost ecstatically, "Like old times" (738).

The dream of "no big bosses" is associated in Gorbag's mind with the formation of a community of "trusty lads"—again, *lads*, a term of great affection—which immediately registers in Shagrat's mind a sort of nostalgia for a time that he can directly remember himself, or else that he imagines was the way that many orcs were able to live prior to their subjugation by "big bosses." Indeed, by imagining the "old times" in this way, Shagrat and Gorbag would appear to be speaking of a state of affairs more suited to their ways of life. As soldiers, in fact, they could simply be thinking of times of relative peace, before they were placed in the unenviable position of fighting against deadly foes, while also taking responsibility for the "lads" in their charge and answering to the "bosses" above them. In a way, the "Northerners" depicted earlier must have felt greater personal freedom, in wanting to avenge their kin and to go back home, rather than being part of the great war and geopolitical conflicts of the time. Shagrat and Gorbag, however, as captains of major garrisons of troops in Mordor, do not have that luxury, but that does not mean that they cease to long for freedom.

Within Tolkien's writings, not to mention in a broader discourse surrounding it and in popular cultural adaptations, orcs are frequently imagined as being inherently evil beings who are "slaves" to the will of their superiors, in particular Morgoth and Sauron (and, perhaps, Saruman). Yet the conversation here not only undermines such a view, but forcefully contradicts it. Gorbag and Shagrat are not slaves to their master's will, whatever that could even mean, and they are not even particularly interested in the cause that motivates Sauron or the other "bosses." Like so many soldiers, they are at war because their military and political leaders had declared and waged war, but they show no great desire to prosecute that warfare. We see no evidence of bloodlust with respect to their enemies, nor any particular desire on their part to attack elves, men, or dwarves. Rather, they wish only to do their duty, ideally to be recognized for doing so (though they are not holding their breath waiting!), and then to be released from it so that they may pursue other interests without the interference of "big bosses." Admittedly, their plans may not be the most wholesome, as it seems they wish to become roving looters of a postwar landscape, to take advantage of a sort of *Pax Mordoriana* to make their fortunes in the world, which—at the risk of stating the obvious—is itself all too realistic, humane, and historically accurate a depiction of what so many humans in various "pax"-times (e.g., Romana, Brittania, Americana) have also attempted and accomplished. That Shagrat likens such a state to "old times" suggests the degree to which this would be preferable norm, in contrast to the dangers of wartime and military service.

Gorbag's optimism does not linger, thus revealing this dream to seem almost unrealistic even to him, the dreamer. He continues:

> But don't count on it. I'm not easy in my mind. As I said, the Big Bosses, ay [...] ay, even the Biggest, can make mistakes. Something nearly slipped, you say. I say, something *has* slipped. And we've got to look out. Always the poor Uruks to put slips right, and small thanks. But don't forget: the enemies don't love us any more than they love Him, and if they get topsides on Him, we're done too [IV.x.739].

The "poor Uruks," in this case, refer to all orcs, and Gorbag is clearly irritated and dismayed that the orcs are "always" the ones who must fix the problems that the "Big Bosses" have created. The very reason he and his men, along with Shagrat and the company from the Tower, are even in this tunnel at that moment is "to put slips right," after all. As is the case with nearly all conflicts and in nearly all countries, the common people, soldiers especially but also workers of all types, are importuned if not also forced to labor in solving problems not of their own making, with the responsibility, but not the credit, being foisted upon them. When Elrond at his Council declared that "such is oft the course of deeds that move the wheels of the world" that "small hands do them because they must, while the eyes of the great are elsewhere" (II.ii.269), readers are probably encouraged to think of hobbits (as Bilbo himself does!) or else "small folk" of other varieties, but it is clear from Gorbag's perspective that the "poor Uruks" are frequently put in such a position as well.

Gorbag's caveat, "don't forget," is itself important. Lest we think that Gorbag, Shagrat, and the other orcs are merely griping about their jobs or criticizing their leaders, we must acknowledge that they hold a terrible stake in the outcome of the war. For them, it is life or death, since "the enemies"—notice that Gorbag does not say *our* enemies—of Sauron, which is to say the elves, men of the West, and so forth, will try to destroy the orcs, even if the orcs themselves are not to blame for the policies about which those enemies are so aggrieved. In fact, as we have seen, those elves and men and their allies think nothing of hunting down and killing orcs who are *not* on the side of Sauron. If anything, Sauron and others seem to offer a better deal to the orcs in their service, since the alternative is to be slain, without trial or even questioning, by the side declaring itself in the right and that readers are given to assume is "good." Gorbag and Shagrat are not happy in their situations as captains in the garrisons of Mordor, but they know that they would be killed immediately by those who oppose Mordor. Indeed, as was the case with the riders of Rohan, who were not at war with Sauron (yet), the orcs would be killed regardless of their allegiances or lack thereof. Any utopian vision of a future for orkish happiness would appear to require the complete and total victory of the forces of Mordor, at least as a first step. No wonder Gorbag is such a pessimist!

As their conversation proceeds, Gorbag and Shagrat compare notes, attempting to figure out what is actually going on. Shagrat says that only about an hour earlier he had received a message, "*Nazgûl uneasy. Spies feared on Stairs. Double vigilance. Patrol to head of Stairs.*" Gorbag reckons this is "Bad business," admitting that "our Silent Watchers were uneasy two days ago," but that "my patrol wasn't ordered out for another day, nor any message sent to Lugbúrz either" (738). He chalks that up to "the great signal going up and the High Nazgûl going off to war," and Shagrat surmises that "the Eye was busy elsewhere," since "Big things are going on away west, they say." Readers of *The Lord of the Rings*, putting together the timeline of events, will recognize the coincidence of Aragorn's revelation of himself to Sauron using the *palantír*, which as luck (or fate or Providence) would have it helps to allow Frodo and Sam to proceed farther than they might otherwise have done. Even these orc captains are surprised by the oversight, and they begin to worry about the "slip" that now likely poses a deadly threat to them and to their companies. Gorbag fears that a mighty elf-warrior is on the loose, an image that grimly amuses Sam, but Shagrat feels more secure in the effectiveness of their surveillance procedures, while also rejoicing in their find, a prisoner that Lugbúrz will be happy to have. Shagrat then reveals that Frodo is alive, as Shelob's venom merely paralyzed him temporarily. He insists that Frodo be kept alive and unharmed, for the prisoner is to be taken to Sauron, but Gorbag, still convinced that a great warrior is at large, warns Shagrat to "catch the big one that's loose, before you send in any report to Lugbúrz. It won't sound too pretty to say you've caught the kitten and let the cat escape" (741). Gorbag's wariness is proven to be quite justified, as Sam will eventually confirm his suspicions, effectively leading to the downfall of the armies of Mordor.

Book IV ends with Sam overhearing a debate between Shagrat and Gorbag over where to store the prisoner before he is transferred to Barad-dûr, with Shagrat insisting that Frodo be placed in the top of the Tower, away from the temptations of the other orcs. "He's going out of harm's way, I tell you [...] See? He's precious. I don't trust all my lads, and none of yours; nor you neither, when you're mad for fun. He's going where I want him" (741). So much for finding some "trusty lads," we might think! As it happens, the two colleagues will come to fatal blows over the disposition of Frodo's mithril shirt, and Shagrat will later reveal that he killed Gorbag in a scene from the first chapter of Book VI later. Needless to say, this illuminating conversation between the captains is hardly a model for friendship, camaraderie, or solidarity, but it does demonstrate in no uncertain terms the degree to which these orcs are quite human, if also nasty, violent, and untrustworthy: traits quite often found in humans, as we all know all too well. In their worries about their jobs, their subordinates, their bosses, the prosecution of the war, and their own futures, Shagrat and Gorbag are rather representative of the common soldiery in wartime, and exemplary figures for a very realistic, earthy, and non-idealized image of humans living and working in dark times.

The Two Towers, more than anywhere else in *The Lord of the Rings* or indeed in Tolkien's entire legendarium, offers a vista into the lives of orcs in Middle-earth toward the end of the Third Age. Perhaps despite himself, Tolkien utterly humanizes these creatures in the scenes in which they appear, demonstrating definitively that they are not demonic or bestial, even if their all-too-human brutality is also on display. They can be loyal and sometimes disloyal, individualistic and communitarian, practical and idealistic, gloomy and yet at times hopeful. Tolkien depicts the orcs as rude, crude, and violent, but also as wary, sensitive, frightened, doubtful, vengeful, dutiful, and above all worried. Orcs worry about their enemies and their supposed allies, about their "bosses," and about the world in which they live. As the War of the Ring comes to its climax in the final volume of *The Lord of the Rings*, these worries among the orcs are only heightened. In *The Return of the King*, readers confront the potential end of the orcs entirely.

CHAPTER 6

Don't You Know We're at War?

The Ends of the Orcs in The Return of the King

War features quite prominently in the third volume of *The Lord of the Rings*, so it is perhaps not surprising that Tolkien, once convinced that the novel would have to be published in installments, wanted to name this one *The War of the Ring* (or else, to give titles to each of Books V and VI, *The War of the Ring* and *The End of the Third Age*).[1] Tolkien initially disapproved of *The Return of the King*, partly on the quite reasonable grounds that it gives away a major element of the plot left still uncertain when that volume's narrative begins. Much of what occurs in these two final Books of the novel is connected to the War, as the story shifts to matters of mustering armies, formulating battle-strategy, engaging in actual military combat, and dealing with the aftermath of the fighting. The hobbits Merry and Pippin become personally engaged in martial activities, eventually becoming military leaders in their own right, while such ostensible non-combatants as Frodo or Sam find themselves among soldiers and soldiery. Needless to say, perhaps, orcs—who have mostly been presented as troops or else heavily armed, more-or-less well-trained marauders throughout *The Hobbit* and *The Lord of the Rings*—here continue to serve as foot soldiers in the enemy armies, but in this last volume we see further depictions of them in their regiments, complete with military hierarchies and discipline (and, at times, lack of discipline). In the War of the Ring, the final disposition of the orcs of Middle-earth is apparently decided, and the representations of orcs in *The Return of the King* is thus all the more significant for allowing readers to get a somewhat conclusive sense of their role in and its importance for Tolkien's world.

Tolkien employment of an *entrelacement* technique continues in *The Return of the King*, which begins with a chapter featuring Gandalf and

Pippin riding to Minas Tirith, thus taking up the storyline where it had been left at the conclusion of Book III. The cliffhanger ending to *The Two Towers* (i.e., Book IV), in which Frodo has been captured by orcs in Mordor and Sam must attempt to rescue him, will not be revisited until the first chapter of Book VI. Meanwhile the movements of various characters—Pippin and Gandalf in Minas Tirith, Merry and the Rohirrim mustering for war, Aragon, Legolas, and Gimli traveling the Paths of the Dead, among others—will be tracked in different chapters, with Frodo and Sam reuniting with the surviving others only in Chapter 4 of Book VI. This makes for a somewhat heterogeneous representation of the places and events encountered, with many things happening at the same time, often serendipitously. Orcs are almost omnipresent in these chapters, but quite unlike their roles in *The Two Towers*, where many individual orcs are featured, in *The Return of the King* they are once again treated as a faceless mass on inhuman enemies for the most part. This itself has consequences for the story, all the more so given the nearly continuous presence of men (humans) working alongside the orcs. Notwithstanding the cooperation and coexistence of orcs and men throughout the war, the post–Sauron world will apparently be a world of men, one in which orcs are not permitted to exist at all.

In this chapter, as in the others, I will discuss key scenes in which orcs appear and make their marks on the narrative as a whole in *The Return of the King*. But I will also examine scenes in which the absence of orcs, or the contrast between orcs and men, is particularly noteworthy. Just as Saruman's army contained orcs and "men," not to mention "half-orcs" (whatever that means), Sauron's forces include any number of different cultures, races, and beings, with several distinctive characters in prominent roles, most of whom are not orcs. However, the defeat of Sauron will presumably entail the destruction of nearly all orcs, if not their complete annihilation, such that afterwards, orcs once again seem to recede into a kind of figurative role, the basis of metaphors that refer to objectionable human behavior or speech. In the end, of course, this serves only to reinforce the idea that orcs are, always have been, and remain human, *all-too-human*, in fact.

Drûgs Are Not Orcs: Varieties of the Humane in the Siege of Gondor

As the great battles begin, Minas Tirith is under siege, Aragorn and his companions seek out an alternative route to Gondor through the Paths of the Dead, and the Rohirrim prepare to join the fray from the northwest.

During the muster of Rohan, the reader is introduced to a new people—arguably a new "race," although these will be classed as "men"—known by the people of Rohan as the *Woses* or the Wild Men. In elfish Sindarin language, they are known as the *Drúedain* (also the *Drûgs*), a terms that appears to mean "Wild Men" as well.[2] In the chapter titled "The Ride of the Rohirrim," Merry first discovers the existence of the Woses by hearing their drums in the darkness, sounds that he mistakes for those of "the enemy." A rider, Elfhelm, disabuses him of this supposition, explaining:

> You hear the Woses, the Wild Men of the Woods: thus they talk together from afar. They still haunt Drúadan Forest, it is said. Remnants of an older time they be, living few and secretly, wild and wary as the beasts. They go not to war with Gondor or the Mark; but now they are troubled by the darkness and the coming of the orcs: they fear lest the Dark Years be returning, as seems likely enough. Let us be thankful that they are not hunting us: for they use poisoned arrows, it is said, and they are woodcrafty beyond compare. But they have offered their services to Théoden [V.v.831].

It is perhaps ironic that Elfhelm gives thanks for not being hunted by these people who are as "wild and wary as beasts," seeing as how the main reason the Drúedain chieftain is offering his services to the King of Rohan is that he wishes his own people not be hunted "like beasts" by the Rohirrim. By introducing the Woses, Tolkien offers an image of a "wild" or "savage" race of humans who are nevertheless on the side of the "good guys." As it happens, their relative goodness is directly associated with their hatred of orcs.

According to Tolkien, the very name Drúedain was conferred upon this "race" of men by the elves in recognition of their anti-orkish *bona fides*. In *Unfinished Tales*, we learn that, "when the Eldar [i.e., the elves] discovered that the Drû-folk were steadfast enemies of Morgoth, and especially of the Orcs, the 'title' *adan* was added, and they were called Drúedain (singular Drúadan), to mark both their humanity and friendship with the Eldar, and their racial difference from the Three Houses of the Edain."[3] The word *adan* means "man," so the elves here effectively *bestowed* humanity onto these creatures who might otherwise have been considered too orc-like in their own character and looks. The description of the appearance of this people in *Unfinished Tales* is not particularly flattering, to say the least.

> To the eyes of Elves and other Men they were unlovely in looks: they were stumpy (some four foot high) but very broad, with heavy buttocks and short thick legs; their wide faces had deep-set eyes with heavy brows, and flat noses, and grew no hair below their eyebrows, except in a few men (who were proud of the distinction) a small tail of black hair in the midst of the chin. Their features were usually impassive, the most mobile being their wide mouths; and

the movement of their wary eyes could not be observed save from those close at hand, for they were so black that the pupils could not be distinguished, but in anger they glowed red.[4]

Clearly, this description is not very different from Tolkien's own representation of the appearance of orcs as "squat, broad, flat-nosed, sallow-skinned, with wide mouths and slant eyes: in fact degraded and repulsive versions of the (to Europeans) least lovely Mongol-types."[5] Indeed, within Middle-earth, one of the theories of the origins of the orcs is that they are themselves an ethnicity within the broader racial category of the Drúedain: "some thought, nonetheless, that there had been a remote kinship, which accounted for their special enmity. Orcs and Drûgs each regarded the other as renegades."[6] Sigmund Freud famously characterized the phenomenon of racism "the narcissism of minor differences," and one might say that the Drûgs' "implacable" hatred of the orcs was based in their own anxieties about appearing orkish themselves.[7]

The "Wild Men" known as the Drúedain are obviously a distinct race or ethnicity from those "wild men" who fought alongside orcs in Saruman's army at the Battle of Helm's Deep. The racism or racialized portrayal of the Drúedain ironically becomes an advantage, since they are so far removed from the other cultures as to not be seen as a rival, particularly so long as they maintain their "place" within their own limited, geographically circumscribed enclave of the Drúadan Forest. In this case, being more absolutely "Othered" is an advantage, for the racial distinction here apparently spares the Woses from the taint of being like the "bad" Dunlendings who also viewed as "wild," but whose opposition to the men of Rohan renders them enemies in *The Lord of the Rings*, despite some evidence that they had legitimate historical grievances against the "Strawheads" who had taken over their lands and forced them into the rugged hill country at their borders. Some of those Dunlendings were undoubtedly among the Southerners making their way up the Greenway and into Breeland, while others may have been part of the purported miscegenation that produced the "half-orcs" or "goblin-men," given the clear signs of cohabitation and fraternization between these "men" and orcs. Hence, the Woses' relative racial purity, their unwillingness to mix with other races of men, is yet another sign of their "goodness" in the elvish and Númenorean racial hierarchies on display in Tolkien's legendarium.

The Drúedain, and particularly their chieftain Ghân-buri-Ghân, play a small but significant role in the narrative. Ghân-buri-Ghân is described as "a strange squat shape of a man, gnarled as an old stone, and the hairs of his scanty beard straggled on his lumpy chin like dry moss. He was short-legged and fat-armed, thick and stumpy, and clad only with grass about his waist," and he reminds Merry of the Púkel-men statues he had seen earlier in Dunharrow (V.v.831). (Indeed, as reported in *Unfinished Tales*, the term *Púkel-men* is another name for the Drúedain, who almost certainly carved the statues years before.) When he speaks, Ghân-buri-Ghân's "voice was deep and guttural, yet to Merry's surprise he spoke the Common Speech, though in a halting fashion, and uncouth words were mingled with it." Théoden had apparently asked the Wild Man for aid in fighting, and the first words Merry hears are those refusing the request: "No, father of Horse-men [...] we fight not. Hunt only. Kill *gorgûn* in woods, hate orc-folk. You hate *gorgûn* too. We help as we can. Wild Men have long ears and long eyes; know all paths. Wild Men live here before Stone-houses; before Tall Men come up out of Water" (832). Robert Stuart refers to this manner of speech as an "appalling 'me Tonto' Westron," markedly contrasted with Théoden's more elevated manner and diction.[8] The language here reinforces the surmise that the Drúedain might be inspired by "Red Indians," for which Tolkien in "On Fairy-Stories" had confessed his childhood enthusiasm, especially with regard to their "bows and arrows," "strange languages," and "glimpses of an archaic mode of life."[9] Indeed, John Garth has gone so far as to suggest that the Woses, silvan "archers who move unseen," are suggestive of Henry Wadsworth Longfellow's Hiawatha and a character like Uncas in James Fenimore Cooper's *The Last of the Mohicans*.[10]

The image of Ghân-buri-Ghân as an American-Indian-like "noble savage" also resolves the paradox of this ostensibly inferior and even somewhat orc-like race's being presented in such a positive light (if that is what it can be called). As Dimitra Fimi has pointed out, the depiction of the Drúedain as "noble savages" allows for a shift in the otherwise relatively consistent moral ordering of the races in Tolkien's legendarium. She notes that "the Woses are a deviation from the strict racial hierarchy of Middle-earth," for "[i]nstead of being classified as an inferior race due to their primitiveness, Tolkien seems to view them as 'noble savages': unlovely in appearance rather than exotically beautiful (as other 'noble savages' in contemporary literature are often portrayed), but still romanticized. Their primitiveness is respected rather than despised."[11] Some might cite Tolkien's presentation of the Drúedain as evidence that he or his work is not racist, yet this depiction still exhibits the hallmarks of bigotry, inasmuch as the infantilizing of the people, along with the celebration of their primitive ways, marks them as a distinctive race *apart* from the "norm." The Woses can thereby be used to further racist or racialist purposes by establishing the "good" savage in contrast to those other unacceptable savages abroad. The rhetoric of the "noble savage" has long been used to pit the vanishing American Indians against the "foreign" cultures and peoples of Asia or Africa, for example.¹² And if the Drúedain remind readers somewhat of the *indigenous* peoples of the Americas, that makes their comparative difference from the Mongol-like orcs, the Turk-like or Near Eastern–seeming Easterlings, and the Black African–like Southrons all the more apparent.

Returning to the conversation between Ghân-buri-Ghân and Théoden, we find that the Drúadan leader offers to guide the Rohirrim along a secret path through the forest, which will allow them to reach the borders of Gondor without fear of being waylaid along the road by orcs and other enemies. This simple act will have major ramifications, enabling the Rohirrim to break the siege of Gondor, to help turn the tide in the Battle of the Pelennor Fields, and to kill the Lord of the Nazgûl (thanks to Merry and Éowyn). As ultimate reward for the aid given to the riders of Rohan by the Drúedain, after the war, Aragorn—now crowned as King Elessar—will give the Forest of Drúadan to "Ghân-buri-Ghân and all his folk, to be their own forever," declaring that hereafter "let no man enter without their leave" (VI.vi.976). While some skeptical readers might question whether granting the Drúedain the right to live in their own homeland is an especially generous reward for helping to restore the kingdom, this is actually far more than the Drûg leader requested, for when Théoden offered to reward him, Ghân-buri-Ghân asks only this: "if you live after the Darkness, then leave Wild Men alone in the woods and do not hunt them like beasts any more" (V.v.833).

Hence, notwithstanding the elves' beneficence in granting some degree of humanity upon the "Wild Men of the Woods," then, some people—including the purportedly noble riders of Rohan—had been hunting them "like beasts" over the years. As far as I can tell, the only other "humane" beings, which is to say in Tolkien's own definition of the term with respect to his tale "all 'speaking creatures,'" who are *hunted* in this way are the orcs. However, as we have seen, the most redeeming quality of these "noble savages" of the woodlands, at least in the eyes the elves and noble men, is their own murderous hatred for orcs, which thus renders them far more like "good guys" from the perspective of the hobbits than the "wild" Dunlendings, Easterlings, and Haradrim, even if those peoples are utterly "humane" and human.¹³ The ultimate reward given to Drúedain by the more elite "humans" in the Fourth Age is to be considered and perhaps even treated as human.

Gothmog and the Mouth of Sauron; or, the State of Mordor

Meanwhile, within the narrative of *The Lord of the Rings*, the Gondorian capital of Osgiliath has been overrun by the forces from Mordor, and the city of Minas Tirith is under siege. As with Saruman's army in the Battle of Helm's Deep, Sauron's forces include both orcs and men, and indeed Sauron's armies are far larger and far more diverse, featuring numerous cultures, ranks, and creatures. The military assault on Gondor includes battalions comprising not only orcs, but also "Easterlings with axes, and Variags of Khand, Southrons in scarlet, and out of Far Harad black men like half-trolls with white eyes and red tongues" (V.vi.846), not to mention trolls and "troll-men," *mûmakil* (also known as Oliphaunts), winged beasts, and Nazgûl, with the Witch-king of Angmar, Lord of the Nazgûl, as the general leading the charge. The seafaring Corsairs of Umbar were also expected to arrive and reinforce Sauron's armies, but as we discover, Aragorn with the aid of the "Dead Men of Dunharrow" intercepted them and took their ships. As impressive as all of this is, the reader will later learn that the tens of thousands of troops fighting in the Battle of the Pelennor Fields were but a fraction of Sauron's larger military forces that were bivouacking and mustering within Mordor, as we see when Frodo and Sam get swept up in some of their movements in Book VI.

Such a multiracial and multi-ethnic coalition is arguably an indication of the well-nigh global antipathy toward the powers of Gondor and of "the West," for these people are clearly not "slaves to the will" of Sauron, just as we have seen the orcs are not. This does not mean they, or Sauron, are in the right, whether morally or politically, but it does give one pause. Sam, looking upon the slain Southron soldier in Ithilien, experiences just such a pause, even if he could not engender in himself the critical thinking necessary to question his own motives for being so very far from home and participating in a war about which he had known nothing just a few months before. The orcs, at least, know well that if they are not victorious, they will be wiped out entirely by peoples who delight in hunting and killing them, but the men of the multiple countries to the east and south are presumably acting in their or their sovereign's interests. The forces of the West also included a varied company, of course, with the sons of Elrond and the Rangers of the North joining Aragorn, Legolas, and Gimli, along with peoples allied with Gondor. What is more, as readers learn later, battles were occurring throughout the known parts of Middle-earth during this time, as elves fought beneath the trees of Mirkwood, while dwarves at Erebor and the men of Dale fought Sauron's forces, among other struggles in various places. Nevertheless, Tolkien presents the War of the Ring as a fight between the "free peoples" in the West—Aragon actually names his sword *Andúril*, "the Flame of the West"—and the multicultural, multiracial forces of the South and the East, as well as the orkish hordes emanating (at least in part) from Gundabad in the North.[14]

Orcs are omnipresent in these chapters, but they are not distinguished by name, characteristics, or personalities, as was the case with Uglúk, Grishnákh, Shagrat, Gorbag, or even some unnamed orcs from the Misty Mountains in *The Two Towers*. In Book V of *The Lord of the Rings*, the orcs are merely a threatening mass of soldiery, or else a retreating body of defeated soldiers to be hunted down from behind. Notably, and unlike the human counterparts with whom they work, fight, and sometimes live, these orcs are not really depicted as having their own homelands, whether in Mordor or elsewhere. They may inhabit strongholds like Gundabad or Moria—tellingly, both of which were founded by dwarves—but even in places like the Goblin-town of *The Hobbit*, orcs are not given the opportunity to live in peace. In any event, there is no sense that orcs *belong* to any land, which makes their extermination by the heroes seem all the more desirable and justified.

Tolkien notes that Sauron's forces during the siege of Gondor were not led by any orc, but rather something far more cunning and perilous. "It was no brigand or orc-chieftain that ordered the assault upon the Lord of Mordor's greatest foe. A power and mind of malice guided it" (V.iv.821), a reference to the Lord of the Nazgûl, a being once known as the Witch-king of Angmar. When that fearsome enemy is defeated by Merry and Éowyn later, Tolkien explicitly names the "lieutenant of Morgul" who now leads the attack on Gondor: Gothmog. This is one of those fascinating little details that makes Tolkien's world so rich, but it is also a curiosity, considering that this person is never again mentioned, and no further information is known of him. We do not even know what sort of "being" Gothmog is.[15] In Peter Jackson's film adaptation, Gothmog is depicted as a particularly gruesome-looking orc, fearless in battle and imperious toward his troops. Yet nothing in the novel itself suggests that an orc would be second-in-command to the Lord of the Nazgûl in so militarily, geographically, and strategically crucial a fortress as Minas Morgul, nor be given the authority to direct the actions of Easterlings, Variags, Southrons, and the "black men" of Far Harad. Indeed, for whatever reason, this passage does not mention Gothmog's issuing of orders to any orcs, only to these varieties of "men," although presumably he would have had command of the orcs of Minas Morgul as well. (The reader later learns that "the Orcs and lesser creatures of Mordor that had dwelt" in the Morgul Vale "had been destroyed in battle" [V.x.885].) Given his level of authority and command, some readers might imagine that Gothmog is himself one of the several otherwise unnamed Nazgûl, hence another Ringwraith with all their awesome power, if also still a subordinate of the Witch-king. But circumstances suggest otherwise (e.g., the absences of winged beasts or pervasive fear amongst those nearby), and it seems most probable that Gothmog is a human being, like so many of those in Sauron's armies. Along with the

Mouth of Sauron, whom we meet later, Gothmog may be one of the Black Númenóreans, those "high" men of Númenor who sided with Sauron long ago. In any event, his named presence in *The Lord of the Rings* as the lieutenant in charge of the armies when the leader is vanquished adds to the sense of Mordor's complex, diverse, and relatively well-organized state.

The introduction of the "Black Númenóreans" adds yet another element to the complex racial hierarchies in the history of Middle-earth. In terms of their actual race, these men would be classified along with Aragon, his ancestors Isildur and Elendil, and the line going all the way back to Elros (i.e., Elrond's brother, who became the first King of Númenor), as the Men of Westernesse. Those labeled as "Black" refer to the Númenóreans who sided with kings of Númenor who had been influenced by Sauron or who became acolytes of Sauron themselves. The Downfall of Númenor, a version of which appears in *The Silmarillion*, is related to this baleful influence, and the climactic end of the Second Age emerges from the defeat of Sauron by the Last Alliance, especially Elendil, as king of the "faithful" Númenóreans (i.e., those who remained elf-friends) and Gil-Galad, the high king of the Noldor. Presumably, many Black Númenóreans supported Sauron in that epochal battle, just as those who remain here toward the end of the Third Age would.

The only person identified as a Black Númenórean in *The Lord of the Rings* is "The Mouth of Sauron," who is also referred to as Sauron's lieutenant, so he is clearly not only a spokesperson of the sort we might associate with a White House press secretary, but a very powerful member of the government of Mordor itself. Appearing in response to Aragorn's summons just outside the Black Gate, the main entrance to the realm of Mordor, the Mouth of Sauron is described as "a tall and evil shape, mounted upon a black horse":

> The rider was robed all in black, and black was his lofty helm; yet this was no Ringwraith but a living man. The Lieutenant of the Tower of Barad-dûr he was, and his name is remembered in no tale; for he himself had forgotten it, and he said: "I am the Mouth of Sauron." But it is told that he was a renegade, who came of the race of those that are named the Black Númenóreans; for they established their dwellings in Middle-earth during the years of Sauron's domination, and they worshipped him, being enamoured of evil knowledge. And he entered the service of the Dark Tower when it first rose again, and because of his cunning he grew ever higher in the Lord's favour; and he learned great sorcery, and knew much of the mind of Sauron; and he was more cruel than any orc [V.x.888].

This last clause is surely intended to highlight the sheer badness of this person—worse than any orc!—but it also indicates the degree to which people *worse than orcs* are handled with diplomacy, even dignity and respect, by the "Captains of the West." This is itself in striking contrast to the treatment of orcs, even those expressly described as serving Sauron against their will, unlike the Mouth of Sauron who is wholeheartedly in favor of Sauron and his plans for the world.

Joined by "only a small company of black-harnessed soldiery" whose racial character is not mentioned, the Mouth of Sauron taunts the embassy from Gondor and offers terms for peace. These include requiring the Gondorians to cede the lands east of the Great River to Mordor and to swear oaths not to take up arms against Sauron again; also, the lands between the river and the Misty Mountains would be self-governing tributaries to Mordor, but that Isengard would be rebuilt with a new overlord stationed there to monitor the region. Tolkien then indicates that the Mouth of Sauron himself is almost certainly to be that ruler of Isengard, who would effectively become a tyrant reigning over the realms of Rohan and the vicinity. It is possible Saruman might have hoped to maintain this role, continuing to inhabit Orthanc, in a world system organized around the victory of Sauron over "the West," but as noted earlier, Saruman never seems to have been a true ally of Mordor, something even Grishnákh indicated was well known to Sauron. More likely, Sauron was happy to *use* Saruman (just as Saruman thought he might be *using* Sauron) to achieve his goals in that region, but he would wish to install his own cabinet members in a postwar administration.

It may be, as Gandalf says, that this "is much to demand," as it would effective granting to Sauron freely "what he must else fight many a war to gain," and I do not wish to suggest that these terms are fair or just. However, I would note that these terms seem to be part of a rational political and military program, one that a reasonable leader might wish to enact, given the persistent threats to his national borders (such as that obviously represented by Faramir's attack on the Haradrim in Ithilien), a long history of hostility with the governments of Gondor and of Rohan, and the strategic importance of the Gap of Rohan and the Misty Mountains in defending against potential invasion by Western powers. After all, as the Mouth of Sauron observes while displaying the items taken by Shagrat from Frodo, "Dwarf-coat, elf-cloak, blade of the downfallen West, and spy from the little rat-land of the Shire [...] here are the marks of a conspiracy" (V.x.889). And as we know from the Council of Elrond, the mission of the Fellowship of the Rings along with its ancillary or proximate quests *is* part of a grand conspiracy of multiple kingdoms, polities, and races based largely in the northwestern regions against Mordor, its leaders, its peoples, and its allies. It is thus understandable that Sauron, as the sovereign of his country, should wish to impose such terms as part of a peace treaty. Moreover, as draconian as these terms might seem, they are clearly not nearly as bad as Gandalf, Elrond, and others would have had their allies believe, when they claimed Sauron wished to "cover all the lands in a second darkness" and "enslave" all who live in the world.

In fact, the encounter with this man who is "crueler than any orc" shows that Mordor is very much like a modern "state," rather than some mythical realm of evil, which is what the propagandists of the West had apparently made it out to be. Even the leaders in the Western forces likely know this fact, for they are formally parleying with an emissary of Sauron rather than battling demons, after all. Shortly before this, moreover, Aragorn took pity on the callow, would-be deserters in his own army, "for these were young men from Rohan, from Westfold far away, or husbandmen from Lossarnach, and to them Mordor had been from childhood a name of evil, and yet unreal, a legend that had no part in their simple life" (V.x.886). This is to say, Aragorn knows Gondor is not at war with "evil," but with an adversary in a struggle for geopolitical hegemony, something that becomes all the more obvious after the war when he deals with the men of Mordor, granting them lands in what at that point had come within his own territorial dominion. The Mouth of Sauron, a human being of the same "race" as Aragorn himself, is merely the messenger from the leader of a country that is ultimately much like Gondor, with its own understandable concerns over matters of national defense and international relations.

The demonization of the enemy remains very much part of the all-too-real world in which we live, and in the United States we have seen how our own political leaders can blithely refer to the Soviet Union as "the Evil Empire" or Iraq, Iran, and North Korea as an "Axis of Evil." Thus, Tolkien's evocation of the way the Captains of the West and those who influence them (e.g., Gandalf, Elrond, and Galadriel) have used such demonization of the leaders and peoples of Mordor is part of the *realism*—perverse as it may be to use this term with respect to a "fantasy" novel—of *The Lord of the Rings*. Within the narrative, Sauron is a Maia (like Gandalf) and hence a being of preternatural power, but even so, Tolkien depicts him in the novel as far more of a political dictator than as a diabolical Satan. Else, why would he need spokespersons, emissaries, bureaucracies, or even armies? Else, why would so many peoples from the East and South, not to mention many who already live nearby, join him in his policies? Sauron may represent a powerful enemy of Gondor and of other Western kingdoms, one who even needs to be defeated perhaps, but it cannot be because he is somehow inherently "evil."

Along those lines, the orcs in Sauron's service, whether among the soldiers or those in the many other jobs his complex society requires (e.g., references to orcs as builders and craftsmen are directly made in these chapters), are also merely citizens of this nation. They may be crude, uncouth, and violent citizens, but they are part of the people of Mordor nonetheless. And, as we have seen, there are very many orcs who have nothing at all to do with Sauron or with Mordor, as they represent different communities and political organizations entirely. Gothmog, the Mouth of Sauron, the Nazgûl (all of whom appear to be "men," technically), many different ethnicities of humans, and other people or creatures work and live alongside the orcs of Mordor, which makes Sauron's realm the most multicultural and "diverse" of the various known societies of Middle-earth.

Book V of *The Lord of the Rings* ends as the Battle of the Morannon gets underway, for when Gandalf rejects the terms offered by the Mouth of Sauron, "Sauron sprang his trap," loosing a "great host" including "a great army of Easterlings," "Orcs innumerable," "a great company of trolls," and other forces to attack the roughly 6,000 in the armies under Aragorn and Gandalf's command (V.x.891). The timing of this is critical, for just as these troops confront one another, Frodo and Sam are reaching Mount Doom, thus coming ever closer to fulfilling the original purpose of the Fellowship of the Ring. In order to get there, these hobbits spend time in the company of orcs, which makes for some of the most vivid scenes involving orcs in *The Return of the King*.

"Where there's a whip there's will": Traversing the Plains of Gorgoroth

Book VI of *The Lord of the Rings* takes up the adventures of Sam in the Tower of Cirith Ungol, where Frodo has been taken by the soldiers under the command of Gorbag and Shagrat. Sam becomes the beneficiary of a rather nasty internecine struggle between these two orc captains, which leads to a murderous row between their respective troops. Shagrat manages to escape, taking Frodo's mithril coat, elven cloak, and Westernesse-forged sword to Barad-dûr—hence, providing the "tokens" that were displayed by the Mouth of Sauron—but nearly all the other orcs in the Tower are killed or else have fled or been called away. Sam and Frodo will still have to confront many orcs, even briefly joining in a company of orc soldiers while disguised as orcs themselves, but they do not have to fight their way through large numbers, as Sam had initially feared. During their journey from Cirith Ungol across the plateau of Gorgoroth to Mount Doom, the hobbits encounter various orcs, and apart from those in the previously discussed chapters (i.e., "The Uruk-Hai" and "The Choices of Master Samwise") these scenes offer the most detailed representation of orcs among their fellow orcs in wartime to be found in *The Lord of the Rings*.

As Sam makes his way to Frodo, he discovers that the orcs in the tower had been "at war with themselves," and "Gorbag and Shagrat had come to blows" (VI.i.899), for there were the bodies of slain orcs everywhere. We learn later from Shagrat himself that Gorbag had attempted to steal "that pretty shirt" (906), which precipitated the melee. Shagrat mentions this to an orc named Snaga,[16] who in his alarm at the events taking place around them refuses to follow orders from the Captain of the Tower. In their querulous exchange, they mention several orcs by name (Radbug, Lagduf, Muzgash, along with Gorbag), which is enough to show that orcs have distinctive individual identities, something Tolkien need not have included had he not wanted to demonstrate definitively the fundamentally "human" nature of orcs, after all. Snaga himself is insubordinate because of his great fear of being killed, a rather reasonable concern, and Shagrat's principal aim is to do his own duty by transporting the spoils from the capture of Frodo to his bosses. "News must get through to Lugbúrz," he exclaims (905).

Snaga's comments indicate that he knows that the Lord of the Nazgûl has already been slain, and thus that the war may not be going as well as their leaders and propagandists have asserted, something Gorbag had surmised earlier. Shagrat's sense of duty may be based, in part, on desperation, as he obviously fears punishment from his superiors, but he still holds out hope that "new lads" will come to help him. Notwithstanding his hardships and actual wounds, Shagrat managed to complete his mission, delivering the goods to Lugbúrz. Let us hope he was rewarded for his good work, even if he would not be able to enjoy it for long.

Speaking of "good" work, Frodo tells Sam that the orcs who captured and questioned him did not cause him any physical harm, and in fact, they actually fed him. Frodo, who had literally been poisoned by Shelob and was completely unconscious when taken by the orcs, even mentions receiving medicinal aid, although he does not quite recognize it as such: he says that the orcs "had just been pouring some horrible burning drink down my throat," which immediately cleared his head (VI.i.910), undoubtedly a reference to the orkish version of *miruvor* that had been administered to Merry by the Uruk-hai in Rohan, or something similar. Needless to say, there is nothing in Tolkien's writings to suggest that orcs would be captured alive, fed, *and* given medical attention, but like the goblins of the Misty Mountains and the orcs in the service of Saruman, these orcs of Mordor are more likely to observe the Geneva Convention than the elves and men of the West. I am joking, of course, but one cannot help but notice the vast discrepancies between the ways that Merry, Pippin, or Frodo were treated by their orkish captors and the way that a single goblin was treated by Beorn, an instance that remains the only example in the entire legendarium of an orc being taken alive by its enemies. If anything, Frodo was not handled much more roughly by Shagrat and Gorbag than he had been by Faramir earlier, even if the behavior was far more rude and the menace somewhat more dreadful. At that point, in fact, Frodo had been made "captive" by elves (in Lothlórien), by men (in Ithilien), and by orcs (in Mordor), and arguably, he had emerged from each equally unscathed.[17]

Sam wisely dresses Frodo in orkish attire—noting with satisfaction, "Well, there you are, Mr. Frodo. A perfect little orc, if I may make so bold" (913)—while also disguising himself so as to blend in more easily amidst the scenery of Mordor. Such camouflage enables them to escape notice for a time as they slowly make their way toward Mount Doom. At one point, attaining a vista upon the scene below, they marvel at the sheer magnitude of the armies they see: "As far as their eyes could reach, along the skirts of the Morgai and away southward, there were camps, some of tents, some ordered like small towns. One of the largest of these was right below them. Barely a mile out into the plain it clustered like some huge nest of insects, with straight dreary streets of huts and long low drab buildings." Sam exclaims that "[t]hese are Men and not Orcs," which leads him to wonder how Sauron could possibly provision such a large population. As Tolkien then explains,

> Neither he nor Frodo knew anything of the great slave-worked fields away south in this wide realm, beyond the fumes of the Mountain by the dark sad waters of Lake Núrnen; nor of the great roads that ran away east and south to tributary lands, from which the soldiers of the Tower brought long waggon-trains of goods and booty and fresh slaves. Here in the northward regions were the mines and forges, and the musterings of long-planned war; and here the Dark Power, moving its armies like pieces on the board, was gathering them together [VI.ii.923].

As always in such references to "slaves," there is no further evidence given of thralldom, and it is in no way certain that the economic order of Mordor involves more or less forced labor or human bondage than those of Gondor, Rohan, Lothlórien, Lake-town, or the Shire. But the fact that Tolkien chooses to provide this information, thus explaining how large armies can be equipped in order to wage war, is another marvelous instance of his desire to produce a "realistic" world system, which only encourages readers to imagine what the "slave-worked fields" of Gondor must look like as well.

Sam and Frodo then encounter two orcs—"One was clad in ragged brown and was armed with a bow of horn; it was of a small breed, black-skinned, with wide and snuffling nostrils: evidently a tracker of some kind. The other was a big fighting-orc, like those of Shagrat's company, bearing the token of the Eye"—and Tolkien explains that "being of different breeds they used the Common Speech after their fashion" (VI.ii.925), which suggests that "breeds" of orcs also represent different nationalities or linguistic communities. It seems these two orcs are searching for Gollum, and they argue over which is to blame for losing track of him. But the larger orc also complains about the mixed messages and confusing information he is receiving from the "big bosses": "That comes from Higher Up. First they say it's a great Elf in bright armour, then it's a sort of small dwarf-man, then it must be a pack of rebel Uruk-hai; or maybe it's all the lot together" (925). The "snuffler" orc then questions the "bosses," averring, "small wonder there's bad news from the battles." The large orc then accuses the other of "rebel-talk," threatening "to give your name and number to the Nazgûl" that is "in charge of the Tower now" (925). The other orc then taunts him, by saying, "You can't do your job, and you can't even stick by your own folk. Go to your filthy Shriekers, and may they freeze the flesh off you! If the enemy doesn't get them first. They've done in Number One, I've heard, and I hope it's true!" (925–926). The "snuffler" thus acknowledges the death of the Witch-king, while also expressing outrage that his fellow *uruk* would side with the loathsome Nazgûl over one of his own people. Whether he does so from a sense of duty to his country (that is, by not standing for "rebel-talk") or from the shame of being accused of disloyalty to his fellow orc, this then leads the larger orc to attack, but he is killed by the other, who runs off. The scene leads Frodo to explain to his companion: "that *is* the spirit of Mordor, Sam; and it has spread to every corner of it. Orcs have always behaved like that, or so all tales say, when they are on their own. But you can't get much hope out of it. They hate us far more, altogether and all the time" (926).

Abrupt and coarse as it is, this bickering between two unnamed orcs is revealing. As with the furtive conversation between Gorbag and Shagrat earlier, it expresses the misgivings of orcs who are ostensibly loyal servants of Sauron in the armies of Mordor. This represents an all too realistic depiction of soldiers in wartime, arguably, as they attempt to do their jobs while also being nervous about their situation and doubtful of the wisdom of their superiors. Again, this hardly sounds like demonic or bestial creatures who are slaves to their master's will, but it sounds quite a lot like regular, ordinary human beings operating in such circumstances. The larger orc's threat to "report" the other is a sign of regimented, bureaucratic officiousness; it is the sort of thing a superior officer might say, but not something a murderous monster would. That he later tries to attack the "tracker" for his insubordination and mockery is a sign of his personal ill humor and violent character, perhaps a sign even of his being ashamed of himself, but otherwise he behaves as a proper soldier throughout.

Later, traveling down a road toward their destination, Frodo and Sam

6. Don't You Know We're at War?   155

are overtaken by a company of marching orcs. They notice that "the leading orcs came loping along, panting, holding their heads down. They were a gang of the smaller breeds being driven unwilling to their Dark Lord's wars; all they cared for was to get the march over and escape the whip. Beside them, running up and down the line, went two of the large fierce *uruks*, cracking lashes and shouting" (930). This reference to "smaller breeds" who have been drafted into the army and who thus have little desire to fight or to serve Sauron is remarkable, as is the reference to "large and fierce *uruks*" who, for whatever reason, are presumably eager to serve or at least to take their leadership positions seriously.[18] As the disguised hobbits hide in the shadows alongside the road, they are discovered by an orc sergeant who takes them for laggards or else soldiers intending to go A.W.O.L. Once he sees the "devices on their shields," the orc recognizes them as deserters, since their legion was to have already reported for battle days earlier, and he too threatens to "report" them (930–931).[19] The orc then orders the hobbits to march with the others and, later "jeered" at the sluggards' sudden ability to run, he sarcastically remarks "Where there's a whip there's a will," adding, "Don't you know we're at war?" (931).

This unnamed "slave-driver" orc clearly represents another dutiful soldier in the armies of Mordor, someone who is committed to doing his job if not also to the grand ideas that the Big Bosses promulgate. Like Gorbag and Shagrat, he likely has hopes for a better world once the war is won, but at present he is focused on making sure that his troops—and those from other companies who are going A.W.O.L. or deserting—arrive in their proper destination, according to military plans and orders. How any reasonable reader could see such a person as a "devil" or "monster" is beyond me, apart from the fact that unpleasant superior officers are likely abhorred by those oppressed by them. Tolkien himself complained of the "huts full of blasphemy and smut" he had endured during World War I, and thus he had strong ideas about the sorts of character and behavior to be found even among his own countrymen in wartime.[20] This scene ends with a collision of soldiers at a crossroads, when "a troop of heavy-armed *uruks* from Barad-dûr charged into the Durthang line and threw them into confusion" (932), thus allowing the hobbits to escape while the orcs violently squabble amongst themselves.

Frodo and Sam's subsequent slog to Mount Doom, as well as the exciting return of Gollum to their adventure, takes place without the presence of orcs. Nearly all the orcs, as well as the many "men" and others in Sauron's armies, are called into battle at the Morannon, for the parley between Gandalf and the Mouth of Sauron is happening at nearly the same moment. The "accidental" destruction of the One Ring, technically accomplished by Gollum himself once Frodo refuses to relinquish it, will have an immediate effect upon that battle, and there the ultimate fate of the entire race of orcs will be decided, improbable as that seems.

Witless and Purposeless: An Unlikely Demise of the Orcs

When last we saw the "Orcs innumerable" attacking the Captains of the West at the end of Book V, the situation seemed grim. But true to Tolkien's theory of the *eucatastrophe*, the sudden and unlooked for reversal of the situation for the better, the eagles appear in time to drive off the Nazgûl on their winged beasts, just as One Ring is destroyed at that very moment, far away at Mount Doom. This is also the final appearance of orcs in *The Lord of the Rings*. Just as Gandalf declares, "[t]he realm of Sauron is ended," we get the following description:

> The Captains bowed their heads; and when they looked up again, behold! their enemies were flying and the power of Mordor was scattering like dust in the wind. As when death smites the swollen brooding thing that inhabits their crawling hill and holds them all in sway, ants will wander witless and purposeless and then feebly die, so the creatures of Sauron, orc or troll or beast spell-enslaved, ran hither and thither mindless; and some slew themselves, or cast themselves in pits, or fled wailing back to hide in holes and dark lightless places far from hope [VI.iv.949].

Not counting material in the Appendices, this is the last time orcs appear in *The Lord of the Rings*. A couple of mentions are made of orcs afterwards, notably Treebeard's retrospective account of fighting orcs near Isengard, plus a metaphorical reference to a human "ruffian" being compared to an orc ("a great squint-eyed brute like a huge orc" [VI.viii.1015]), but actual orcs do not appear again in the story. The destruction of the One Ring, and with it the defeat of Sauron, apparently entails the end of orcs as well.

Even by the standards of post-battle "mopping up" operations, as we had seen before in the Battle of Helm's Deep or in the Battle of Five Armies in *The Hobbit*, this is rather abrupt. It is also shocking. Nothing in the prior materials, nearly a thousand pages into the novel, not to mention the three-hundred pages of *The Hobbit*, would have suggested that orcs were incapable of consciousness, purpose, or ultimately existence itself in the absence of Sauron's ringed power. Readers have already experienced orcs who frequently operate independently of Sauron, sometimes even in opposition to his will, as when Uglúk specifically renounces Sauron in favor of Saruman, when the unnamed northern orcs reject any allegiances to Sauron or to a "dirty little wizard," or when Shagrat and Gorbag express their desire to be rid of all "big bosses."[21] Normally, as all fans know, Tolkien goes to some lengths to ensure the consistency, logic, and for want of a better term *realism* of his imaginary world, but this scene reveals a major and perhaps unconscionable inconsistency. Given everything Tolkien had revealed to his readers about orcs, it is clear that orcs simply would *not* behave like this.

In fact, the "ant" metaphor seems especially inapt. It may be pedantic to point this out, but one need not be an entomologist or myrmecologist to know that even ants would not behave this way when deprived of their queen. Although there are variations among species, in general, "worker ants" can live many months after the death of the "queen," and in most cases would simply continue living their lives without much of a difference. Because a queen is the only ant laying eggs, reproduction ends, so the remaining ants will not be able to sustain the colony beyond their own lifetimes. But for the span of those lifetimes, they are "free" to do as they will, which mostly means that they will continue to behave as they had done before. If orcs are really to be likened to such insects, then it seems clear that they would continue with their lives as before, which might mean continuing to fight in battle, but which also could me exiting the battle field to return home (like those northern orcs in *The Two Towers* wished to do) or find other, more pleasurable or profitable activities to engage in (as Gorbag expressed interested in doing). What they would *not* do is "wander witless and purposeless," and it certainly seems even more unlikely that they would "then feebly die."

It is also interesting that Tolkien chose to use the term "brooding" to characterize the "thing" that holds ants (or orcs) in its sway. As a philologist, Tolkien well knew that the word comes from the verb *to breed*; a *brood* was the progeny or offspring, especially of creatures hatched from eggs. It was traditionally associated with hens, and a "brooding thing" was thus a creature in the process of sitting upon or hovering over its eggs. According to the *Oxford English Dictionary*, this sense of *sheltering* leads to the broader, more metaphorical sense of looming or shading, which in turn leads to a commonly used but all the more figurative sense of obsessive, often melancholic thinking: effectively *nursing* a morbid idea. Hence, in Tolkien's extended metaphor regarding the ultimate disposition of Sauron's orcs, Tolkien's "swollen brooding thing" suggests Sauron himself, here figured as an insect queen who gives birth to such offspring, while also perhaps mentally dwelling upon them. But even as a metaphor, this idea that Sauron's active will was required for the orcs to have any wit or purpose is farfetched, and given that orcs reproduced sexually amongst themselves (as Tolkien makes clear in several places, not to mention its simple, logical sense), there is not even the figurative idea of Sauron as a "father" (or "mother") of orcs in Tolkien's legendarium. As I discussed in Chapter 2, the idea that Sauron or Melkor before him "bred" orcs in any literal sense is fairly absurd, and it is all the less probable that these god-like beings occupied the roles of egg-laying, insect queens. The character of Bolg alone, among many other clues, indicates that orcs had families, and reproduced "after the manner of the Children of Ilúvatar," and so on.

Although nothing in Tolkien's published writings would have prepared readers for this bizarre and seemingly inappropriate *ant* analogy, Tolkien was undoubtedly thinking about it as a possible solution to the Orkish Question he had posed for himself by representing orcs as "rational, incarnate creatures," capable of reasoning and speech, and yet utterly disposable and nearly irredeemable beings. As I discussed in Chapter 2, in the aftermath of *The Lord of the Rings*, Tolkien entertained a number of different ideas concerning the origins and characters of orcs. In a September 1954 draft letter to Peter Hastings, the same one in which Tolkien compared the creation of orcs to "the calculated dehumanizing of Men by tyrants that goes on today," Tolkien suggested that "[t]here might be other 'makings' all the same which were more like puppets filled (only at a distance) with their maker's mind and will, or ant-like operating under the direction of a queen-centre."[22] In an unpublished essay written around 1959–1960, Tolkien imagines that "Morgoth held the Orcs in dire thraldom; for in their corruption they had lost almost all possibility of resisting the domination of his will." Hence, "when Morgoth was at last removed from Arda the Orcs that survived in the West were scattered, leaderless and almost witless, and were for a long time without control or purpose." Tolkien then notes, "[t]his servitude to a central will that reduced the Orcs almost to an ant-like life was seen even more plainly in the Second and Third Ages under the tyranny of Sauron."[23] Yet even granting these revisionist notions, most readers would find it difficult to square the appearance and behavior of the orcs in *The Hobbit* and *The Lord of the Rings* with this description of mindless insects dependent on a "queen-centre." To do so would require ignoring nearly every scene in which orcs speak, for example.

Intriguingly, among the *Letters* can be found one other reference to ants used in this figurative way. Referring to the way that even the quarrelsome Greeks were eventually able to defeat the Persians, Tolkien writes: "but the abominable chemists and engineers have put such a power into Xerxes' hands, and all ant-communities, that decent folk don't seem to have a chance."[24] In this letter, Tolkien had already asserted that his "political opinions lean more and more toward Anarchism (philosophically understood), meaning abolition of control not whiskered men with bombs," and his critique of centrally controlled "ant-communities" is thus here connected to his opposition to "the State"—as he puts it, "I would arrest anybody who uses the word State (in any sense other than the inanimate realm of England and its inhabitants), a thing that has neither power, rights, nor mind"—and to "the frightful landslide into Theyocracy." Here Tolkien sounds much more like Gorbag and Shagrat, one might argue, than he does like a hobbit. Indeed, in his Gorbag-like desire to be free of the centralized authority of big bosses, such as that of an ant-queen, Tolkien even seems to retreat a bit from his parenthetical caveat regarding "whiskered men with bombs," as he concludes: "There is only one bright spot and that is the growing habit of disgruntled men of dynamiting factories and power-stations; I hope that, encouraged now as 'patriotism,' may remain a habit!"[25]

In his later revisionary versions of the orc origin story, as discussed in Chapter 2 above, Tolkien mooted the farfetched possibility that orcs were like "puppets," whose movements and speech was completely controlled by the will of Morgoth. In that case, orcs, "with no independent life or will, would simply cease to move or do anything at all when the will of their maker was brought to nothing." This clearly is not what happens in *The Lord of the Rings*. But Tolkien in *Morgoth's Ring* goes on to suggest that for Morgoth (or Sauron) to "hold them in absolute servitude required a great expense of the will," and that therefore many orcs "were only intermittently objects of his immediate thought and concern, and while that was removed they relapsed into independence."[26] Such a conception helps to explain why orcs like Gorbag and Shagrat could complain about their bosses, or perhaps even why Uglúk or the unnamed northern orcs could maintain such disdainful disregard of Sauron entirely, but it still would not explain how, in the total absence of Sauron's active will, orcs would somehow "wander witless and purposeless and then feebly die."

Regarding his tentative and dubious "puppet" theory of the orcs, Tolkien himself concedes that "the Orcs were not of this kind," but follows by saying that "[t]he *orks*, it is true, sometimes appear to have been reduced to a condition very similar, though there remains actually a profound difference." Tolkien explains that orcs "who dwelt long under the immediate attention of his [Morgoth's] will" would behave in an almost herd-like manner, seemingly with little independent will or purpose of their own. Lacking that immediate attention, however, the orcs—or men, who Tolkien observes can be "reduced to a like condition"—would reclaim their autonomy, even to the degree of resisting or rebelling against their "master." Because it took an enormous effort of will for Morgoth (or Sauron) to "hold them in absolute servitude," "the number of *orks* that were thus 'absorbed' was always only a small part of their total."[27] Tolkien reasons that Sauron may have exerted even greater control over the wills of orcs than Melkor had, but even so, it would have been impossible for him to control them, puppet-like, entirely. Without his authority, in other words, it seems extraordinarily unlikely, even by the standards of Tolkien's revised visions of the orcs and their fundamental being, that they would suddenly "wander witless and purposeless and then feebly die." In fact, on the contrary, Tolkien suggests that without the "will" of Sauron to guide or dominate them, the orcs would be entirely free to do as they themselves willed.[28] If anything, their reaction to the destruction of Sauron would be quite the opposite of what is described in the paragraph cited above.

That said, it is not entirely clear what such newly liberated orcs would do with their suddenly acquired freedoms. Presumably, whatever orcs were not currently in Sauron's service, such as those in Goblin-town or in Moria, would be largely unaffected and go on with their lives as they had done before. We learn that many orcs were at this time fighting in various places (e.g., along the river near Fangorn Forest, near Dale and on the slopes of Erebor, under the trees of northern Mirkwood, and at Dol Guldur), and we cannot know how they would have responded to the sudden, unexpected defeat of Sauron, apart from our knowledge of their total defeat. As for the orcs on the battlefield in the Morannon, we are told that "some slew themselves, or cast themselves in pits, or fled wailing back to hide in holes and dark lightless places far from hope," while the "Men of Rhûn and Harad, Easterling and Southron," either "gathered themselves for a last stand of desperate battle" or "fled eastward," or else "cast down their weapons and sued for mercy" (VI.iv.949). As we have discussed, orcs are never shown to "sue for mercy," although they are often depicted as fleeing for the lives, and all evidence in Tolkien's writings suggest that orcs would never be shown mercy by their enemies if they did so.[29]

"Orc-Talk": In the Aftermath of the War of the Ring

As mentioned above, following the curious scene in which orcs "ran hither and thither mindless; and some slew themselves, or cast themselves in pits, or fled wailing back to hide in holes and dark lightless places far from hope," orcs are never seen again. Mention is made of orcs elsewhere, but as I discuss below, even those orcs are referred to definitively in the past tense, with little to no suggestion that orcs still exist. Remarkably, even in scenes of further battle against foes both familiar and strange during "the scouring of the Shire," the final chapters of *The Lord of the Rings* feature no orcs. It is as if the defeat of Sauron, contrary to all expectation, brings with it the final extermination of the orcs as well.

Bizarre as it would seem in a fantasy world, one can imagine that the destruction of Sauron's fantastically "evil" creatures is somehow related to the more general disenchantment of the world following the epoch of the rings of power. Tolkien strikes an elegiac tone when referring to the departure of the "high" elves, like Galadriel and Elrond, who take with them so much that seemed magical and awe-inspiring. But the magically otherworldly aspects of the "enemies" also disappear, as its seems that dragons, balrogs, Nazgûl, trolls, giant spiders, and other creatures will also no longer haunt Middle-earth in the Fourth Age. Orcs might be listed among their number, but given the fundamental humanity of orcs in their depiction in the texts, it seems less probable. Perhaps the idea is that fantastic bogeymen or hobgoblins fade into the shadows, and orkishness becomes more metaphorical, designating attitudes or behaviors rather than actual people or modes of being. Although readers see no more orcs in person or "on camera" after the destruction of the One Ring, there is a sense that human beings identified with or characterized as *orcs* must remain.

Still, given their nigh omnipresence elsewhere in *The Lord of the Rings*, the orcs' absence in the final chapters is noteworthy. For example, as Aragorn organizes his postwar affairs, no orcs are mentioned at all. Now crowned king of Gondor, Aragorn (i.e., King Elessar) begins the administration of a postwar world system, and one of his first acts as "Lord of the West" is to deal with his former enemies, who would presumably have included many orcs. But as Tolkien writes,

> the King sat on his throne in the Hall of the Kings and pronounced his judgements. And embassies came from many lands and peoples, from the East and the South, and from the borders of Mirkwood, and from Dunland in the west. And the King pardoned the Easterlings that had given themselves up, and sent them away free, and he made peace with the peoples of Harad; and the slaves of Mordor he released and gave to them all the lands about Lake Núrnen to be their own [VI.v.968].

Incidentally, King Elessar's peace with the Easterlings and Haradrim may have itself been relatively short-lived. In Appendix A of *The Lord of the Rings*, Tolkien mentions the wars he and King Éomer of Rohan fought together against the peoples of those lands: "For though Sauron had passed, the hatreds and evils that he bred had not died, and the King of the West had many enemies to subdue before the White Tree could grow in peace. And wherever King Elessar went with war King Éomer went with him; and beyond the Sea of Rhun and on the far fields of the South the thunder of the cavalry of the Mark was heard" (App. A, 1071). No reference is made to orcs fighting with the Easterlings or Southrons in those battles, as the orcs have presumably been annihilated at that point.

There never any reference to or suggestion of anyone's "making peace" with orcs, even though the orcs in the War of the Ring obviously fought alongside the Dunlendings, Easterlings, Southrons, and men of Mordor. Some readers might imagine that "the slaves of Mordor" here could include orcs, but in the context of this scene and given everything else we know of Aragorn's treatment of orcs in *The Lord of the Rings*, this seems improbable. But the reference to these people in Mordor does demonstrate once again that the country was not a hellscape ruled by a devil and inhabited by demons, but rather a country like others, only with a large and diverse population. All the rhetoric about poisonous fumes and desolate lands were clearly part of the Western anti–Sauron propaganda.[30] Moreover, that King Elessar is in a position to grant the citizens of Mordor lands within their own country suggests that a result, if not an explicit goal, of Gondor's participation in the War of the Ring was territorial conquest, a mere fact that thus retroactively establishes Sauron's (and the Mouth of Sauron's) expressed terms for peace as both legitimate and even reasonable.

King Elessar's empire stretches throughout the western lands, of course, and the northern counterpart to Gondor, Arnor, is to be reestablished during his reign. Thus he will be the ruler not only of Gondor, but of such realms as Rohan, Dunland, Breeland, and the Shire. As a benevolent ruler, King Elessar and his successors (presumably) grant the lords of those lands—almost all of whom have personal, sometimes familial ties to Gondor—a high degree of self-governance, but all are subjects of the one King.[31] As it happens, King Elessar's sovereign control stretches well beyond the regions that Sauron had hoped to gain, not that Sauron would have stopped there, of course. Some skeptics of the Gondorian or Númenórean cause, such as those who had allied themselves with Mordor in the first place, might note that Aragorn had accomplished this victory and its attendant territorial expansion with the aide what appeared to be a sorcerer of fearsome abilities, a powerful being of the same order as Sauron, one who wielded a mighty "ring of power" to boot. Aragorn acknowledges this assistance by having Gandalf be the one to formally "crown" him king (VI.v.968), a supplement to the ritual which presumably confers an additional degree of "divine" sanction upon King Elessar's right to rule. None of this is considered a problem. However, one does not have to brush history "against the grain" too vigorously to imagine that some in this world may not wish to see such absolute rule ordained by powerful wizards from far way and by the fading aristocracy of the elves, many of whom are eager to leave this world behind them.

Reading "with the grain," however, most readers will celebrate the end of the orcs and the apparent peace and prosperity to come in the days following the return of the king. Part of the brilliance of Tolkien, I think, lies in his quite realistic reckoning of the painful aftermath of even victorious adventures. Just as he had wisely understood that the slaying of the dragon in *The Hobbit* could not serve as the triumphant climax of that narrative, given the world-historical situation and the geopolitics of the day, in *The Lord of the Rings* the end of Sauron, the annihilation of the orcs (improbable as that seems), or even the restoration of the king to his ancestral throne, cannot be the end of the story. As the hobbits make their long way back from Minas Tirith to the Shire, they encounter many people along the way, most notably Saruman, who had been permitted by Treebeard to leave Orthanc, a place that now "belongs" to the King.[32] The company meets Saruman, along with his lackey Gríma Wormtongue, on the road, and it seems that he has been reduced to a beggar; in fact, he does "beg" for some pipe-weed, which Merry gives him (V.i.vi.984). In this exchange there is the ominous suggestion that Saruman knows far more of the Shire and its burgeoning tobacco industry than the hobbits care for. The final battle in the War of the Rings, in fact, takes place many months after the fall of Sauron, as the hobbits will have to "scour" the Shire of the influence of Saruman there.

When the four hobbits arrive at the border of the Shire, they find a gate has been erected, barring entry, and soon discover more bad news. As Sam puts it, "[n]o welcome, no beer, no smoke, and a lot of rules and orc-talk instead" (V.i.viii.1000). What he means exactly by "orc-talk" in this context is not clear, unless in refers to suspicious or unfriendly discourse in general, but it quickly become apparent that no orcs are involved in the business of the Shire at all. It turns out Saruman, using the nickname "Sharkey," has taken control of the Shire: quite rapidly, too, considering that he had appeared as a beggar on the road near the Gap of Rohan just two months earlier. This may be a sign of the degree to which his influence had been spreading over time, hence the alarming sight of "squint-eyed Southerner" and other "ruffians" nearly a year earlier. Saruman reveals that "Sharkey" was an affectionate name given to him by his "people," stating, "[a]ll my people used to call me that in Isengard" (1018), and Tolkien informs us in a footnote that *Sharkey* was "probably Orkish in origin: *sharkû*, 'old man.'" Thus, even with no orcs to be found, Saruman's "people"—which, as readers saw in *The Two Towers*, included both orcs and men—still use this "sign of affection" for him in the Shire.

Sam observes that conditions in the Shire are "worse than Mordor," to which Frodo responds, "Yes, this is Mordor," adding, "Saruman was doing its work all along, even when he thought he was working for himself" (1018). The complete lack of actual orcs in any of this is perhaps evidence of the thoroughness of the genocidal ents and Huorns of Fangorn Forest, who had apparently allowed some "men" to escape while slaying all orcs. In any event, everyone involved in the besmirchment of the Shire is either a man or a hobbit (or Saruman himself), and any apparent *orkishness* to be found there is thus either metaphorical or a tacit admission that orcs have never been anything other than a race (or rather multiple races) of men in the first place. If Bill Ferny or Lotho Sackville-Baggins can be considered orc-like, then it is much harder to imagine Uglúk, Grishnákh, or Shagrat as somehow more inherently monstrous. Memorably, Frodo takes pity on Saruman, refusing to allow the hobbits to kill him: "I do not wish him to be slain in this evil mood. He was great once, of a noble kind that we should not dare to raise our hands against. He is fallen, and his cure is beyond us; but I would still spare him, in the hope that he may find it" (1019). The "noble kind" that Saruman was of once is exactly the same as that of Sauron (i.e., an angelic being, one of the Ainur active in the cosmogonic music of creation itself, and a Maia of Aulë), but presumably Frodo's compassion, and the reader's, cannot be expected to extend that far. Still the pity for an implacable enemy, one who has done devastating and lasting harm to one's friends and country, shows that Frodo's (and again, the reader's) sympathies ought to be quite expansive, which makes their lack of care for orcs all the more noteworthy. Orcs, ever since Golfimbul's troops centuries earlier at least, have done no harm to the Shire whatsoever, yet the peoples of the Shire do not pity them.

There is the question of the "half-orcs," people specifically mentioned in connection with Saruman, and sure enough, among the first "big" folk that the returning hobbits encounter are "large ill-favoured Men lounging against the inn-wall; they were squint-eyed and sallowfaced," reminding Sam of the "squinted-eyed Southerner" in Bree and reminding Merry of "many that I saw in Isengard" (1004). Pippin names these adversaries "half-orcs and ruffians" (1006). During the battle that ensues against the "ruffians," Merry slays "the leader, a great squint-eyed brute like a huge orc" (1015), which turns out to be the last time the word *orc* appears in *The Lord of the Rings* (not counting the Appendices). Although many of Saruman's "ruffians" are depicted as having orkish or half-orkish features, there are no people identified as orcs present in the scouring of the Shire.

The ultimate defeat of Saruman's ruffians and their allies among the hobbits in the Battle of Bywater is cited as "the last battle fought in the Shire, and the only battle since the Greenfields" over 270 years before, the one in which Golfimbul and his fellow orcs were destroyed. The death of Saruman by Gríma's hand, and the slaying of Gríma by hobbit archers in response, are the final shots fired in the War of the Ring. Orcs play no role at all in the struggles following the destruction of the Ring itself, as far as the text reveals, but the pervasive sense of orkishness in the world of all-too-human nature remains. Perhaps it is symbolic of Tolkien's relatively pessimistic view of the "long defeat" that is humane existence in the mundane world that, in the final chapter of *The Lord of the Rings*, Frodo joins Bilbo, Gandalf, Elrond, and Galadriel at the Grey Havens, where they board a ship bound for Aman, the Blessed Realm, thus leaving this world and its residual orkishness behind. But famously, in the final lines, Sam returns home to his wife and child at Bag End, thus concluding the tale of "the hobbit" in the very place where it began, in a hole in the ground.

Conclusion

*In a Hole in the Ground
There Lived an Orc*

At the end of *The Lord of the Rings,* orcs appear to have been completely eradicated from the western lands in Middle-earth, with there being no further mention of orcs after the destruction of the One Ring or in the aftermath of the battles with Sauron's forces. Those fighting elsewhere, such as the ones mentioned by Treebeard, appear to have been totally wiped out as well. The only hint of their continued existence in the text lies in the comment that, while "some slew themselves, or cast themselves in pits," others "fled wailing back to hide in holes and dark lightless places far from hope" (VI.iv.949). This is a rather anticlimactic and ignominious end to a race of beings thought to be fearsome adversaries, and given all the information Tolkien had provided about orcs in the foregoing pages, it is also hardly credible. Nearly everything readers of *The Hobbit* and *The Lord of the Rings* had learned about orcs militates strongly against the very possibility of such an outcome. The convenient evanescence of orcs in the waning days of the Third Age is potentially more meaningful still for the Fourth Age of Middle-earth. In an "age of men," when the enchantments of the elves and wizards have faded from the "real world," and when such fabled monsters as dragons, trolls, and giants have also left the scene, the *literal* demonization of the enemy might disappear as well, leaving what once were orcs to be recognized at last for what they had always been: regular, ordinary, often marginalized, and mostly oppressed people, *les damnés de la terre du milieu.*

I have maintained throughout this book that Tolkien's orcs are in fact human beings, and my argument is based on evidence from Tolkien's own writings rather than on revisionist speculations or on a desire to rewrite the tales from an alternative perspective.[1] Admittedly, in reading Tolkien's work "against the grain," as it were, I have tried to illuminate the degree to which his personal correspondence, the posthumously published

"Silmarillion" materials and their manifold revisions, and his published novels offer a far more nuanced and potentially sympathetic vision of the orcs than most readers, fans, and scholars acknowledge. The racialist and, indeed, racist characterizations of the orcs have become increasingly difficult to avoid, as it has become clearer to some in recent years that orcs appear to be nothing other than non-white human beings, with physical features and cultural attributes readily ascribable to non–European civilizations or stereotypes. Moreover, projection of a moral character onto these features has served to undergird various forms of xenophobia and bigotry in our all-too-real world, as some white supremacists and neofascists have attempted to enlist Tolkien's writings in their own odious ideological battles, in which the depiction of orcs has played an enormous role.[2] As we have seen, ultimately Tolkien may have viewed orkishness as more a matter of behavior than as a cultural or racial attribute, for he found vices like cruelty and violence, but also less obviously objectionable attitudes, like favoring technology, modern machinery, or cosmopolitanism, as signs of that a given person might be an orc. Factory workers riding motorcycles or using chainsaws could be classed as orcs, at least metaphorically. What becomes relatively clear throughout his work and despite his own misgivings, however, is that Tolkien envisions orcs *as* humans.

As many fans probably know, Tolkien had intended to include an Epilogue to *The Lord of the Rings*, versions of which are now available in *Sauron Defeated*. The scene is set some seventeen years after the defeat of Sauron, long after Frodo, Bilbo, Gandalf, Galadriel, and Elrond had sailed from the Grey Havens to the uttermost West, and it depicts the *paterfamilias* Sam talking with his own children about the events that had taken place, while also preparing for a visit from King Elessar and Queen Arwen to the borders of the Shire. In each version of the Epilogue, Sam indicates that he believes orcs still exist. In one, his son Frodo-lad, who is very fond of the stories of the dwarves, asks whether he can soon have an axe, pointedly following up the request with, "Are there any orcs left?" His father responds, "I daresay there are if you know where to look. […] But not in the Shire, and you won't have an axe for chopping off heads."[3] Thus, the only reference to the existence of orcs is also a reference to the desire to chop their heads off with an axe. In the second version, Sam mentions Moria directly, stating: "Dark places still need a lot of cleaning up. I guess it will take a lot of trouble and daring deeds yet to root out the evil creatures from the halls of Moria. For there are certainly plenty of Orcs left in such places. It is not likely that we shall ever quite get rid of them."[4] Here, Sam is confident in the continuing existence of orcs, but he clearly laments the inability to complete the genocide.

In the 1960s, Tolkien nearly succumbed to the temptation to write a sequel to *The Lord of the Rings*, going so far as to draft a first chapter titled "The New Shadow." Set in Gondor during the reign of Aragorn's son Eldarion, it hints at the stirrings of a Satanic (or perhaps Sauronic) cult, while describing the youth of Gondor "playing at" being orcs. It features a conversation between a young man, offended at having had his own childhood antics—specifically, stealing apples, including unripe ones, from his neighbor's trees—referred to as "Orc-work," and an older man trying to explain what makes orkish behavior so objectionable. Yet there are no references to actually existing orcs, which makes the conversation turn on issues of ethics rather than of race. That is, it is a question of which sorts of actions performed by "men" can be deemed "Orc-work," such that the term *orc* functions as a way of passing judgement on one's moral character.⁵ Thus "orcs" have become, if they were not already, merely human persons who are deemed immoral.

In a 1964 letter, Tolkien mentions this tale and why he decided not to pursue it further. As he put it,

> I did begin a story placed about 100 years after the Downfall [of Mordor], but it proved both sinister and depressing. Since we are dealing with *Men* it is inevitable that we should be concerned with the most regrettable feature of their nature: their quick satiety with good. So that the people of Gondor in times of peace, justice and prosperity, would become discontented and restless—while the dynasts descended from Aragorn would become just kings and governors—like Denethor or worse. I found that even so early there was an outcrop of revolutionary plots, about a centre of secret Satanistic religion; while Gondorian boys were playing at being Orcs and going round doing damage. I could have written a "thriller" about the plot and its discovery and overthrow—but it would be just that. Not worth doing.⁶

Tolkien discusses something similar in a late letter from 1972, in which he says he "discovered that the King's Peace would contain no tales worth recounting; and his wars would have little interest after the overthrow of Sauron; but that almost certainly a restlessness would appear about then, owing to the (it seems) inevitable boredom of Men with the good: there would be secret societies practising dark cults, and 'orc-cults' among adolescents."⁷ Tolkien's concerns about the rise of dark cults and adolescents behaving like orcs may have been related to his increasing dismay over his own fandom, especially among young adults in the United States, whom he referred to in the 1960s as "my deplorable *cultus*."⁸

So, to review: In *The Lord of the Rings* itself we are told of the apparent disappearance of the orcs entirely, with the remaining survivors of their folk hiding in holes and "dark lightless places devoid of hope" (VI. iv.949). In an unpublished Epilogue to the novel, Sam surmises that orcs must still exist, and perhaps will always exist, even as he wishes they could be exterminated once and for all. And in the aborted sequel to the novel, Tolkien presents orkishness as a label for immoral human behavior but gives no indication that a distinctive "race" of beings called *orcs* still exists during the reign of King Eldarion in the Fourth Age. As it turns out, arguably, all of these moments are further indications of the view that orcs are nothing other than human people, marked by their racial character (and, indeed, by a rather racist presentation of that character) but also by their apparently moral deficiencies with respect to those peoples deemed to be "good." Hence, to the extent that the "good" wins in the final chapters of *The Lord of the Rings*, the orcs—which is to also say the figural representation in incarnate forms of orkishness in human beings—as "bad" people must disappear. However, Tolkien's lament that men's "satiety with the good" diminishes all too rapidly suggests that a more pervasive and diffuse quality of orkishness, if not the beings demonized as orcs in the novels, would reemerge in due course.

One of the most cogent and perhaps even sympathetic pop-cultural representations of an orc in recent years can be found in the first season of the Amazon Prime series, *The Lord of the Rings: The Rings of Power* (2021), which is loosely based on materials from the novel's Appendices and set in the Second Age of Middle-earth.[9] Adar, a mysterious character invented for the show, is the leader of the orcs in the southern lands that will become Mordor, and viewers learn that he is one of the original elves—perhaps *the* original elf—who were taken by the dark powers and transformed into orcs, an idea consistent with the somewhat "canonical" view in Tolkien's world that orcs were made from elves. In a memorable scene, Adar is captured and subjected to a cruel interrogation by Galadriel, who says, "When I was a child, I heard stories of elves taken by Morgoth. Tortured. Twisted. Made into a new and ruined form of life. You are one of them, are you not? The Moriondor. The Sons of the Dark. The first orcs."

Speaking slowly and *sotto voce*, Adar replies, "*Uruk* … we prefer 'uruk.'" By supplying the preferred term for his people, Adar is striking back at the racialist and imperialist program involved in being named by one's enemies, just as a member of the Wampanoag or Narragansett nations may not wish to be referred to as "Indian" (or later "Native American"). Adar is also insisting that his people be recognized *as* a people, referring to other uruks as his "children" and declaring that they have "no master." Galadriel spits back at him, "They are not children, they are *slaves*." Here, as in many places in Tolkien's original texts, the term *slave* is used as an insult, used without a modicum of sympathy for those presumably in bondage, and moreover, used to suggest they because they are "slaves" they are undeserving of kindness or even of life. Adar rejects that characterization immediately, asserting that "each one has a name.

A heart. [...] We are creations of The One, Master of the Secret Fire, the same as you. As worthy of the breath of life, and just as worthy of a home." These references are well known to Tolkien aficionados, as "the One" refers to Eru Ilúvatar, and the "Secret Fire" is invoked by Gandalf when facing the balrog in Moria in *The Lord of the Rings* (II.v.330). Indeed, Adar's comments about orcs' being "worthy of the breath of life" have some basis in Tolkien's own views, for as the author himself expressed it, "by accepting or tolerating their making—necessary to their actual existence—even Orcs would become part of the World, which is God's and ultimately good."[10] The very existence of orcs, in other words, suggests that they belong here in this world.

It is remarkable that this television series would offer viewers a somewhat sympathetic orc (or *uruk*) character, even if orcs will remain the "bad guys" elsewhere in most other episodes. Still, by challenging the view that orcs are demonic beings, mindless slaves to the will of diabolical overlords, *The Rings of Power* is actually truer in some ways to Tolkien's own presentation in *The Lord of the Rings*, even if Tolkien's fictional heroes rarely if ever acknowledge what readers can see clearly from the text itself. Orcs are people, often nasty and cruel people, but people nonetheless. If they have been dehumanized, that process has been facilitated as much by their enemies who delight in hunting and killing them as it has been by despots who press them into service. The visceral fear orcs have of elves, for example, even though Tolkien suggests that the two "races" are actually one, with orcs being mutilated and thus victimized elves, is sign enough of their innocence in a strict ontological sense; that is, they are not *inherently* evil, and elves have no right to treat them as such. The fact that they live, work, and fight alongside humans in multiracial, multicultural societies demonstrates that not all people consider orcs to be monsters. The orcs' personalities, families, communities, and cities, along with their hopes and dreams, render them as *humane* as any beings in Middle-earth. In their simple humanity, in fact, the orcs are probably far more like hobbits than they are to the elite elves or "high" men of Westernesse. For readers who are not members of a powerful, hereditary castes of overlords, orcs might be all the more "relatable" precisely because of their many flaws and faults, which may render them far more *human* than many other characters in Tolkien's legendarium.

As the famous story goes, Tolkien was suddenly inspired to pen the first line of *The Hobbit* whilst grading papers, and upon a blank page he "scrawled" the line, "In a hole in the ground there lived a hobbit," which became the origin of the novel.[11] Over twenty years and some 500,000 published words later, Tolkien would deposit his remaining orcs in a hole in the ground as well, although unlike hobbit holes typified by their comforts, orcs are relegated to "dark lightless places devoid of hope." Yet a principle message of *The Hobbit* and *The Lord of the Rings* is that hopelessness is never really an option, and just as Uglúk, Grishnákh, Gorbag, and Shagrat had hopes of fulfilling their duties, completing their missions, and winning favor or reward from their superiors, thereby achieving some degree of happiness, hope must remain in some form or other for the remaining orcs of Middle-earth. Gorbag had expressed perhaps the most lofty goal for those who love freedom, a life without interference from "big bosses," which seems largely consistent with the relatively modest dreams of the orcs of the Misty Mountains, whether in Moria, Goblin-town, or Gundabad, to return home and be left in peace. Indeed, nearly all orcs that readers encounter in Tolkien's writings, and perhaps the many more that are not directly encountered but implied in the texts, seem to crave freedom as well.

If the putative happy ending of *The Lord of the Rings* lies in the restoration of a person like Sam to the simple pleasures of life in the Shire, then we can at least speculate upon a orkish version whereby the decommissioned soldiery or others among the orc-folk—the many women, children, artisans, technicians, educators, laborers, and others that are not depicted but who must exist—may seek lives worth living, apart from any tyrannical "bosses" and their agendas. Only, one suspects, in the orcs' case, they have been so vilified and demonized by those who consider them enemies that they would necessarily have to fight for this cause. It is almost unimaginable that the powers that be in the Fourth Age would stand idly by while communities of orcs developed thriving societies in which they could live without anxiety. Under such circumstances, orcs are ultimately forced into the role of revolutionaries, ones who would benefit from the solidarity of their erstwhile allies (e.g., "wicked" dwarves, "wild" men, Easterlings, Southrons, and the men of Mordor, not to mention others who might rally to their side) in order to help reshape Middle-earth into a place that all races can inhabit. As with the tongue-in-cheek philosophical satire of the *Existential Comics* version of The Council of Elrond, the organization of a multiracial coalition of radicals could seek "to end all domination, and ensure that the people, be they men, elves, or orcs, or anything else, will be able to govern themselves."[12]

I realize that my arguments throughout this book may not convince everyone to become orc-sympathizers, and I certainly do not expect readers to abandon their support for the Fellowship of the Ring and its goals in favor of joining Team Gorbag in seeking out nice and handy loot. My goal has not been to convince readers of *The Silmarillion*, *The Hobbit*, and *The Lord of the Rings* that they should cheer for the goblins and orcs. But I believe very strongly that the inability to sympathize with one's fellows, with persons of other "races" or "nations," is debilitating not only to political solidarity or multicultural exchange, but to what a more religious person might call our very souls. Demonizing others effectively turns us into demons as well, and only someone who has become "soulless" can delight in the dehumanization of others. On that score, I would add more positively that the ability to see the value in others—even, or perhaps especially, in one's enemies—can only be beneficial to ourselves as well. As the brilliant fantasist Ursula K. Le Guin has put it,

> If you deny any affinity with another person or kind of person, if you declare it to be wholly different from yourself—as men have done to women, and class has done to class, and nation has done to nation—you may hate it, or deify it, but in either case you have denied its spiritual equality, and its human reality. You have made it into a thing, to which the only possible relationship is a power relationship. And thus you have fatally impoverished your own reality. You have, in fact, alienated yourself.[13]

With Le Guin, I am opposed to policies that would impoverish our own reality and alienate us further from both ourselves and our fellows. By recognizing the basic humanity of the orcs, we reinforce our own humanity.

Notes

Preface and Acknowledgments

1. See Corey Mohler, "The Council of Elrond," *Existential Comics*: https://existentialcomics.com/comic/175.

Introduction

1. J.R.R. Tolkien, *The Lord of the Rings*, 50th Anniversary ed. (Boston: Houghton Mifflin, 2004), II.ii.267. Subsequent citations to this novel include Book, chapter, and page number for ease of reference for those using different editions and appear parenthetically in the text.

2. See Tolkien, *The Letters of J.R.R. Tolkien*, ed. Humphrey Carpenter (Boston: Houghton Mifflin, 2000), 243.

3. I have throughout the book opted not to capitalize a number of words that in Tolkien's writings are frequently capitalized, including the word "orc." Just as we do not in common usage capitalize the word *human*, I believe that *orc*—as well as *elf*, *dwarf*, *man*, etc.—ought to remain lowercase. However, in my direct quotations, I follow the conventions of the text in question.

4. Tolkien, *Letters*, 241.

5. See Mary Ellmann, "Growing Up Hobbitic," *New American Review* 2 (1968), 225.

6. "This then, as it may appear, was my father's final view of the question: Orcs were bred from Men." See Tolkien, *Morgoth's Ring*, ed. Christopher Tolkien (New York: HarperCollins, 1993), 421.

7. See Charles W. Mills, "The Wretched of Middle-earth: An Orkish Manifesto," *The Southern Journal of Philosophy* 60 (Suppl. 1).S1 (September 2022), 105–135.

8. Tolkien, *Letters*, 274.

9. Following a widely used convention in Tolkien Studies, I distinguish the 1977 book *The Silmarillion* from the many notes, drafts, revisions, and other materials comprising Tolkien's lifelong "Silmarillion" project.

10. See, e.g., my "Three Rings for the Elven Kings: Trilogizing Tolkien in Print and Film," in *Representing Middle-earth: Tolkien, Form, and Ideology* (Jefferson, NC: McFarland, 2024), 64–78.

Chapter 1

1. J.R.R. Tolkien, *The Letters of J.R.R. Tolkien*, ed. Humphrey Carpenter (Boston: Houghton Mifflin, 1981), 82.

2. *Ibid.*, 78, 90.

3. *Ibid.*, 90.

4. *Ibid.* 89.

5. *Uruk-hai*, as used in *The Lord of the Rings*, simply means "orc-people" or "orc-folk" in the Black Speech, although the orcs who refer to themselves as such appear to see it as value-laden, placing themselves at a higher level of authority or accomplishment than those other orcs not recognized as Uruk-hai, for instance.

6. Tolkien, "Guide to the Names in *The Lord of the Rings*," in *A Tolkien Compass*, ed. Jared Lobell (New York: Del Rey, 1975), 184.

7. As I write this in 2023, the news is in a flurry with tales of killer whales (a.k.a. orcas) attacking sailboats and other craft at sea. Given their own terrible forms and their emergence from the depths, one might make the case for a demon-like casting of the great sea mammals as aquatic orcs, now wreaking vengeance upon those

who, like the Númenóreans, presume to be "sea-lords" while cowering along the oceans' most superficial superficies.

8. See Christopher Tolkien's comments in J.R.R. Tolkien, *The Book of Lost Tales, Part I*, ed. Christopher Tolkien (New York: Del Rey, 1992), 24.

9. Tolkien famously speaks of his audacious desire to develop a distinctively English mythology in his letter to Milton Waldman, part of which has been reproduced as the Preface to *The Silmarillion* in later editions. There, and elsewhere, he also distinguishes between the English and British (or Celtic) culture; as he put it in a letter to his son, "For I love England (not Great Britain and certainly not the British Commonwealth [grr!])." See *Letters*, 144, 65.

10. See Dimitra Fimi, *Tolkien, Race, and Cultural History: From Fairies to Hobbits* (London: Palgrave Macmillan, 2009).

11. Tolkien, *The Book of Lost Tales, Part I*, 75–76, 268, 272, and 279.

12. Tolkien, *Letters*, 177–178; technically, the word *orc* appears at least twice in *The Hobbit*. Also, the disavowal of "soft feet" here may be connected to Tolkien's repudiation of his "Goblin Feet" poem, where the "padded," "padding," "happy little feet" of the gnomish goblins are directly referenced.

13. J.R.R. Tolkien, "Guide to the Names in *The Lord of the Rings*," in *A Tolkien Compass*, ed. Jared Lobell (New York: Del Rey, 1975), 184. Tolkien adds: "It should be spelt *ork* (so the Dutch translation) in a Germanic language, but I had used the spelling *orc* in so many places that I have hesitated to change it in the English text, though the adjective is necessarily spelt *orkish*."

14. Tom Shippey, *J.R.R. Tolkien: Author of the Century* (Boston: Houghton Mifflin, 2000), 87–88.

15. Tolkien, *Letters*, 185.

16. Here one might also mention the figure of "Orc" in William Blake's writings. As Northrop Frye put it in *Fearful Symmetry*, "gigantic energies still remain in men, imprisoned, but struggling to be free. The revolt of Prometheus nearly destroyed Olympus; and in the Eddas it is prophesied that some day the chained Loki will burst free and begin the destruction of the world. The imprisoned Titanic power in man, which spasmodically causes revolutions, Blake calls *Orc*." See Frye, *Fearful Symmetry: A Study of William Blake* (Princeton: Princeton University Press, 1969), 128–129.

17. Tolkien, *The Book of Lost Tales, Part II*, ed. Christopher Tolkien (New York: Del Rey, 1984), 161.

18. Friedrich Klaeber, "Notes," in *Beowulf and the Finnesburg Fragment*, rev. ed., trans. John R. Clark Hall, ed. C L. Wrenn (London: George Allen and Unwin, 1950), 183 (182–194). This edition contains a lengthy essay, "Prefatory Remarks on Prose Translation of *Beowulf*," by J.RR. Tolkien himself (ix–xliii).

19. Shippey, *J.R.R. Tolkien*, 88.

20. Tolkien, *The Nature of Middle-earth: Late Writings on the Lands, Inhabitants, and Metaphysics of Middle-earth*, ed. Carl Hostetter (New York: Houghton Mifflin Harcourt, 2021), 272.

21. Shippey, *J.R.R. Tolkien*, 88.

22. The more "monstrous" depictions of orcs in film adaptations of Tolkien's work, whether in the visions of Rankin and Bass, Ralph Bakshi, or Peter Jackson, are perhaps ways of getting around the questions of race and racism in the novels, but even there, the human and "humane" qualities of the creatures as we encounter them onscreen are apparent.

23. Tolkien, *The Silmarillion* (New York: Del Rey, 2002), 47.

24. See my *J.R.R. Tolkien's* The Hobbit: *Realizing History Through Fantasy* (New York: Palgrave Macmillan, 2022), 101; see also Sigmund Freud, *Civilization and Its Discontents*, trans. James Strachey (New York: W.W. Norton, 1989), 72.

25. For a discussion of this article and its significance, see Robin A. Reid, Bianca Beronio, Robert T. Tally Jr., Cait Coker, Cami Agan, Robert Stuart, Charlotte Krausz, Tom Ue, and Helen Young, "Nine Tolkien Scholars Responded to Charles W. Mill's 'The Wretched of Middle-earth: An Orkish Manifesto,'" *Mythlore* 42.1 (Fall/Winter 2023), 183–197, which includes my "Orcs and Revolution."

26. Charles W. Mills, "The Wretched of Middle-earth: An Orkish Manifesto," *The Southern Journal of Philosophy* 60 (Suppl. 1).S1 (September 2022), 116, 128.

27. *Ibid.*, 135.

28. Tolkien, *Letters*, 274.

29. Robert Stuart, *Tolkien, Race, and Racism in Middle-earth* (New York: Palgrave Macmillan, 2022), 150.
30. Humphrey Carpenter, *J.R.R. Tolkien: A Biography* (Houghton Mifflin, 2000), 149.
31. Michael Moorcock, *Wizardry and Wild Romance: A Study of Epic Fantasy* (London: Victor Gollancz, 1987), 125.
32. Tolkien, *Letters*, 107.
33. *Ibid.*, 215, 246.
34. *Ibid.*, 63–64.
35. *Ibid.*, 65.
36. *Ibid.*, 78.
37. Quoted in Richard Wolin, *Heidegger in Ruins: Between Philosophy and Ideology* (New Haven: Yale University Press, 2023), 109.
38. Wolin, *Heidegger in Ruins*, 109.
39. See Tolkien, *Letters*, 241.
40. Stuart, *Tolkien, Race, and Racism in Middle-earth*, 237. Stuart is referring to a comment made by Tolkien in an irate letter sent to a German publisher: "if I am to understand that you are enquiring whether I am *of Jewish* origin, I can only reply that I regret that I appear to have *no* ancestors of that gifted people"; see Tolkien, *Letters*, 37.
41. Tolkien, *The Hobbit* (New York: Del Rey, 1982), 62.
42. Tolkien, *Morgoth's Ring*, ed. Christopher Tolkien (New York: HarperCollins, 1993), 418. There are three Elf-Man "breedings" in Tolkien's legendarium (Lúthien-Beren, Idril-Tuor, and Arwen-Aragorn), in which the couples produce all the more noble children, but even so, the rarity of such intermarriage in a sign of its departure from norms. Throughout Tolkien's work, "bloodlines" and the overall quality of people are seen as diminishing thanks to "breeding" with "lesser" folk.
43. In fact, this crisis did lead to the resignation of the Prime Minister, who was replaced by a more moderate Tory, Harold Macmillan, in early 1957.
44. Tolkien, *The Letters of J.R.R. Tolkien: Revised and Expanded Edition*, ed. Humphrey Carpenter with Christopher Tolkien (New York: William Morrow, 2023), 366–367.
45. *Ibid.*, 367.
46. *Ibid.*, 567; see also, Carpenter, *J.R.R. Tolkien: A Biography*, 233.
47. Tolkien, *Letters*, 450; in the same letter Tolkien expresses gratitude that his work "has good friends to defend it against the malice of its enemies," but points out that "all the fools are not in the other camp."
48. Upon hearing of the formation of the New York Tolkien Society, for example, Tolkien worried that the Society would attract lunatics, but even if "real lunatics don't join them," such things filled him "with alarm and despondency"; see *Letters*, 359.
49. Tolkien, *Letters*, 111.
50. In an October 21, 1963, letter to a Mrs. Munby, Tolkien writes: "There must have been orc-women. But in stories that seldom if ever see the Orcs except as soldiers of armies in the service of the evil lords we naturally would not learn much about their lives. Not much was known." Indeed, apart from Éowyn (who had to disguise herself as Dernhelm), Tolkien rarely depicted women of any race among soldiers, so the "absence" of female orcs is not so much an omission as a lack of interest in or awareness of those aspects of orkish life not devoted to martial activities. See https://tolkiengateway.net/wiki/Letter_to_Mrs_Munby.
51. Tolkien, *Letters*, 89.
52. *Ibid.*, 195.

Chapter 2

1. J.R.R. Tolkien, *The Letters of J.R.R. Tolkien*, ed. Humphrey Carpenter (Boston: Houghton Mifflin, 1981), 26.
2. Following the convention used by Christopher Tolkien and adopted in Tolkien Studies more generally, my use of the "Silmarillion" (in quotation marks) refers to all the stories, in their multiple and sometimes discrepant versions, associated with Tolkien's legendarium outside of *The Hobbit* and *The Lord of the Rings*, whereas *The Silmarillion* (italicized) refers to the volume first published in 1977.
3. Tolkien, *Letters*, 138, 139, 110.
4. Shippey, *The Road to Middle-earth* (Boston: Houghton Mifflin, 2003), 233. The phrase "infantry of the old war" comes from Tolkien, "*Beowulf*: The Monsters and the Critics," *The Monsters and the Critics and Other Essays*, ed. Christopher Tolkien (New York: HarperCollins, 1983), 22.

5. Tom Shippey, "Orcs, Wraiths, Wights: Tolkien's Images of Evil," in *J.R.R. Tolkien and His Literary Resonances*, eds. George Clark and Daniel Timmons (Westport, CT: Greenwood, 2000), 186.

6. See my *Representing Middle-earth: Tolkien, Form, and Ideology* (Jefferson, NC: McFarland, 2024), 17–19.

7. Tolkien, *Letters*, 24, 137.

8. Tolkien, *The Silmarillion* (New York: Del Rey, 2002), 23.

9. As I discuss in the next section, there were at least a few named orcs in the earlier "Silmarillion" materials, so the decision to exclude named orcs from *The Silmarillion* seems to have Christopher's own, and his reasoning for doing so is not known. In *The Lays of Beleriand*, for example, an Orc-captain named Boldog who leads the army involved in Morgoth's raid on Doriath is mentioned several times.

10. Tolkien, *The Lord of the Rings*, 50th Anniversary ed. (Boston: Houghton Mifflin, 2004), III.iv.486.

11. Tolkien, *The Silmarillion*, 47.

12. See https://tolkiengateway.net/wiki/Letter_to_Mrs_Munby.

13. Tolkien, *The Silmarillion*, 87.

14. *Ibid.*, 103–104.

15. *Ibid.*, 107, 121.

16. Robin A. Reid, "Making or Creating Orcs: How Thorinsmut's Free Orcs AU Writes Back to Tolkien," *Journal of Tolkien Research* 11.2 (2020), [1–17], 2 [https://scholar.valpo.edu/journaloftolkienresearch/vol11/iss2/3/].

17. Tolkien, *The Lords of the Rings*, VI.i.914.

18. Tolkien, *Letters*, 190.

19. Tolkien, *The Silmarillion*, 37.

20. *Ibid.*, 38.

21. Tolkien, *Letters*, 195.

22. For an interesting analysis of the materials used to put together *The Silmarillion*, see Douglas Kane, *Arda Reconstructed: The Creation of the Published Silmarillion* (Bethlehem, PA: Lehigh University Press, 2011).

23. Christopher Tolkien, "Foreword," in J.R.R. Tolkien, *The Book of Lost Tales, Part I*, ed. Christopher Tolkien (London: George Allen and Unwin, 1983), xii.

24. See Verlyn Flieger, "The Arch and the Keystone," *Mythlore* 38.1 (Fall/Winter 2019), 5–17; see also Flieger, "But What Did He Really Mean?" *Tolkien Studies* 11 (2014), 149–166.

25. Tolkien, *The Book of Lost Tales, Part II*, ed. Christopher Tolkien (London: George Allen and Unwin, 1984), 12, 159.

26. Tolkien, *The Book of Lost Tales, Part I*, 75–76, 268, 272, and 279.

27. Tolkien, *The Book of Lost Tales, Part II*, 161. Compare this with a passage, written around 1930, in which Tolkien writes: "The hordes of Orcs he made of stone, but their hearts of hatred. Glamhoth, people of hate, the Gnomes have called them"; see *The Shaping of Middle-earth*, ed. Christopher Tolkien (London: George Allen and Unwin, 1986), 100.

28. Tolkien, *The Book of Lost Tales, Part II*, 221.

29. *Ibid.*, 166.

30. *Ibid.*, 99.

31. Dimitra Fimi, *Tolkien, Race, and Cultural History: From Fairies to Hobbits* (New York: Palgrave Macmillan, 2009), 46, 47.

32. Tolkien, *Morgoth's Ring*, ed. Christopher Tolkien (New York: HarperCollins, 1993), 409.

33. Dimitra Fimi, *Tolkien, Race, and Cultural History*, 155.

34. Tolkien, *Morgoth's Ring*, 80.

35. *Ibid.*, 73–74.

36. *Ibid.*, 369.

37. *Ibid.* 409.

38. As it happens, dogs (but not wolves!) tend to be presented in a rather favorable light in Tolkien's view, while cats do not fare so well. A very early version of the character who would become Sauron, arguably, was a cat: Tevildo, the "Prince of Cats" see Tolkien, *The Book of Lost Tales, Part I*, 42, 49. In a 1959 letter to a cat-breeder who had wished to give *Lord of the Rings*-inspired names to the kittens in her litter, Tolkien responded: "to me Siamese cats belong to the fauna of Mordor"; see Tolkien, *Letters*, 300.

39. Tolkien, *Morgoth's Ring*, 410, the interpolated "[become]" in the original (i.e., supplied by Christoper Tolkien). The reference to Melian involves a Maia who married an elf, then became effectively a queen of the elvish realm, giving birth to an elvish daughter (Lúthien) and remaining in this elf-like form thereafter.

40. *Ibid.*, 410.

41. *Ibid.*, 411.

42. *Ibid.*, 414.

43. For example, compare the ways in which indigenous populations have been associated with Satan, as in early Puritan writings in New England in the seventeenth century.

44. Tolkien, *Morgoth's Ring*, 415–418.

45. In a text apparently from the early 1930s, "The Earliest Annals of Beleriand," Tolkien asserts that the orcs were not brought into being until after Melkor's return from Valinor, which would have taken place long after the "awakening" of the elves; see *The Shaping of Middle-earth*, 375–376.

46. Tolkien, *Morgoth's Ring*, 417–418.

47. *Ibid.*, 418–419.

48. *Ibid.*, 420–421. Citing an even later fragment, Christopher adds: "But, as always, it is not quite so simple." In a note written (apparently) around November 1969, Tolkien expanded on the specious notion that Orcs could be like puppets, but here offering the somewhat more realistic view that, like armies well trained to follow orders blindly and without question, orcs long under the direct supervision of Morgoth or really Sauron would become almost like creatures without independent wills of their own. "Other originally independent creatures, and Men among them (but neither Elves nor Dwarves), could also be reduced to a like condition." That paragraph breaks off, but the next paragraph states: "men could (and can still be) reduced to such a condition. 'Puppets' would simply cease to move or 'live' at all, when not set in motion by the direct will of their maker" (421–422). But again, even in this iteration of the theory or orc origins, it is remarkable that Tolkien, when resurrecting this "puppet" speculations, folds both orcs and men into the same category; that is, orcs are no *more* puppet-like than men, and it is a sign of their basic humanity that they can be subject to the same "dehumanizing" power by those who rule them.

49. Tolkien, *Morgoth's Ring*, 390–391.

50. *Ibid.*, 400.

51. *Ibid.*, 405–406.

52. Tolkien, *The Silmarillion*, 8–9.

53. Tolkien, *Letters*, 195.

54. Tolkien, *The Silmarillion*, 7.

55. Tolkien, *Letters*, 195.

56. See, e.g., my *Representing Middle-earth*, 131–144.

57. Erich Auerbach, "Philology and Weltliteratur," trans. M. and E. W. Said, *Centennial Review* 13.1 (1969), 17.

Chapter 3

1. See J.R.R. Tolkien, *The Hobbit* (Del Rey, 1982); subsequent references to the novel in this chapter are cited parenthetically in the text.

2. Tolkien, *The Letters of J.R.R. Tolkien*, ed. Humphrey Carpenter (Boston: Houghton Mifflin, 1981), 24.

3. Dimitra Fimi, *Tolkien, Race, and Cultural History: From Fairies to Hobbits* (London: Palgrave Macmillan, 2009), 120.

4. This is not to say that all orcs look the same or have the same features, any more than all humans do. One can certainly imagine racial or ethnic subdivisions *within* the orcdom, but that is not designated in Tolkien by the use of the terms *goblin* or *orc*.

5. In the revised 1951 edition and subsequently, a second use of the word *orc* appears in the scene following Bilbo's escape from Gollum, as he notes the low ceiling in the tunnels: "'A bit low for goblins, at least the big ones,' thought Bilbo, not knowing that even the big ones, the orcs of the mountains, go along at great speed stooping low with their hands almost on the ground" (88). This does suggest that orcs could be thought of as goblins of large stature, but given that Bilbo is already in the mountains, its is not entirely clear how this distinction between relatively smaller "goblins" and "orcs of the mountain" holds up.

6. See Tolkien, *Letters*, 178, 185; see also, Tolkien, *The Lord of the Rings*, 50th Anniversary ed. (Boston: Houghton Mifflin, 2004), Appendix F, 1131.

7. See Douglas A. Anderson, ed. *The Annotated Hobbit*, 2nd ed. (Boston: Houghton Mifflin, 2002), 27.

8. Tolkien, *Letters*, 406.

9. *Ibid.*, 177–178, 185.

10. *Ibid.*, 90.

11. On the "intrusions" of history in the novel, see my *J.R.R. Tolkien's 'The Hobbit': Realizing History Through Fantasy* (New York: Palgrave Macmillan, 2022).

12. Tolkien, *Letters*, 110–111. "Niggle" is a reference to Tolkien's brief, allegorical

tale "Leaf by Niggle," in which the titular character attempts to complete a grand painting of a tree, only to render a single leaf in nearly perfect form. For more on Tolkien's untold tales, see Peter Grybauskas, *A Sense of Tales Untold: Exploring the Edges of Tolkien's Literary Canvas* (Kent: Kent State University Press, 2021).

13. Tolkien, *Letters*, 333.

14. As Robert Stuart has pointed out, by establishing orcs as mostly nameless, faceless masses of soldiers, the narratives "enable genocidal fantasy." See Stuart, *Tolkien, Race, and Racism in Middle-earth* (New York: Palgrave Macmillan, 2022), 133.

15. John D. Rateliff, *The History of The Hobbit* (Boston: Houghton Mifflin, 2007), 15.

16. Needless to say, part of the dehumanizing of the enemy lies in making them are almost supernatural or inhuman collective threat—swarming like insects, for instance—while also maintaining that they are somehow inferior as fighters, thus denying them the valor or skill associated with the "good" soldiers. See my "Demonizing the Enemy: Monstrosity, Ethics, and the Sense of the World Wars," *Representing Middle-earth: Tolkien, Form, and Ideology* (Jefferson, NC: MacFarland, 2024), 131–144.

17. Karen Wynn Fonstad, *The Atlas of Middle-earth*, rev. ed. (Boston: Houghton Mifflin, 1991), 75, 80.

18. Rateliff, *The History of The Hobbit*, 8, 712.

19. Needless to say, like the Vikings, the orcs could still be raiders.

20. Tom Shippey, *J.R.R. Tolkien: Author of the Century* (Boston: Houghton Mifflin, 2000), 15.

21. Rateliff, *The History of The Hobbit*, 712. *Gundabad* is apparently a dwarvish name, but its meaning is unknown; see Tolkien, *The Peoples of Middle-earth*, ed. Christopher Tolkien (New York: HarperCollins, 1996), 301.

22. Most readers assume that Legolas and Gimli enjoy a playing competition to see who can slay the most *orcs*, but in the Battle of Helm's Deep the enemy army comprises both orcs and human men (Dunlendings), so the competitors' tallies of their kills almost certainly included the fallen of both "races."

23. See Tolkien, *Letters*, 111. Some years ago at a conference of Tolkien scholars—*scholars*, mind you!—I witnessed grown men and women batting about a grotesque, mutilated, plastic doll's head with a club on the hotel lawn, thus playing "golf" as hobbits might with the head of an orc. Apparently, it is a tradition at this annual gathering to engage in such grisly sport. Marveling at the sheer stupidity of the scene, I could not help but also wonder what these hobbit-admiring people imagined might constitute *orkish* behavior.

24. Rateliff, *The History of The Hobbit*, 785.

25. This situation leads to one of the more amusing anachronisms in *The Hobbit*: "'This won't do at all,' said Thorin, 'If we don't get blown off, or drowned, or struck by lightning, we shall be picked up by some giant and kicked sky-high for a football'" (57).

26. It is possible the anthropomorphic trolls named William, Bert, and Tom are somewhat anarchic, living apart from the company of others with no sign of a troll-king or community nearby (although they seem to recognize William as the leader of their small group); they too are obviously social beings, working together to pursue their trollish business.

27. Rateliff, *History of the Hobbit*, 131, 163.

28. In fact, part of Gandalf's misgivings about the safety of their journey depended on there *not* being a king in that region: "he hardly dared to hope that they would pass without fearful adventure over those great tall mountains with lonely peaks and valleys where no king ruled" (56). But the, needless to say, Gandalf was probably not thinking of an *orc* king amid these considerations.

29. It is not at all certain that Sauron is even capable of "peopling" a region, but if this is meant to indicate that he sent peoples under his own rule to live in this region (as, say, King James I could be said to have "peopled" the Jamestown Colony in Virginia in 1609 and thereafter), then perhaps it is to be imagined as such. Which "creatures" these annalists have in mind is not specified, but given the subsequent history, orcs seem be the most likely "people," although Sauron clearly had many "men" in his service as well.

30. One might argue that the current inhabitants of Virginia or the United States have no inherent right to claim this lands as theirs now, given the vexed historical realities of colonialism, settlement, and the taking of land from Indigenous peoples to be found in those places at those times. But in theory, the goblins of the Misty Mountains have at least as much right to imagine theirs as a homeland.

31. If so, this would simply register the degree to which orkish cultures are similar to many hundreds of human cultures, from antiquity to the modern era, in this regard.

32. Hence, perhaps, the lyrics "Work, work! Nor dare to shirk / While Goblins quaff, and Goblins laugh, / Round and round far underground / Below, my lad!" express an odious orkish desire for slave laborers to relieve them of their own toil, but do not depict the reality of their own living conditions. However, even as Tolkien often refers to the "slaves" of the evil enemies, his own characters—or even the narrative voice itself—seems to have much pity or sympathy with those so victimized either. Certainly Gandalf or the others show no desire to liberate or otherwise aid any such enslaved persons in *The Hobbit*.

33. Stuart, *Tolkien, Race, and Racism in Middle-earth*, 133.

34. Tolkien, *Letters*, 145–146. See also my "'You cannot press the One Ring too hard': Tolkien, Ethics, and the Ambiguities of Magic," in *Magic in Fantasy Literature: Definitions, Manifestations, Functions*, eds. Tetiana Riazantseva and Yevheniia Kanchura (Kyiv: Shevchenko Institute of Literature, National Academy of Science of Ukraine, 2024), 224–239.

35. See, e.g., Stuart, *Tolkien, Race, and Racism in Middle-earth*, 136.

36. Ibid., 147.

37. The orcs' "recognition" of a blade that had killed many and was used by the elves of Gondolin (a city that had ceased to exist thousand of years earlier) to "hunt" their kind raises a perplexing question, never quite resolved in Tolkien's legendarium. Although Tolkien cannot imagine orcs to be immortal or particularly long-lived, notwithstanding their potential origins *as* elves, he nevertheless makes reference to orcs who "remember" ancient times. A logical way of viewing this would be to say that these orcs know their history, legends, and myths, which is to say that they too value "lore."

38. Tolkien himself was obviously concerned with the ways that the eagles could be viewed as unrealistically convenient *mechanisms* in the plot. As he wrote in a letter: "The Eagles are a dangerous 'machine.' I have used them sparingly, and that is the absolute limit of their credibility or usefulness"; see *Letters*, 271.

39. Perhaps Tolkien had this scene in mind when he later wrote that Orcs "must not be dealt with on their own terms of cruelty and treachery. Captives must not be tormented, not even to discover information for the defense of the homes of Elves and Men. If any Orcs surrendered and asked for mercy, they must be granted it, even at a cost." See *Morgoth's Ring*, ed. Christopher Tolkien (New York: HarperCollins, 1993), 419.

40. Tolkien states that the prisoners were treated better by the elves than by the orcs, "for Wood-elves were not goblins, and were reasonably well-behaved even to their worst enemies, when they captured them. The giant spiders were the only living things that they had no mercy upon" (169). These elves seem to show no mercy toward orcs either, nor any desire to "capture" or even to spare the lives of orcs, whom they actively hunt and slay, even when the orcs are" fugitives" no longer putting up a fight (292).

41. In an earlier draft of *The Hobbit*, one in which Bilbo himself slays Smaug, the "battle" takes place only on the return journey, near Beorn's home along the river, with the goblins fighting "essentially to avenge the Great Goblin's death" rather than to conquer or plunder Erebor; see Rateliff, *The History of The Hobbit*, 375.

42. The *greed* of the Elvenking, for example, is explicitly mentioned: "If the elf-king had a weakness it was for treasure, especially for silver and white gems; and though his hoard was rich, he was ever eager for more, since he had not yet as great a treasure as other elf-lords of old. His people neither mined nor worked metals or jewels, nor did they bother much with trade or with tilling the earth. All this was well known to every dwarf" (168). In Tolkien's earlier draft of *The Hobbit*, the elf-king explicitly craves "the treasure"

of the Lonely Mountain; as Ratliff puts it, "he had decided to seize any treasure the dwarves might gain from Smaug," which "prompts Gandalf to remark, 'Your own acts condemn you,' a judgement in keeping with Tolkien's earlier observation that although the wood-elves share in the treasure Bilbo gives to the Lake Men, they 'may not deserve' it"; see Rateliff, *The History of The Hobbit*, 573.

43. According to the *OED*, the use of the phrase "three parts" in this context would indicate three-out-of-four, or 75 percent.

44. Qtd. in Mikal Gilmore, "George R.R. Martin: The Rolling Stone Interview," *Rolling Stone* (April 23, 2014): https://www.rollingstone.com/culture/culture-news/george-r-r-martin-the-rolling-stone-interview-242487/.

45. Tolkien, *The Silmarillion* (New York: Del Rey, 2002), 47.

46. See https://tolkiengateway.net/wiki/Letter_to_Mrs_Munby.

47. Shippey, *The Road to Middle-earth: How J.R.R. Tolkien Created a New Mythology* (Boston: Houghton Mifflin, 2003), 233.

Chapter 4

1. As Tom Shippey has put it, "the orcs entered Middle-earth originally just because the story needed a continual supply of enemies over whom one need feel no compunction." See Shippey, *The Road to Middle-earth* (Boston: Houghton Mifflin, 2003), 233.

2. Tolkien, *The Lord of the Rings*, 50th Anniversary ed. (Boston: Houghton Mifflin, 2004), 27. References to this edition are hereafter cited parenthetically in the text. For the convenience of those using other editions and where the location may be unclear, I follow the Book, chapter, page convention: that is, I.i.27 = Book I, Chapter 1, page 27.

3. And, as we have seen, Tolkien desperately wanted to published a version of the "Silmarillion" alongside *The Lord of the Rings*, in fact, as a single tales ("the Saga of the Jewels and the Rings"), and thus Allen & Unwin was confronted with what Tolkien himself estimated to be a roughly 1,000,000-word work that would be the "sequel" to *The Hobbit*. See *The Letters of J.R.R. Tolkien*, ed. Humphrey Carpenter (Boston: Houghton Mifflin, 1981), 136–137.

4. See Shippey, *J.R.R. Tolkien: Author of the Century* (Boston: Houghton Mifflin, 2000), 16–17.

5. Tolkien, *Letters*, 184.

6. Robert Stuart, *Tolkien, Race, and Racism in Middle-earth* (New York: Palgrave Macmillan, 2022), 90 91.

7. Of course, the fact of such cohabitation is a sign that orcs *are* men, which is my contention throughout the book.

8. Tolkien, *Letters*, 274.

9. Stuart, *Tolkien, Race, and Racism*, 90.

10. Or rather, the apparent menace comes from the "wrong" kind of newcomers. Many of the most noble races of elves and men, such as the Noldor (including Galadriel) or the Númenoreans (including Aragorn's ancestral line) came to where they now live as straightforwardly imperialist colonizers, but Tolkien views their settlement in different parts of Middle-earth a wholly ennobling and beneficial development. It is not clear that the conquered populations of those occupied territories would always agree, and in any event, as with so much of the history of imperialism in our own world, their "voices" are rarely heard in the texts.

11. Helen Young, *Race and Popular Fantasy Literature: Habits of Whiteness* (London: Routledge, 2016), 24.

12. Virginia Luling, "An Anthropologist in Middle-earth," *Mythlore: A Journal of J.R.R. Tolkien, C.S. Lewis, Charles Williams, and Mythopoeic Literature* 21.1 (1996), 56.

13. One would imagine the race of hobbits might be an exception, but in the Prologue to *The Lord of the Rings*, we learn that their race is divided into three distinctive ethnicities or kinship groups, the Harfoots ("browner of skin, smaller, and shorter"), the Stoors ("broader, heavier in build"), and the Fallohides, who "were fairer of skin and also of hair, and they were taller and slimmer than the others." Tolkien then observes that the Fallohides "mingled with the other kinds," and thus "they were often found as leaders or chieftains among clans of Harfoots or Stoors. Even in Bilbo's time the strong Fallohidish strain could still be noted among the greater

families, such as the Tooks and the Masters of Buckland" (3–4). Hence, even with the rather small and mostly brunette hobbits, those taller and "fairer" of their race were likely to reign over others.

14. Apparently, some orkish "baby boom" had occurred in the interim. More likely, however, the lack of information about orcs—just like the lack of interest in their welfare—hides the fact that there were many orc families still alive after the Battle of Five Armies, and it is probable that many more arrive from other areas at this time.

15. Tolkien makes clear that, in addition to "the Black Speech," there must be multiple languages amongst the different orc cultures and communities, for he includes a scene in which orcs are "using ordinary speech"—that is, the Common Speech understood by unworldly hobbits—because "members of two or three quite different tribes were present, and they could not understand one another's orc-speech" (III.iii.445).

16. Tolkien, *The Hobbit* (New York: Del Rey, 1982), 90.

Chapter 5

1. See, e.g., my "Three Rings for the Elven Kings: Trilogizing Tolkien in Print and Film," in *Representing Middle-earth: Tolkien, Form, and Ideology* (Jefferson, NC: McFarland, 2024), 64–78.

2. See Mieke Bal, *Narratology: Introduction to the Theory of Narrative*, 3rd ed. (Toronto: University of Toronto Press, 2009), 145–164.

3. See Joseph Frank, *The Idea of Spatial Form* (New Brunswick: Rutgers University Press, 1991).

4. See Shippey, *The Road to Middle-earth: How J.R.R. Tolkien Created a New Mythology* (Boston: Houghton Mifflin, 2003), 94–134.

5. Tolkien, *The Letters of J.R.R. Tolkien*, ed. Humphrey Carpenter (Boston: Houghton Mifflin, 1981), 177.

6. From a Marxist perspective, as Fredric Jameson has suggested, these ideas "may function to rewrite certain religious concepts—most notably Christian historicism and the 'concept' of providence, but also the pretheological systems of primitive magic—as anticipatory foreshadowings of historical materialism within precapitalist social formations." See Jameson, *The Political Unconscious: Narrative as a Socially Symbolic Act* (Ithaca: Cornell University Press, 1981), 285.

7. Tolkien, *Letters*, 238.

8. See Tolkien, *The Silmarillion* (New York: Del Rey, 2002), 352.

9. Carl F. Hostetter, in "Uglúk to the Dung-pit," has identified the speaker as Grishnákh, but that is certainly incorrect (see Hostetter, "Uglúk to the Dung-pit," *Vinyar Tengwar* 26 [November 1992]: 16). Grishnákh is introduced on the next page as a new "voice, softer than the others but more evil," which would seem to indicate that Pippin had not yet heard the voice before. Moreover, shortly thereafter one of Uglúk's soldiers actually kills the "yellow-fanged guard" with the "saw-edged knife" who had threatened Pippin, and obviously that was not Grishnákh, but rather one of his fellow orcs of Mordor.

10. In Appendix F of *The Lord of the Rings*, Tolkien discusses the invention of the Black Speech by Sauron, and—making reference to this scene—he explains that "the curse of the Mordor-orc was in the more debased form used by the soldiers of the Dark Tower, of whom Grishnákh was the captain" (App. F, 1131), which lends further weight to the argument that Grishnákh was not the "Mordor-orc" in question. Tolkien does not translate the line, but in an earlier version he renders it as *Uglúk to the cesspool, sha! the dungfilth; the great Saruman-fool, skai!* (see *The Peoples of Middle-earth*, 83). Later, in his "Words, Phrases, and Passages in *The Lord of the Rings*," a guide for use by translators, Tolkien provided a slightly different translation: "Uglúk to the torture (chamber) with stinking Saruman-filth, dung-heap, skai!"; he also notes that *skai* is an interjection "of contempt" ("Words, Phrases, and Passages," 78–79.) Observing just how different these translations are, Christopher concludes that "it seems clear that my father was at this time devising interpretations of the words, whatever he may have intended them to mean when he wrote them" (*The Peoples of Middle-earth*, xii).

11. See Virginia Luling, "An Anthropologist in Middle-earth," *Mythlore: A Journal of J.R.R. Tolkien, C.S. Lewis, Charles*

Williams, and Mythopoeic Literature 21.1 (1996), 56.

12. Tolkien seems somewhat ambivalent on the matter. On the one hand, he says that *uruk-hai* simply means "orc-folk" or "orc-kind," thus not representing a distinctively "higher" form of orc. On the other hand, he does elsewhere suggest that the term was normally applied "only to the great soldier-orcs that at this time issued from Mordor and Isengard" (*The Lord of the Rings*, App. F, 1131).

13. According to the Tale of Years, nearly two and a half months have passed since the Fellowship's escape from Moria on January 15. The fellowship leaves Lorien on Feb 16, Merry and Pippin are captured on March 26, and escape from the orcs during the attack by the Rohirrim on March 29.

14. Indeed, almost immediately after proposing to Gandalf that they join with "the Power" in order to guide its policies for the better, Saruman proposes that he and Gandalf take "the Ruling Ring" for themselves, prompting Gandalf to observe that "only one hand at a time can wield the One," and shortly after, Gandalf notes that "Saruman was mustering a great force on his own account, in rivalry of Sauron and not in his service" (II.ii.260). There is little evidence in *The Lord of the Rings* to prove that Saruman was *ever* sincerely in cahoots with Sauron.

15. See my *Representing Middle-earth: Tolkien, Form, and Ideology* (Jefferson, NC: McFarland, 2024), 110–116.

16. Shippey, *J.R.R. Tolkien: Author of the Century* (Boston: Houghton Mifflin, 2000), 133.

17. Merry and Pippin are also later given meat and bread to eat. Pippin "ate the stale grey bread hungrily, but not the meat. He was famished but not yet so famished as to eat flesh flung to him by an Orc" (450).

18. As Uglúk had already been described as "a large black Orc," and all the orcs are characterized by their swart, swarthy, or sallow skin, the reference by Uglúk to "Whiteskins" would seem to reinforce the *racial* difference between these peoples (in the modern ways that the word *race* is used, I mean). The "brown" Dunlendings' disdain for the "Strawheads" (i.e., the blond Rohirrim) adds to this general sense as well, which demonstrates that both orcs and men are well aware of their situation within a system of racial difference, even if they are also treated rather differently within that system. These hierarchies need not have been marked by light-versus-dark distinctions, but they tend to appear this way in Tolkien's legendarium.

19. Judging the tracks left from this scene, Aragorn later imagines that "some large and bold Orc may have been trying to escape with the prize alone, for his own ends" (III.v.490), but the text suggests that Grishnákh, even if he did manage to secure the "prize" for himself, was always planning to take it straight back to his superiors. Admittedly, he would have probably been richly rewarded for that service, so the plan may not have been in any way selfless, but it still indicates a loyalty to Mordor.

20. Tolkien, "Words, Phrases, and Passages," 79.

21. Treebeard slips in some Quenya (elvish) words, *morimaite* and *sincahonda*, which mean "blackhanded" and "flinthearted," terms he had already said using the "Common Speech."

22. Treebeard later refers to Gríma as "a dragged rat" is "grimly delighted" to learn of his unhappy fate (III.ix.574).

23. Notwithstanding Tolkien's (or Sam's) sense of this, the orcs were likely speaking in the "Common" language that Sam already knew, for he is also able to understand the speech of many orcs in Mordor without wearing or holding the Ring.

24. Tolkien, *Letters*, 89.

25. Verlyn Flieger, "The Orcs and the Others: Familiarity as Estrangement in *The Lord of the Rings*," in *Tolkien and Alterity*, eds. Christopher Vaccaro and Yvette Kisor (New York: Palgrave Macmillan, 2017), 206–207.

26. Tolkien, *The Letters of J.R.R. Tolkien: Revised and Expanded Edition*, ed. Humphrey Carpenter with Christopher Tolkien (New York: William Morrow, 2023), 367.

27. Brian Rosebury, *Tolkien: A Cultural Phenomenon* (New York: Palgrave, 2003), 82–83.

Chapter 6

1. Tolkien, *The Letters of J.R.R. Tolkien*, ed. Humphrey Carpenter (Boston: Houghton Mifflin, 1981), 167.
2. See Tolkien, "Words, Phrases and Passages in Various Tongues in *The Lord of the Rings*," ed. Christopher Gilson, *Parma Eldalamberon* 17 (2007), 99.
3. Tolkien, *Unfinished Tales of Númenor and Middle-earth*, ed. Christopher Tolkien (New York: Del Rey, 1988), 402.
4. *Ibid.*, 394.
5. Tolkien, *Letters*, 274.
6. Tolkien, *Unfinished Tales*, 401–402.
7. Sigmund Freud, *Civilization and Its Discontents*, trans. James Strachey (New York: W.W. Norton, 1989). 92. Interestingly enough, Tolkien seems to have been worried that readers might try to associate the Drúedain with *hobbits*, leading him to write a substantial passage "contrasting Drûgs and Hobbits," in Christopher's words. See Tolkien, *The Peoples of Middle-earth*, ed. Christopher Tolkien (New York: HarperCollins, 1996), 309–316.
8. Robert Stuart, *Tolkien, Race, and Racism in Middle-earth* (New York: Palgrave Macmillan, 2022), 91. This is, of course, a reference to the execrable caricature of the American Indian sidekick from the radio and later television show *The Lone Ranger*, in which Tonto's broken English frequently omits articles, prepositions, and so on.
9. Tolkien, "On Fairy-Stories." *The Monsters and the Critics and Other Essays*, ed. Christopher Tolkien (New York: HarperCollins, 1983), 134.
10. John Garth, *The Worlds of J.R.R. Tolkien: The Places That Inspired Middle-earth* (Princeton: Princeton University Press, 2020), 116. See also Bianca Beronio, "'Red Indians Are Better': Indigeneity, Race, and Representation in Tolkien's Middle-earth," M.A. Thesis, Texas A&M University–Commerce, 2024.
11. Dimitra Fimi, *Tolkien, Race, and Cultural History: From Fairies to Hobbits* (London: Palgrave Macmillan, 2009), 151.
12. The sense that the indigenous peoples of the Americas are "vanishing" lends a elegiac aspect to their character as "noble savages," of course, making theirs a race to be admired in its very evanescence.
13. As Tolkien writes, "It seems clear to me that Frodo's duty was 'humane' not political. He naturally thought first of the Shire, since his roots were there, but the quest had as its object not the preserving of this or that polity, such as the half republic half aristocracy of the Shire, but the liberation from an evil tyranny of all the 'humane'—including those, such as 'easterlings' and Haradrim, that were still servants of the tyranny." Tolkien then explains that, in his tale, the term *humane* "includes of course Elves, and indeed all 'speaking creatures.'" See *Letters*, 240–241.
14. Needless to say, perhaps, it is precisely this aspect of *The Lord of the Rings* which appeals so powerfully to many white supremacists, neofascists, and others on the far-right in Europe and the Americas who claim to be defending "Western civilization" from the encroachments of variously "foreign" threats. See, e.g., my "Tolkien's Deplorable Cultus."
15. *Gothmog* is also the name given to "the Lord of the Balrogs" in *The Silmarillion*, but it is obvious that no balrog is present in the Battle of the Pelennor Fields. This Gothmog may have been named in honor of the First Age's terror, or more likely was a name Tolkien had in mind from his large body of unpublished "Silmarillion" materials, such as the use of the name *Grond* to denote the great battering ram of the forces of Mordor, for *Grond* was also the name of Morgoth's mace, "the Hammer of the Underworld," in the First Age, according to *The Silmarillion*.
16. In Appendix F to *The Lord of the Rings*, Tolkien explains that *snaga* is the word for "slave" in the Black Speech of the orcs (1131), but here this particular character's name (Snaga) is capitalized, and he seems to be a distinct person, not merely a member of the category of servant, even in Shagrat's view. The confusion need not be resolved here, but it is notable that the descriptor and the proper name coincide for this orc, who is clearly a subordinate of Shagrat and exhibiting insubordination, actively calling into question Shagrat's leadership and decision-making, just as Shagrat and Gorbag had been skeptical of the competence of their own superior officers. If Snaga be a "slave" (*snaga*), he is undoubtedly a bold and canny one. (As I have noted earlier, the term *slave* seems

to be used in *The Lord of the Rings*, by characters as well as by the narrator, as a term of opprobrium more than as the name for one's station, and even among the "good" few characters express sympathy for "slaves," even as they may express there opposition to being enslaved themselves. As such, it may be that for orcs, *snaga* is used more as an insult than as a way of indicating a person's condition of freedom or bondage.)

17. Undoubtedly the experience with the orcs was traumatic in its own way, but then Galadriel herself felt the need to apologize to Frodo for the psychological torment she had willfully caused him.

18. Needless to say, there is no way that Frodo or Sam could have known which soldiers were drafted or pressed into service against their will and which were not. All they can see is which ones are likely "privates" and which are "sergeants," for example.

19. Specifically, the orc sergeant orders them to "fall in, or I'll have your numbers and report you" (VI.ii.931), which suggests a complex bureaucratic infrastructure in which soldiers are assigned numbers and records are kept. In other words, the orcs of Mordor live in a society much like that of the modern United States or United Kingdom.

20. Tolkien, *Letters*, 78.

21. In a late addition to the legendarium, in a note written sometime after January 19, 1970, Tolkien mentions "Eastern Orcs" who were "long masterless" and "yet wild and ungovernable"; these "Eastern orcs […] were not subservient to Sauron," and for some time at least "they despised him and laughed at him." *These* orcs, most certainly, would not mourn the loss of Sauron, nor find it difficult to live without him. See Tolkien, *The Nature of Middle-earth: Late Writings on the Lands, Inhabitants, and Metaphysics of Middle-earth*, ed. Carl Hostetter (New York: Houghton Mifflin Harcourt, 2021), 370.

22. Tolkien, *Letters*, 195.

23. Tolkien, *Morgoth's Ring*, ed. Christopher Tolkien (New York: HarperCollins, 1993), 419.

24. Tolkien, *Letters*, 64.

25. *Ibid.*, 63.

26. Tolkien, *Morgoth's Ring*, ed. Christopher Tolkien (New York: HarperCollins, 1993), 421–422.

27. *Ibid.*, 420–421.

28. *Ibid.*, 418–420.

29. In his later essays on orcs, Tolkien does write that orcs "must not be dealt with on their own terms of cruelty and treachery. Captives must not be tormented, not even to discover information for the defense of the homes of Elves and Men. If any Orcs surrendered and asked for mercy, they must be granted it, even at a cost. This was the teaching of the Wise, though in the horror of the War it was not always heeded." See Tolkien, *Morgoth's Ring*, 419.

30. Tolkien described the regions around Lake Núrnen in the southern parts of Mordor as being more agricultural, whereas northern region contained mines and forges, so Mordor is much like other countries in having both industrial and agricultural regions (see *The Lord of the Rings*, VI.ii.923). Indeed, at that point Sam and Frodo had already risked drinking the "poisonous" water of Mordor, and while they found the taste bitter, they were able to drank their fill with no adverse effects.

31. Technically, Rohan is an independent kingdom, ruled in that day by King Éomer who "took again the Oath or Eorl," prerequisite to King Elessar's "renewal" of "the gift" of Gondor's ruler in the past. But again, if King Elessar has the power to "grant" these lands to the people of Rohan, then he must have viewed them as *his* to bestow. See Tolkien, *The Lord of the Rings*, Appendix A, 1071.

32. Indeed, the ents literally hand the keys to the Tower of Orthanc to Aragorn (VI.vi.980). Treebeard also recounts how the ents had killed nearly all the invading orcs of that region: "not many escaped alive, and the River took most of those" (979).

Conclusion

1. For example, I am not interested in the project of something like Kirill Yeskov's *The Last Ringbearer*, a 1999 work of "fan fiction" written in Russian and purporting to depict the events of *The Lord of the Rings* from the point of view of those on the side of Sauron. Notably, in that novel, there are no orcs at all; rather "orc" is just an insulting and dehumanizing

racial slur used by their enemies to refer to the (human) people of Mordor.

2. See, e.g., my "Tolkien's Deplorable Cultus," *Spectre* (August 20, 2024).

3. Tolkien, *Sauron Defeated*, ed. Christopher Tolkien (New York: HarperCollins, 1992), 116.

4. *Ibid.*, 122.

5. Tolkien, *The Peoples of Middle-earth*, ed. Christopher Tolkien (New York: HarperCollins, 1996), 411–414.

6. Tolkien, *The Letters of J.R.R. Tolkien*, ed. Humphrey Carpenter (Boston: Houghton Mifflin, 1981), 344. As Christopher Tolkien points out, the timeline here is a bit confusing, since Aragorn (King Elessar) would still be alive and ruling 100 years after the fall of Sauron. Elsewhere, Tolkien mentions that the story takes place 100 years into the reign of Eldarion. Perhaps because "The New Shadow" remained in draft form, it did not need to be definitively settled yet. See Tolkien, *The Peoples of Middle-earth*, 419–420.

7. Tolkien, *Letters*, 419.

8. Quoted in Humphrey Carpenter, *J.R.R. Tolkien: A Biography* (Boston: Houghton Mifflin, 2000), 233.

9. See J.D. Payne and Patrick McKay, creators, *The Lord of the Rings: The Rings of Power*, Season 1 (Amazon Studios and New Line Cinema, 2022).

10. Tolkien, *Letters*, 195. In the same letter, Tolkien notes that orcs "would be creatures begotten of sin, and naturally bad" but *not* "irredeemably bad," likening their condition to that of "the calculated dehumanising of Men by tyrants that goes on today."

11. Tolkien, *Letters*, 215.

12. See Corey Mohler, "The Council of Elrond," *Existential Comics*: https://existentialcomics.com/comic/175.

13. Ursula K. Le Guin, "American SF and The Other," *Science-Fiction Studies* 2.3 (November 1975), 209–210.

Bibliography

Selected Works by J.R.R. Tolkien

Beowulf: A Translation and Commentary. Ed. Christopher Tolkien. Houghton Mifflin, 2014.

"*Beowulf*: The Monsters and the Critics." *The Monsters and the Critics and Other Essays.* Edited by Christopher Tolkien. HarperCollins, 1983. 5–48.

The Book of Lost Tales, Part I. Ed. Christopher Tolkien. *The History of Middle-earth*: Vol. 1. George Allen and Unwin, 1983.

The Book of Lost Tales, Part II. Ed. Christopher Tolkien. *The History of Middle-earth*: Vol. 2. George Allen and Unwin, 1984.

"Guide to the Names in *The Lord of the Rings*." In *A Tolkien Compass.* Ed. Jared Lobell. New York: Del Rey, 1975. 168–216.

The History of Middle-earth (12 volumes).

The Hobbit. Del Rey, 1982.

The Lays of Beleriand. Ed. Christopher Tolkien. *The History of Middle-earth*: Vol. 3. George Allen and Unwin, 1985.

"Leaf By Niggle." *The Tolkien Reader.* Del Rey, 1966. 100–120.

The Letters of J.R.R. Tolkien. Ed. Humphrey Carpenter. Houghton Mifflin, 1981.

The Letters of J.R.R. Tolkien: Revised and Expanded Edition. Ed. Humphrey Carpenter with Christopher Tolkien. William Morrow, 2023.

The Lord of the Rings. 50th Anniversary ed. Houghton Mifflin, 2004.

The Lost Road and Other Writings. Ed. Christopher Tolkien. *The History of Middle-earth*: Vol. 5. Unwin Hyman, 1987.

Morgoth's Ring. Ed. Christopher Tolkien. *The History of Middle-earth*: Vol. 10. HarperCollins, 1993.

"Mythopoeia." *Tree and Leaf.* HarperCollins, 2001. 85–90.

The Nature of Middle-earth: Late Writings on the Lands, Inhabitants, and Metaphysics of Middle-earth. Ed. Carl Hostetter. Houghton Mifflin Harcourt, 2021.

"On Fairy-Stories." *The Monsters and the Critics and Other Essays.* Edited by Christopher Tolkien. HarperCollins, 1983. 109–161.

The Peoples of Middle-earth. Ed. Christopher Tolkien. *The History of Middle-earth*: Vol. 12. HarperCollins, 1996.

The Return of the Shadow. Ed. Christopher Tolkien. *The History of Middle-earth*: Vol. 6. Unwin Hyman, 1988.

Sauron Defeated. Ed. Christopher Tolkien. *The History of Middle-earth*: Vol. 9. HarperCollins, 1992.

The Shaping of Middle-earth. Ed. Christopher Tolkien. *The History of Middle-earth*: Vol. 4. George Allen and Unwin, 1986.

The Silmarillion. Del Rey, 2002.

The Treason of Isengard. Ed. Christopher Tolkien. *The History of Middle-earth*: Vol. 7. Unwin Hyman, 1989.

Unfinished Tales of Númenor and Middle-earth. Ed. Christopher Tolkien. Del Rey, 1988.

The War of the Jewels. Ed. Christopher Tolkien. *The History of Middle-earth*: Vol. 11. HarperCollins, 1994.

The War of the Ring. Ed. Christopher Tolkien. *The History of Middle-earth*: Vol. 8. Unwin Hyman, 1990.

"Words, Phrases and Passages in Various Tongues in *The Lord of the Rings*." Ed.

Christopher Gilson. *Parma Eldalamberon* 17 (2007).

Other Works

Anderson, Douglas A., ed. *The Annotated Hobbit*. 2nd ed. Boston: Houghton Mifflin, 2002.

Aristotle. *The Poetics*. Trans. S.H. Butcher. Boston: Hill and Wang, 1961.

Ashford, David. "'Orc Talk': Soviet Linguistics in Middle-earth." *Journal of the Fantastic in the Arts* 29.1 (2018): 26–40.

Auerbach, Erich. "Philology and *Weltliteratur*," trans. M. and E.W. Said, *Centennial Review* 13.1 (1969): 1–17.

Bates, Brian. *The Real Middle-earth: Exploring the Magic and Mystery of the Middle Ages, J.R.R. Tolkien, and* The Lord of the Rings. New York: Palgrave Macmillan, 2003.

Beronio, Bianca. "'Red Indians are Better': Indigeneity, Race, and Representation in Tolkien's Middle-earth." M.A. Thesis, Texas A&M University–Commerce, 2024.

Birns, Nicholas. *The Literary Role of History in the Fiction of J.R.R. Tolkien*. London: Routledge, 2024.

Bogost, Ian. "Where in the World is Middle Earth [sic]?" (June 20, 2007): https://bogost.com/writing/blog/where_in_the_world_was_middle/.

Burger, Peter. *The Political Unconscious of the Fantasy Sub-Genre of Romance*. Lewiston, NY: The Edwin Mellen Press, 2001.

Carpenter, Humphrey. *The Inklings: C.S. Lewis, J.R.R. Tolkien, Charles Williams, and Their Friends*. New York: HarperCollins, 2006.

_____. *J.R.R. Tolkien: A Biography*. Houghton Mifflin, 2000.

Chance, Jane. "'In the Company of Orcs': Peter Jackson's Queer Tolkien." In *Queer Movie Medievalisms*. Eds. Kathleen Coyne Kelly and Tison Pugh. Farnham, Surrey: Ashgate, 2009, 79–96.

_____. "Subversive Fantasist: Tolkien on Class Difference." In *The Lord of the Rings, 1954–2004: Scholarship in Honor of Richard E. Blackwelder*. Eds. Wayne Hammond and Cristina Scull. Milwaukee: Marquette University Press, 2006, 153–168.

Chance, Jane, and Alfred K. Siewers, eds. *Tolkien's Modern Middle Ages*. New York: Palgrave Macmillan, 2005.

Chesterton, G.K. *Charles Dickens: A Critical Study*. New York: Dodd Mead and Co., 1906.

Colebatch, Hal. *Return of the Heroes: The Lord of the Rings, Star Wars, Harry Potter, and Social Conflict*. Second edition. Christchurch, NZ: Cybereditions, 2003.

Conley, Tom. "*The Lord of the Rings* and the Fellowship of the Map." In *From Hobbits to Hollywood: Essays on Peter Jackson's* Lord of the Rings. Eds. Earnest Mathijs and Murray Pomerance. Amsterdam: Rodopi, 2006, 215–229.

Croft, Janet Brennan. "Barrel-Rides and She-Elves: Audience and Anticipation in Peter Jackson's *Hobbit* Trilogy." Guest lecture, Marquette University Libraries Special Collections (March 26, 2015): https://www.academia.edu/13050712/Barrel_rides_and_She_elves_Audience_and_Anticipation_in_Peter_Jacksons_Hobbit_Trilogy.

_____. "Mithril Coats and Tin Ears: 'Anticipation' and 'Flattening' in Peter Jackson's *The Lord of the Rings* Trilogy." In *Tolkien on Film: Essays on Peter Jackson's* The Lord of the Rings. Ed. Janet Brennan Croft. Altadena, CA: Mythopoeic Press, 2004, 63–80.

_____. *War in the Works of J.R.R. Tolkien*. Westport, CT: Praeger, 2004.

Croft, Janet Brenan, and Leslie A. Donovan, eds. *Perilous and Fair: Women in the Works and Life of J.R.R. Tolkien*. Altadena, CA: Mythopoeic Press, 2015.

Crown, Sarah. "What the Booker Prize Really Excludes." *The Guardian* (October 17, 2011): https://www.theguardian.com/books/booksblog/2011/oct/17/science-fiction-china-mieville.

Echo-Hawk, Roger. *Tolkien in Pawneeland: Essays on the Inner Secrets of Middle-earth*. 2nd ed. CreateSpace Independent Publishing, 2016.

Ekman, Stefan. *Here Be Dragons: Exploring Fantasy Maps and Settings*. Middletown, CT: Wesleyan University Press, 2013.

Ellmann, Mary. "Growing Up Hobbitic." *New American Review* 2 (1968): 217–29.

Fimi, Dimitra. *Tolkien, Race, and Cultural History: From Fairies to Hobbits*. London: Palgrave Macmillan, 2009.

Firchow, Peter E. "The Politics of Fantasy: The Hobbit and Fascism." *Midwest Quarterly* 51.1 (Autumn 2008): 15–27.

Flieger, Verlyn. "The Arch and the Keystone." *Mythlore* 38.1 (Fall/Winter 2019), 5–17.

———. "But What Did He Really Mean?" *Tolkien Studies* 11 (2014), 149–166.

———. "The Orcs and the Others: Familiarity as Estrangement in *The Lord of the Rings*." In *Tolkien and Alterity*. Eds. Christopher Vaccaro and Yvette Kisor. New York: Palgrave Macmillan, 2017, 205–222.

———. "A Postmodern Medievalist?" In *Tolkien's Modern Middle Ages*. Eds. Jane Chance and Alfred K. Siewers. New York: Palgrave Macmillan, 2005, 17–28.

———. *A Question of Time: J.R.R. Tolkien's Road to Faërie*. Kent: Kent State University Press, 1997.

———. *There Would Always Be a Fairy Tale: More Essays on Tolkien*. Kent: Kent State University Press, 2017.

Fonstad, Karen Wynn. *The Atlas of Middle-earth*. Rev. ed. Boston: Houghton Mifflin, 1991.

Foucault, Michel. *Discipline and Punish*. Trans. Alan Sheridan. New York: Vintage, 1977.

Frank, Joseph. *The Idea of Spatial Form*. New Brunswick: Rutgers University Press, 1991.

Freud, Sigmund. *Civilization and Its Discontents*, trans. James Strachey. New York: W.W. Norton, 1989.

Frye, Northrop. *Fearful Symmetry: A Study of William Blake*. Princeton: Princeton University Press, 1969.

Fussell, Paul. *The Great War and Modern Memory*. 25th Anniversary edition. Oxford: Oxford University Press, 2000.

Garth, John. *Tolkien and the Great War: The Threshold of Middle-Earth*. London: HarperCollins, 2003.

———. *The Worlds of J.R.R. Tolkien: The Places That Inspired Middle-earth*. Princeton: Princeton University Press, 2020.

Gilmore, Mikal. "George R.R. Martin: The Rolling Stone Interview." *Rolling Stone* (April 23, 2014): https://www.rollingstone.com/culture/culture-news/george-r-r-martin-the-rolling-stone-interview-242487/.

Groot, Jerome de. *The Historical Novel*. London: Routledge, 2010.

Grybauskas, Peter. *A Sense of Tales Untold: Exploring the Edges of Tolkien's Literary Canvas*. Kent: Kent State University Press, 2021.

Hartog, François. *The Mirror of Herodotus: The Representation of the Other in the Writing of History*. Trans. Janet Lloyd. Berkeley: University of California Press, 2009.

Hawthorne, Nathaniel. *The House of the Seven Gables*. Ed. Milton R. Stern. New York: Penguin, 1986.

Honegger, Thomas, and Frank Weinreich, eds. *Tolkien and Modernity*. Zollikofen, Switzerland: Walking Tree, 2006.

Hostetter, Carl F. "Uglúk to the Dung-pit." *Vinyar Tengwar* 26 (November 1992): 16.

Houghton, John Wm., Janet Brennan Croft, Nancy Martsch, John D. Rateliff, and Robin Anne Reid, eds. *Tolkien in the New Century: Essays in Honor of Tom Shippey*. Jefferson, NC: McFarland, 2014.

Hume, Kathryn. *Fantasy and Mimesis: Responses to Reality in Western Literature*. London: Methuen, 1984.

Jameson, Fredric. *The Political Unconscious: Narrative as a Socially Symbolic Act*. Ithaca: Cornell University Press, 1981.

Kane, Douglass Charles. *Arda Reconstructed: The Creation of the Published Silmarillion*. Bethlehem, PA: Lehigh University Press, 2011.

Kellner, Douglas. "*The Lord of the Rings* as Allegory: A Multiperspectivist Reading." In *From Hobbits to Hollywood: Essays on Peter Jackson's* Lord of the Rings. Eds. Earnest Mathijs and Murray Pomerance. Amsterdam: Rodopi, 2006, 17–39.

Kermode, Frank. *The Sense of an Ending: Studies in the Theory of Fiction*. Oxford: Oxford University Press, 1967.

Kisor, Yvette. "'Poor Sméagol': Gollum as Exile in Middle-earth." In *Tolkien in the New Century: Essays in Honor of Tom Shippey*. Eds. John Wm. Houghton, Janet Brennan Croft, Nancy Martsch, John D. Rateliff, and Robin Anne Reid. Jefferson, NC: McFarland, 2014, 153–168.

Komornicka, Jolanta N. "The Ugly Elf: Orcs Bodies, Perversion, and Redemption in *The Silmarillion* and *The Lord of the Rings*," in *The Body in Tolkien's Legendarium: Essays on Middle-earth Corporeality*. Ed. Christopher Vaccaro. Jefferson, NC: McFarland, 2013, 83–96.

Lakowski, Romuald I. "The Fall and Repentance of Galadriel." In *Perilous and Fair: Women in the Works and Life of J.R.R. Tolkien*. Eds. Janet Brennan Croft and Leslie A. Donovan. Altadena, CA: Mythopoeic Press, 2015, 153–167.

Landa, Ishay. "Slaves of the Ring: Tolkien's Political Unconscious." *Historical Materialism* 10.4 (2002): 113–133.

Le Guin, Ursula K. "American SF and The Other," *Science-Fiction Studies* 2.3 (November 1975), 208–210.

The Lord of the Rings: The Fellowship of the Ring. Dir. Peter Jackson. New Line, 2001.

The Lord of the Rings: The Return of the King. Dir. Peter Jackson. New Line, 2003.

The Lord of the Rings: The Two Towers. Dir. Peter Jackson. New Line, 2002.

Lukács, Georg. *The Historical Novel*. Trans. Hannah and Stanley Mitchell. Lincoln: University of Nebraska Press, 1983.

———. *The Theory of the Novel*. Trans. Anna Bostock. Cambridge: MIT Press, 1971.

Luling, Virginia. "An Anthropologist in Middle-earth." *Mythlore: A Journal of J.R.R. Tolkien, C.S. Lewis, Charles Williams, and Mythopoeic Literature* 21.1 (1996): 53–57.

Marx, Karl. *Grundrisse: Foundations of the Political Economy*. Trans. Martin Nicolaus. New York: Penguin, 1973.

Marx, Karl, and Friedrich Engels, *The Communist Manifesto*. Trans. Samuel Moore. New York: Signet, 1998.

Mendlesohn, Farah, and Edward James. *A Short History of Fantasy*. London: Middlesex University Press, 2009.

Miéville, China. "Cognition as Ideology: A Dialectic of SF." *Red Planets: Marxism and Science Fiction*. Eds. Marc Bould and China Miéville. Middletown, CT: Wesleyan University Press, 2009, 231–248.

———. "Editorial Introduction: Marxism and Fantasy." *Historical Materialism* 10.4 (2002): 39–49.

Mills, Charles. "The Wretched of Middle-earth: An Orkish Manifesto," *The Southern Journal of Philosophy* 60(Suppl. 1).S1 (September 2022), 105–135.

Mitchell, Sebastian. *Utopia and Its Discontents: Plato to Atwood*. New York: Bloomsbury 2020.

Mohler, Corey. "The Council of Elrond," *Existential Comics*: https://existentialcomics.com/comic/175.

Moorcock, Michael. *Wizardry and Wild Romance: A Study of Epic Fantasy*. London: Victor Gollancz Ltd., 1987.

Moretti, Franco. *The Modern Epic: The World System from Goethe to Garcia-Márquez*. London: Verso, 1994.

Nicolay, Theresa Freda, *Tolkien and the Modernists*. Jefferson, NC: McFarland, 2014.

Nietzsche, Friedrich. "On the Uses and Disadvantages of History for Life." *Untimely Meditations*. Ed. Daniel Breazeale. Trans. R.J. Hollingdale. Cambridge: Cambridge University Press, 1997, 57–124.

Pearce, Joseph. *Tolkien, Man and Myth: A Literary Life*. New York: HarperCollins, 1998.

Pratchett, Terry. "Why Gandalf Never Married" (1985): http://www.ansible.co.uk/misc/tpspeech.html.

Rabkin, Eric S. *The Fantastic in Literature*. Princeton: Princeton University Press, 1976.

Rateliff, John D. *The History of the Hobbit*. 2 vols. Boston: Houghton Mifflin, 2007.

———. "Inside Literature: Tolkien's Exploration of Medieval Genres." In *Tolkien in the New Century: Essays in Honor of Tom Shippey*. Eds. John Wm. Houghton, Janet Brennan Croft, Nancy Martsch, John D. Rateliff, and Robin Anne Reid. Jefferson, NC: McFarland, 2014, 133–152.

Reid, Robin A. "Making or Creating Orcs: How Thorinsmut's Free Orcs AU Writes Back to Tolkien," *Journal of Tolkien Research* 11.2, article 3 (2020), 1–17. [https://scholar.valpo.edu/journaloftolkienresearch/vol11/iss2/3/].

———. "Race in Tolkien Studies: A Bibliographic Essay." In *Tolkien and Alterity*. Eds. Christopher Vaccaro and Yvette Kisor. New York: Palgrave Macmillan, 2017, 33–74.

Rosebury, Brian. *Tolkien: A Cultural Phenomenon*. New York: Palgrave, 2003.

Schürer, Norbert. "Second Age, Middle Age." *Journal of Tolkien Research* 15.2, Article 6 (2022): https://scholar.valpo.edu/journaloftolkienresearch/vol15/iss2/6.

Shippey, Tom. *J.R.R. Tolkien: Author of the Century*. Boston: Houghton Mifflin, 2000.

———. "Orcs, Wraiths, Wights: Tolkien's Images of Evil." *J.R.R. Tolkien and his Literary Resonances*. Ed. George Clark and Daniel Timmons. Westport, CT: Greenwood, 2000, 183–98.

———. *The Road to Middle-earth: How J.R.R. Tolkien Created a New Mythology*. Boston: Houghton Mifflin, 2003.

Sofge, Erik. "Orc Holocaust: The Reprehensible Moral Universe of Gary Gygax's Dungeons & Dragons." *Slate Magazine*. Posted Monday, March 10, 2008. http://www.slate.com/id/2186203.

Stanton, Michael N. *Hobbits, Elves, and Wizards: Exploring the Wonders and Worlds of J.R.R. Tolkien's* The Lord of the Rings. New York: Palgrave, 2001.

Stuart, Robert. *Tolkien, Race, and Racism in Middle-earth*. New York: Palgrave Macmillan, 2022.

Suvin, Darko. *Metamorphoses of Science Fiction: On the Poetics and History of a Literary Genre*. New Haven: Yale University Press, 1979.

Tally, Robert T, Jr. *J.R.R. Tolkien's* The Hobbit: *Realizing History Through Fantasy*. New York: Palgrave Macmillan, 2022.

———. "Let Us Now Praise Famous Orcs." *Mythlore* 29.1/2 (2010): 17–28.

———. *Representing Middle-earth: Tolkien, Form, and Ideology*. Jefferson, NC: McFarland, 2024.

———. "Tolkien's Geopolitical Fantasy: Spatial Narrative in *The Lord of the Rings*." In *Popular Fiction and Spatiality: Reading Genre Settings*. Ed. Lisa Fletcher. New York: Palgrave Macmillan, 2016, 125–140.

———. "'Uruk … We prefer *Uruk*": Representing the Orc in *The Rings of Power*." *Tolkien, Race, and Racism*. Ed. Robin Anne Reid. Jefferson, NC: McFarland, forthcoming.

———. "'You cannot press the One Ring too hard': Tolkien, Ethics, and the Ambiguities of Magic." *Magic in Fantasy Literature: Definitions, Manifestations, Functions*. Eds. Tetiana Riazantseva and Yevheniia Kanchura. Kyiv: Shevchenko Institute of Literature, National Academy of Science of Ukraine, 2024, 224–239.

Terkel, Studs. *The Good War: An Oral History of World War II*. New York: New Press, 1984.

Thomas, Paul Edmund. "Some of Tolkien's Narrators." In *Tolkien's "Legendarium": Essays on "The History of Middle-earth."* Edited by Verlyn Flieger and Carl F. Hostetter. Westport, CT: Greenwood Press, 2000. 161–181.

Vaccaro, Christopher, ed. *The Body in Tolkien's Legendarium: Essays on Middle-earth Corporeality*. Jefferson, NC: McFarland, 2013.

Vaccaro, Christopher, and Yvette Kisor, eds. *Tolkien and Alterity*. New York: Palgrave Macmillan, 2017.

Wilson, Edmund. "Oo, Those Awful Orcs!" *The Bit Between My Teeth: Literary Chronicles, 1950–1965*. New York: Farrar, Strauss, and Giroux, 1965. 326–332.

Wise, Dennis Wilson. "On Ways of Studying Tolkien: Notes Toward a Better (Epic) Fantasy Criticism." *Journal of Tolkien Research* 9.1 (2020): https://scholar.valpo.edu/journaloftolkienresearch/vol9/iss1/2.

Yeskov, Kirill. *The Last Ringbearer*. Trans. Yisroel Markov. Minneapolis: Tenseg Press, 2011.

Young, Helen. *Race and Popular Fantasy Literature: Habits of Whiteness*. London: Routledge, 2016.

Index

Agee, James 10
Anderson, Douglas A. 177*n*7
Auerbach, Erich 61

Benjamin, Walter 12
Beronio, Bianca 174*n*25, 183*n*10
Blake, William 1, 174*n*16

Carpenter, Humphrey 29, 173*n*1
Chomsky, Noam 1, 2
Croft, Janet Brennan 4

Echo-Hawk, Roger 26
Ellmann, Mary 173*n*5
Evans, Walker 10

Fanon, Franz 1
Fimi, Dimitra 21, 26, 51, 52, 62, 144
Flieger, Verlyn 48, 134
Fonstad, Karen Wynn 68–69
Foucault, Michel 1
Frank, Joseph 110
Freud, Sigmund 26, 143
Frye, Northrop 174*n*16

Garth, John 144
Grybauskas, Peter 178*n*12

Heidegger, Martin 32–33
Hesiod 23
Hostetter, Carl F. 40, 181*n*9
Hugh of Saint Victor 60–61

Jameson, Fredric 181*n*6

Kane, Douglass Charles 176*n*22
Klaeber, Friedrich 23

Le Guin, Ursula K. 172

Lewis, C.S. 30
Luling, Virginia 101

MacDonald, George 21, 64
Martin, George R.R. 89
Marx, Karl 2
Mills, Charles 10, 26–27
Mohler, Corey 1, 185*n*12
Moorcock, Michael 30

Nietzsche, Friedrich 12, 19, 60, 107

Perrault, Charles 22

Rateliff, John D. 67, 69–70, 178*n*21, 179*n*42
Reid, Robin Anne 26, 46, 174*n*25, 176*n*16
Rios, Mariana 26
Rosebury, Brian 134–135

Shippey, Tom 22–23, 24, 40, 69, 91, 96, 110, 120, 175*n*4, 180*n*1
Stuart, Robert 26, 29, 32–33, 76, 78, 98, 100, 116, 144, 175*n*40, 178*n*14, 183*n*8

Tolkien, Christopher 10, 17–18, 21, 29, 30–31, 37, 38, 39, 40, 46, 48–49, 51, 52–55, 57, 66, 134, 173*n*6, 174*n*8, 175*n*2, 176*n*9, 177*n*48, 181*n*10, 183*n*7, 185*n*6
Troyes, Chrétien de 22

Waldman, Milton 76
Wolfe, Gene 21
Wolin, Richard 32, 175*n*37

Yeskov, Kirill 184*n*1
Young, Helen 26, 101

Zimmerman, Morton Grady 28

www.ingramcontent.com/pod-product-compliance
Ingram Content Group UK Ltd.
Pitfield, Milton Keynes, MK11 3LW, UK
UKHW042011140426
5217IPUK00015B/1101